A MANUAL OF GOOD ENGLISH

By the Same Author

A REFRESHER COURSE IN ENGLISH

A REFRESHER COURSE IN PUNCTUATION AND
SPELLING

QUESTIONS AND ANSWERS ON ENGLISH

QUESTIONS AND ANSWERS ON SPELLING AND
PUNCTUATION

A
Manual of
Good English

By

W. J. WESTON, M.A., B.Sc.

LONDON
GEORGE NEWNES LIMITED
TOWER HOUSE, SOUTHAMPTON STREET
STRAND, W.C.2

First published .   .   . 1950
Second Impression   .   . 1953

PRINTED IN GREAT BRITAIN

PREFACE

THIS book has been planned to show how the masters of English literature have used our language to express their thoughts with clarity and precision and to demonstrate to the reader, by means of the examples given and the discussion of them, that everyone can write and speak English lucidly and easily.

The writing of good English depends not upon a pedantic use of unassailable grammatical rules, but upon the happy choice of words and phrases which present the writer's thoughts vividly and precisely. The grammar in Acts of Parliament is above reproach but the meaning, or perhaps, more strictly the intention, of the author is frequently, alas, more than a little obscure.

The value of this book lies in the choice of the examples and the clarity of the explanation and discussion of them, thus guiding the reader to the formation of a writing technique based upon the best models.

W. J. W.

A

A or An ?   (See also " **Article** ")

(*a*) A rose by any other name would smell as sweet.

(*b*) An apple a day keeps the doctor away.

(*c*) An old man broken with the storms of state,
Is come to lay his weary bones among ye,
Give him a little earth for charity.

(Wolsey in *King Henry VIII.*)

The rule is this : *a* is replaced by *an* before a vowel *sound*—
" An oak is more hardy than a beech." This includes words
beginning with a silent *h*. (" But ", said Mr. Squeers, " when
the *h* is sounded, the *a* only is to be used, as a 'and, a 'art, a
'ighway.")

The sound, you note, may vary though the same letter represents it : and it is the sound, not the letter, that determines
whether *a* or *an* is the better word. Thus we say " an urn "
but " a unique specimen " ; we say " an hour ", but " a house ",
we say " an unusual occurrence ", but " a usual thing " (for
usual begins with a *y* sound). Better write " a usurer " and
" a unit " even though Ruskin writes, " I know myself to be
an usurer as long as I take any interest on any money ", and
though Browning writes—

> That low man goes on adding one to one,
> His hundred's soon hit,
> This high man, aiming at a million,
> Misses an unit.

The affected " such an one ", too, has the authority of Browning :

> All prudent counsel, as to what befits
> The golden mean, is lost on such an one.

Perhaps, however, we do well to avoid " an one " and say
" a one ".

The doubt about *a* or *an* results from the fact that in their
speech people play all manner of pranks with their language.

7

The *n* was originally always present. It was often ignored when another consonant sound followed it, *an year* became *a year*. We have frequent instances where forms with and without *n* survive, *my* and *mine*, *eve* and *even*, *maid* and *maiden*. Moreover, we have curious results of this playing with *n*. *Adder*, *apron*, *umpire*, have all lost an initial *n* ; they were once *a nadder*, *a naperon*, *a numpire*. *Newt* and *nickname*, on the other hand, have captured from the preceding *an* the lost *n* : the words were *an ewt*, *an ekename*. And you have the pet names *Nan* for " *mine Ann* ", *Ned* for " *mine Edward* " and *Nell* for " *mine Ellen* ".

We use *a* in *a history*, *a ewe*, *a European*, but *an* in *an antique vase*, *an honour*, *an artist*. But though the *h* is sounded, *an historian* and *an historical novel* are found, the syllable followed by *an* being unaccented, and—except in very careful speech— the *h* having little value.

Note the instances of *a* and *an* in these two sentences from *Tom Brown's Schooldays* :

> Now they pull up at a lodge, and take on board a well-muffled-up sportsman, with his gun-case and carpet-bag. An early up-coach meets them, and the coachmen gather up their horses, and pass one another with the accustomed lift of the elbow, each team doing eleven miles an hour, with a mile to spare behind if necessary.

ABBREVIATION

(*a*) *Madame* (the saleswoman's) : *ma'am* (most people's) : *m* (in the housemaid's " *Yes'm* "). [The full form becomes ever shorter.]

(*b*) Pisky, Pisky, loud Amen,
Down on your knees and up again :
Presby, Presby, dinna bend,
But set ye doon on Man's Chief End.
  [*Episcopalian* and *Presbyterian* are rather cumbrous for controversy.]

(*c*) Hodges & Sons v. Hackbridge Park Residential Hotel Ltd., K.B., 1940. [*&*, the ampersand is for *and*, *v* for *versus*, against, *Ltd.* for Limited, *K.B.* for King's Bench Division of the High Court of Justice.]

An ABBREVIATION is a shortening, an abridgment either by

cutting off a part—(*exam.* for *examination*)—or by contracting (*ransom*, like many of our English words, is a contracted form; its doublet is *redemption*). Thus *piano* (the soft instead of the soft-and-strong) is an abbreviation of *pianoforte*, *brig* of *brig-antine*, *drawing-room* of *with-drawing-room*, *still* (in the sense of "an apparatus for distilling") of *distillery*. In these times, too, there is an ever-swelling flood of initials doing duty for full words. Thus we are to understand U.N.R.R.A. as the United Nations Relief and Rehabilitation Administration.

So long as the shortened form is neither a trap nor an ob-scurity, the abbreviation is the natural development of language; for it conveys thought with greater economy. There seems to be no valid objection to shortenings like *phone* for *telephone*, or *photo* for *photograph*: perhaps there is in those of the example (*b*). "Episcopalian" and "Presbyterian" would doubtless be more dignified; but, of course, these lines are only a little fun.

The great point is that we are all well advised in this matter of language—which concerns others as well as ourselves—to conform to custom. We make ourselves slightly ridiculous when we insist on "consolidated annuities" when all around us say "consols"; or "cinematograph" when others say "cinema"; or "costermonger" when others are saying "coster". But we should think twice before using "phiz" for "physiognomy", even though Browning has (in *Fra Lippo Lippi*):

"How looks my painting, now the scaffold's down?"
I ask a brother: "Hugely!" he returns—
"Already not one phiz of your three slaves
That turn the Deacon off his toasted side,
But's scratched and prodded to our hearts' content."

"Coon" has replaced "racoon"; "curio" is heard more frequently than "curiosity" for the things sold in an antique shop. "Dynamo" for "dynamo-electric machine" and "mag-neto" for "magneto-electric machine" are well understood; "gym" and "zoo" are useful variants for "gymnasium" and "Zoological Gardens". A curious development is to make a new word from the initials of a well-known phrase, illustrated by our saying, "It's a question of £ s. d." ("el-es-dee", not "pounds, shillings and pence"), "He's an M.P." ("em-pee",

9

not " Member of Parliament "), " So the B.B.C. announces " (the " bee-bee-cee ", not the " British Broadcasting Corporation "). Here is a little of *The Times* comment upon our habit of forming new names from initials :

It is when the names of institutions are abbreviated that their study becomes interesting. L.M.S., for instance, is an admirable name for a railway ; the train pulls in on the first two letters and lets out steam with a complacent hiss. L.N.E.R. gallops to the right rhythm ; but G.W.R. is hopeless and does not sound like a railway at all. . . . G.P.O. is as brisk, cheerful, and efficient as a postman's knock ; and the L.P.T.B. has the hurried, bumpy cadence that we should expect.

When the abbreviation (whether initial word or opening syllable) is not yet regarded as a word in itself, a stop similar to the full stop at the end of a sentence follows it. Thus : " The gallant action of H.M.S. *Jervis Bay* (Captain E. S. F. Fegen, R.N.) enabled a large proportion of the convoy to escape."

The matter of importance in regard to the using of abbreviations seems to be this : we should write and say the full form unless we are quite certain that our readers or our hearers will readily interpret the short form in its intended meaning. Courtesy, however,—as well as prudence—asks us not to impose burdens upon our readers or our hearers ; it may well be that, instead of writing " A.B.C.A." we should submit to a little more trouble and write " Army Bureau of Current Affairs ". There has been waste, not economy, when our shortened forms cannot be interpreted by those for whom we meant them—waste of our time as writers, and waste of our readers' time and patience.

ABSOLUTE PHRASE. (See **Nominative Absolute**)

ABSTRACT and CONCRETE

(*a*) (i) Though justice be thy plea consider this—
That in the course of justice none of us
Should see salvation.

(*Merchant of Venice.*)

(ii)   Beauty's ensign yet
Is crimson in thy lips and in thy cheeks,
And death's pale flag is not advanced there.
                              (*Romeo and Juliet.*)
(*b*) (i)   And then the justice
In fair round belly with good capon lined
With eyes severe and beard of formal cut,
Full of wise saws and modern instances.
                              (*As You Like It*, II, VII.)
(ii) The beauty of Israel is slain upon thy high places:
How are the mighty fallen !

                              (2 *Samuel* i.)

An ABSTRACT NOUN names a thing of the mind ; a CONCRETE NOUN names a thing of the senses. *Justice* and *beauty* in (*a*) are Abstract Nouns ; in (*b*) they are Concrete Nouns. It needs some development of mind to abstract. Fire, water when shining in the sun, the moon, the stars in " this brave, o'erhanging firmament, this majestical roof fretted with golden fire "—all these are *bright* ; and in time we can think of *brightness* apart from the concrete objects in which it exists. We have then abstracted from those concrete things the quality of brightness that they have in common.

Where choice is possible we are probably well advised to prefer the Concrete to the Abstract—" Then shall ye bring down my grey hairs with sorrow to the grave " is more effective than " Then shall ye bring my old age with sorrow to death." We must, indeed, have abstractions. It is by means of these that we reason. To grasp an abstract idea, however, calls for mental effort ; and people do not care for effort, for protracted effort at any rate. Our hearers are lethargic when we assert that " Division of labour means increase of production " ; they rouse themselves when we say " Many hands make light work." And " Too many cooks spoil the broth " probably makes a deeper impression than " Unity of command is desirable."

When a teacher would impress on his students a general state-ment—an abstraction, he takes care to give a concrete instance of that general statement—maybe more than one. Here is an instance from Lord Morley's *Introduction to Wordsworth's Poetical Works* :

To find beautiful and pathetic language, set to harmonious

numbers, for the common impressions of meditative minds, is no small part of the poet's task. That part has never been achieved by any poet in any tongue with more complete perfection and success than in the immortal *Elegy*, of which we may truly say that it has for nearly a century and a half given to greater multitudes of men more of the exquisite pleasure of poetry than any other single piece in all the glorious treasury of English verse. It abounds, as Johnson says, " with images which find a mirror in every mind, and with sentiments to which every bosom returns an echo." These moving commonplaces of the human lot, Gray approached through books and studious contemplation ; not, as Wordsworth approached them, by daily contact with the lives and habits of men and the forces and magical apparitions of eternal nature.

ACCENT. (See also "Stress in Words ")

Hóspitable : Desúltory : Sédentary : Ábject : Advértisement : Advértise : Áspirant ; Décadence : Laméntable : Ímpious.

To ACCENT a syllable or a word is to give that syllable or word prominence over its companions. Thus in *bróther* you place stress on the first syllable : you speak, therefore, of this first syllable as the accented one.

In English words the strong accent is near the beginning, on the first or the second syllable : *beáutiful, sómething, bútton, ánimal, immédiate, intélligible.* And when we introduce words from other languages, the accent of the newcomers tends to conform to English usage : these newcomers may, for a while, retain in their new surroundings the accent they had in the old surroundings. But time brings changes. Thus, we hear *cánine* more often than *caníne* though the latter is closer to the original Latin. It is this conflict between the custom of the original tongue and the custom of English that often gives rise to uncertainty in the manner of accenting some of our words.

When the same letters stand for both noun and verb, discrimination is at times effected by variation of accent. This word *accent* itself, for instance, has one sound when a noun, another sound when a verb. Used as a noun—" The accent in English words is usually at the beginning of the word "— we pronounce it *ac-cent*. Used as a verb—" We often accent the verb differently from the noun "—we pronounce it as *ac-cent*. We talk of " *a compound* " but " *to compound* a felony " ; we " give a testimony of good *conduct* ", " we *conduct* operations " ; we notice " a *decrease* in the number of births ", through careful observation we " *decrease* the number of errors in our spelling " ; we make " an *extract* of a favourite passage " ; we " ask the dentist to *extract* an aching tooth " ; we " compose a *digest* of a number of documents ", we " *digest* the information we gather ". So with *pro-duce* (noun), *pro-duce* (verb) ; *essay* (noun), *es-say* (verb), *in-sult* (noun), *in-sult* (verb), *al-ly* (noun), *ally* (verb).

Occasionally, when the same letters represent both noun and adjective, we get a similar change in accent. The strong accent falls on the first syllable in the noun, on a later syllable in the adjective. We have the noun *August*, the name of the month, and the adjective *august*, meaning " majestic " or " venerable " ; we have the noun *compact* (an agreement—" the compact between the parties was scrupulously observed ") and the adjective " *compact* ", knit closely together ; we have the noun *expert* (" the expert gave evidence "), and the adjective *expert* (" You are now an expert writer ") ; we have the noun *minute* (" Sixty minutes make an hour "), and the adjective *minute*, the change of accent being here accompanied by a change in the vowel sound (" Minute additions in course of time mean much ") ; we have the noun *invalid* and the adjective *invalid* (" An invalid contract will not be enforced ").

ACCIDENCE. (See also **" Parse "** and **" Syntax "**)

Man :   Plural, *men*
            Possessive Singular, *man's*
            Possessive Plural, *men's*.

To carry : Present Tense, *I carry*, etc.
Past Tense, *I carried*, etc.
Past Participle, *I have carried*, etc.

To rise : Present Tense, *I rise*, etc.
Past Tense, *I rose*, etc.
Past Participle, *I have risen*, etc.

The ACCIDENCE of a word comprises its variations, its inflexions; these are the " accidents " as distinct from the " essence " of the word. In a language like Latin accidence is of much importance; in a language like English, which has shed most of its inflexions, accidence is of little importance. " Sir Hugh," says Mrs. Page, " my husband says my son profits nothing in the world at his book; I pray you, ask him some questions in his accidence." For " schooling " meant once the learning of (Latin) grammar : " Thou hast most traitorously corrupted the youth of the realm in erecting a grammar school ", was Jack Cade's complaint against Lord Say.

Several influences have brought about the simplifying of English grammar. The chief influence, perhaps, was the mingling of peoples speaking different dialects. It is, for example, a great boon that we have come to regard the gender of nouns and pronouns as corresponding to sex; we are not called upon to combat with such extraordinary troubles as confront us in German nouns. In German, though *Hand* is feminine, *Fuss* (foot) is masculine, and *Bein* (leg) is neuter; both *Weib* (woman) and *Mädchen* (girl) are neuter.

ACTIVE VOICE. (See under " Passive Voice ")

The noble Brutus hath told you Cæsar was ambitious.

In the active voice of the verb the doer is made prominent, being made the Subject of the sentence : here *Brutus*, the Subject, is the active agent. In the passive voice either the Direct Object of the sentence, or the Indirect Object, is made prominent. Thus, contrast the effect of these sentences with that above :

You have been told by the noble Brutus that Cæsar was ambitious. [Indirect Object made the Subject.]

That Cæsar was ambitious has been told you by the noble Brutus. [Direct Object, that is " That Cæsar was ambitious ", made the Subject.]

14

ADJECTIVE, ATTRIBUTE or PREDICATE. (See also "Adjectives and Adverbs")

(*a*) Ah me ! for aught that ever I could read,
    Could ever hear by tale or history,
    The course of true love never did run smooth.
                (*A Midsummer Night's Dream.*)

(*b*) Fame is the spur that the clear spirit doth raise
    (That last infirmity of noble mind)
    To scorn delights and live laborious days.
                  (MILTON, *Lycidas.*)

Note that *smooth* in (*a*) is an adjective, coupled with its noun " course " by the verb " run ". The adjective is part, therefore, of the predicate of the sentence ; and we say that it is used PREDICATIVELY. It is used ATTRIBUTIVELY when the statement made by it is compressed into the single word. In this sentence of Burke's, for example, the adjectives are used as attributes, not as predicates : " When bad men combine, the good must associate ; else they will fall, one by one, an unjustified sacrifice in a contemptible struggle." (Notice *bad, unjustified, contemptible.*) In (*b*) the words *clear, last, noble, laborious,* are attributes, not predicates.

Some adjectives are used as predicates, rarely as attributes. Among them are *aware, afraid, sorry* (when used as an attribute as in " This is a sorry sight " there is a deviation from the usual meaning), *ill* (used as an attribute as in " 'Tis an ill wind that blows nobody good " we have again a departure from the usual meaning), *glad* (but there is the current phrase " glad news "), *alone, alike.*

The predicative *aware* corresponds to the attribute *wary*

,,	,,	*afraid*	,,	,, ,,	,,	*frightened*
,,	,,	*alone*	,,	,, ,,	,,	*lonely*
,,	,,	*alike*	,,	,, ,,	,,	*like*

(" Like master, like man ; Like mistress, like Nan ").

ADJECTIVES and ADVERBS. (See also "Noun")

(*a*) (i) You look cold.
    (ii) That which we call a rose
        By any other name would smell as sweet.
    (iii) He married young.

(*b*)   (i) You look coldly upon the plan.
       (ii) Sweetly rose the sound.
       (iii) He married early.

Cold, sweet, young are ADJECTIVES. *Coldly, sweetly, early* are ADVERBS.

Shall we say " The snow fell thick ", and " The course of true love never did run smooth " ? Or shall we replace the adjectives by the adverbs *thickly* and *smoothly* ? Your sense of what is fit tells you at once that the adjective, not the adverb, conforms to English idiom. For we must note that a good many verbs, besides the usual coupling verb *be*, attach an attribute to a preceding noun or pronoun. " This seems conclusive," you say, rightly using the adjective and not the adverb *conclusively.* " The butter tastes rancid," you say ; or, " The milk has turned sour." It would be an excessive, and a quite erroneous, devotion to grammar to use *rancidly* and *sourly* merely because the words follow the verbs.

Consider the question a little. An adjective is an attribute to a noun or pronoun ; it is dependent upon the noun or pronoun. Read this extract :

My present letter will be given to a single figure. When I entered at Oxford, John Henry Newman was beginning to be famous. The responsible authorities were watching him with anxiety ; clever men were looking with interest and curiosity on the apparition among them of one of those persons of indisputable genius who are likely to make a mark upon his time. His appearance was striking. He was above the middle height, slight and spare.

Clearly, the words *present, single, famous, responsible, clever, those, indisputable, striking, middle, slight, spare* are all adjectives. They are attributes to the substantives *letter, figure* and so on. An adverb, on the other hand, is nearly always an attribute of an attribute. Look at this extract :

His head was large, his face remarkably like that of Julius Cæsar. The forehead, the shape of the ears and nose, were almost the same. The lines of the mouth were very peculiar, and I should say exactly the same. I have often thought of the resemblance, and believed that it extended to the temperament.

You recognise as adverbs the words *remarkably, almost, very, exactly, often* : they are attributes, they modify the meaning, of the attributes *like, same, peculiar*, and so on.

The end syllable *-ly* is, you note, frequent in adverbs : the adjective *bold* becomes the adverb *boldly* ; the adjective *high* becomes the adverb *highly* (" We here highly resolve that these dead shall not have died in vain "). You would, however, be wrong to regard *-ly* as the infallible sign of the adverb. Many adjectives end in *-ly*. In " the daily paper " *daily* is an adjective ; in " With bended knees I daily beseech God " *daily* is an adverb. In Wordsworth's " Choice word and measured phrase, a stately speech ", *stately* is an adjective ; in Shakespeare's " A figure appears before them, and with solemn march goes slow and stately by them ", *stately* is clearly an adverb. *Statelily* is possible for the adverb ; but what an awkward word to sound it is ! There is, indeed, a modern tendency to attach *-ly* for the adverb in spite of the troublesome repetition of sounds—to write *livelily* as the adverb from *lively* ; and *comelily* as the derivation from *comely*. But *lively* seems preferable and is well sanctioned by authority : " We must act lively " is the injunction, not *livelily*.

We should note, too, that the one word in many instances serves for adjective and adverb. In our proverb, " Fast bind, safe find ", *fast* is the adverb. It would be silly pedantry to write *fastly* simply because *fast* is the adjective in " England must be the fast friend of France." In " She is well " *well* is an adjective ; in " She sings well " *well* is an adverb. *Hard* is another instance. You speak of your " hard earned wages " and *hard* is certainly an adverb. If you altered it to *hardly*, you might suggest doubt of your deserts. Notice, in conclusion, these instances in " I saw now that ' Right away ' and ' Directly ' were one and the same thing." In " Keep Right ", *right* is the adverb ; it would be against English idiom to have " rightly ", though of course *rightly* is called for in sentences like " He cannot see rightly " and in Hamlet's " Rightly to be great is not to stir without great argument, but greatly to find quarrel in a straw."

ALLEGORY. (See "Metaphor")

" The bridge thou seest," said he, " is human life ; consider it attentively." Upon a more leisurely survey of it, I found that it consisted of threescore and ten entire arches, with several broken arches, which, added to those that were entire, made up the number to about a hundred. As I was counting the arches, the genius told me that this bridge consisted at first of a thousand arches : but that a great flood swept away the rest, and kept the bridge in the ruinous condition I now beheld it. " But tell me further," said he, " what thou discoverest on it."—" I see multitudes of people passing over it," said I, " and a black cloud hanging on each end of it." As I looked more attentively, I saw several of the passengers dropping through the bridge into the great tide that flowed beneath it : and, upon further examination, perceived there were innumerable trap-doors that lay concealed in the bridge, which the passengers no sooner trod upon, but they fell through them into the tide, and immediately disappeared.

(ADDISON.)

An ALLEGORY is an extended Metaphor, a description of one thing under the image of another resembling it. " Fierce wars and faithful loves shall moralize my song ", wrote Spencer, introducing his great verse allegory, *The Faerie Queene*. Bunyan's *Pilgrim's Progress* is our great example of an allegory in prose. This is what Macaulay writes :

Bunyan is indeed as decidedly the first of allegorists, as Demosthenes is the first of orators, or Shakespeare the first of dramatists. Other allegorists have shown equal ingenuity ; but no other allegorist has ever been able to touch the heart ; and to make abstractions objects of terror, of pity, and of love.

In his allegory, you very likely remember, Bunyan tells you of " a castle, called Doubting-Castle, the owner whereof was Giant Despair ", that " Giant Despair had a wife, and her name was Diffidence ", of how " They came to the Delectable Mountains ", of Mr. Worldly-Wise-Man and Mr. Standfast and Mr. By-Ends and " a man that could look no way but downwards with a muckrake in his hands."

ALLITERATION. (See also "Echoes")

(*a*) Apt alliteration's artful aid.

(*b*) To scorn delights and live laborious days.

(c) After life's fitful fever he sleeps well.

(d) Mere prattle without practice is all his soldiership.

(e) Lord Shaftesbury, who aimed at the same easy, dégagé mode of communicating his thoughts to the world, has quite spoiled his matter, which is sometimes valuable, by his manner, in which he carries a certain flaunting, flowery, figurative, flirting style of amicable condescension to the reader, to an excess more tantalizing than the most starched and ridiculous formality of the age of James I. There is nothing so tormenting as the affectation of ease and freedom from affectation.

(WILLIAM HAZLITT.)

(f) There twice a day the Severn fills ;
    The salt sea-water passes by,
And hushes half the babbling Wye,
    And makes a silence in the hills.

(TENNYSON, In Memoriam.)

ALLITERATION is the effective use of words having syllables beginning with the same sound. See how, in the Tennyson example, the *s* and *h* sounds recur and delight, how Hazlitt plays upon the *f* sound, how the liquid *l* runs through the line, " To scorn delights and live laborious days."

Language is a tool ; it is a capital vehicle of thought. But language is also a toy : it is a plaything in which from the earliest times men and women have taken delight. And one of the best language games is the gathering together of like sounds. " I will something affect the letter, for it argues facility." So says one of Shakespeare's characters, and he proceeds to compose a sonnet describing the hunting exploits of the princess, the sonnet beginning, " The praiseful princess pierced and pricked a pretty pleasing pricket." So he shows how, in speech as in dress, an excess of ornament is a blemish.

The technical name for this hunting of the letter is ALLITERATION. The child delights in it. " Peter Piper picked a peck of pickling pepper." Writers great and small delight in it, too. " Apt alliteration's artful aid " fixes in the memory numbers of our proverbs : " Waste not, want not " ; " Penny wise, pound foolish " ; " Be not made a beggar by banqueting upon borrowing." Early English verse made noticeable and effective use of words containing the same sound : the great poem, *Piers*

Plowman, begins, " In a summer season, when soft was the sun ". Look at a few instances.

Miss Mitford, in her charming account of *Our Village*, contrasts the two umpires. The village team had been beaten at cricket ; and

> a fourth imputed our defeat to the over-civility of our umpire, George Gosseltine, a sleek, smooth, silk, soft-spoken person, who stood with his little wand under his arm, smiling through all our disasters—the very image of peace and good humour ; whilst their umpire, Bob Coxe, a roystering, roaring, bullying blade, bounced, and hectored, and blustered from his wicket, with the voice of a twelve pounder.

The very letters of the descriptive adjectives seem to belong to the different men. And see what fine sport old Burton has in his catalogue of beauties :

> Modest Matilda, pretty pleasing Peggy, sweet-singing Susan, mincing, merry Moll, dainty, dancing Doll, neat Nancy, jolly Joan, nimble Nell, kissing Kate, bouncing Bess with black eyes, fair Phyllis with fine white hands, fiddling Frank, tall Tib, slender Sid—all will lose their grace and grow out of fashion.

And here is Mrs. General's advice in *Little Dorrit* : " ' Father ' is rather vulgar, my dear. The word ' Papa ', besides, gives a pretty form to the lips. Papa, potatoes, poultry, prunes and prisms, are all very good words for the lips ; especially prunes and prisms."

Alliteration is maybe a childish toy, and we should not seek industriously after the jingle of like beginnings,—in our serious writings at any rate. Perhaps you agree with the critic : " Some ", he writes, " use overmuch repetition of one letter as, ' Pitiful poverty prayeth for a penny, but puffed presumption payeth not a point.' " But how haunting are phrases in which alliteration is skilfully used ; how they linger in the memory ! " After life's fitful fever he sleeps well " ; doesn't that owe some of its beauty to the repetition of the *f* sound ? So natural it is to seek after similar sounds that we are sometimes led astray : that line of Milton's " Tomorrow to fresh woods and pastures new " is as often quoted wrongly as rightly. The alliterative " fresh fields " becomes a substitute for the correct term.

The alliteration is peculiarly effective when the sounds used suggest the sense. Thus Coleridge's—

> The fair breeze blew, the white foam flew,
> The furrow followed free ;
> We were the first that ever burst
> Into that silent sea.

Or those famous lines of Tennyson—

> Come ; for all the vales
> Await thee ; azure pillars of the hearth
> Arise to thee ; the children call, and I
> Thy shepherd pipe, and sweet is every sound,
> Sweeter thy voice, but every sound is sweet ;
> Myriads of rivulets hurrying thro' the lawn,
> The moan of doves in immemorial elms,
> And murmuring of innumerable bees.

Alliteration is the more effective when not obtrusive. Ruskin's prose every now and then presents us with delightful instances. Look, for example, at the masterly manner in which this paragraph plays upon the sounds of *f* and *r* and *m*, of *n* and *c*. The paragraph is from a description in *The Stones of Venice*—of a statue :

> It is the face of a man in middle life ; for there are two deep furrows right across the forehead, dividing it like the foundations of a tower. The height of it above is bound by the fillet of the ducal cap. The rest of the features are singularly small and delicate, the lips sharp, the sharpness of death perhaps being added to that of the natural lines. But there is a sweet smile upon them, and a deep serenity upon the whole countenance.

We need not quarrel with the statement that the sense of your words is more to be considered than the sounds. Very likely it is. But the sound matters also. Don't you, for example greatly admire Campbell's poem *Hohenlinden* : don't you remember many of its lines too ? And isn't your admiration great and your memory retentive, in some measure, because of the cunning alliteration running through the poem ?

> On Linden, when the sun was low,
> All blood-less lay the untrodden snow,
> And dark as winter was the flow
> Of Iser, rolling rapidly.

Look at the effective instances of alliteration in these lines from Robert Browning's poems.   In the first he plays upon the liquid *l* sound :

> From the sprinkled isles,
> Lily on lily, that o'erlace the sea,
> And laugh their pride when the light-wave lisps Greece.
>
> *(Cleon.)*

The lip-unvoiced-stop *p* is prominent here :

> How could you ever prick those perfect ears
> Even to put the pearl there !

The voiceless-spirant *f* governs the line from *Bishop Blougram's Apology* :

> So free we seem, so fettered fast we are.

And look at the way in which one letter sings to another in Fuller's note :

> I find this Chaucer fined in the Temple two shillings for striking a Franciscan friar in Fleet Street, and it seems his hands ever after itched to be revenged, and have his penny-worths out of them, so tickling religious Orders with his tales and yet so pinching them with his truths that friars, in reading his books, knew not how to dispose their faces betwixt crying and laughing.   He lies buried in the south aisle of St. Peter's, Westminster ; and since hath got the company of Spencer and Drayton, a pair royal of poets, enough almost to make passengers' feet to move metrically, who go over the place where so much poetical dust is interred.

ALLUSION

(*a*) " Wot I like in that 'ere style of writin'," said the elder Mr. Weller, " is, that there ain't no callin' names in it, —no Wenuses, nor nothin' o' that kind.   Wot's the good o' callin' a young 'ooman a Wenus or a angel, Sammy ? "
" Ah ! what, indeed ? " replied Sam.
" You might jist as well call her a griffin, or a unicorn, or a king's arms at once, which is werry well known to be a collection o' fabulous animals," added Mr. Weller.
(Pickwick Papers.)

(*b*) I know they are so lively and as vigorously productive as those fabulous dragons' teeth and, being sown up and down, may chance to spring up armed men.

(So MILTON says of Books.)

An ALLUSION is a passing reference : for illustration or orna-ment you direct attention to what will make your statement more impressive. You assume that your hearer or reader will readily recall the person or place or occurrence to which you allude ; you pay him the compliment of knowledge. " Every schoolboy knows ", says Macaulay ; and then he ushers in names with which, we may be pretty certain, few of us, school-boys or others, are quite familiar. Therein lies the danger of allusion ; the writer's knowledge is not shared by the reader. Are we all, for instance, able to interpret fully in (b) " those fabulous dragons' teeth " ? Perhaps we should be shy of parad-ing our knowledge by way of allusions. If our hearers or readers cannot place them directly, the allusions irritate ; if our hearers or readers know at once to what you allude, the allusion may appear hackneyed and pointless. Mr. Weller's objection is too large. For it would be a heavy handicap to be deprived in our speaking and our writing of the privilege of allusion. But we are to exercise temperance in the matter.

We should note too, that delight in the sound rather than the aptness of the allusion may prompt to the use of a name. Here, in Rossetti's *The Blessed Damozel* :

> " We two," she said, " will seek the groves
>   Where the lady Mary is
> With her five handmaidens, whose names
>   Are five sweet symphonies—
> Cecily, Gertrude, Magdalene,
>   Margaret and Rosalys."

Musical ornament and not instruction gives rise to the catalogue of proper names. And Kipling in " Our Fathers of Old " brings together the names because, as he says, they " sing themselves " ; it is not because he would have us learn a lesson in botany :

> Excellent herbs had our fathers of old—
>   Excellent herbs to ease their pain—
> Alexanders and Marigold,
>   Eyebright, Orris and Elecampane.
> Basil, Rocket, Valerian, Rue,
>   (Almost singing themselves they run)
> Vervain, Dittany, Call-me-to-you—
> Cowslip, Melicot, Rose of the Sun.

Anything green that grew out of the mould
Was an excellent herb to our fathers of old.

We need not, you see, lose our enjoyment of the music of the verse even though we remain ignorant of the allusion.

As to this, Mr. Crothers in *The Gentle Reader*, writes :

The poets who delight us with their verses are not always serious-minded persons with an important thought to communicate. When I read

In Xanadu did Kubla Khan
A stately pleasure-dome decree,

I am not a bit wiser than I was before, but I am a great deal happier ; although I have not the slightest idea where Xanadu was, and only the vaguest notion of Kubla Khan.

And perhaps you will be amused by this outburst of his :

Suppose these lines from *Paradise Lost* to be taken for study :

Thick as autumnal leaves that strow the brooks
In Vallombrosa, where th' Etrurian shades,
High over-arched embower, or scattered sedge
Afloat, when with fierce winds Orion armed
Hath vexed the Red Sea coast, whose waves o'erthrew
Busiris and his Memphian chivalry.

What an opportunity this presents to the schoolmaster ! " Come, now," he cries with pedagogic glee, " answer me a few questions. Where is Vallombrosa ? What is the character of its autumnal foliage ? Bound Etruria. What is sedge ? Explain the myth of Orion. Point out the constellation on the map of the heavens. Where is the Red Sea ? Who was Busiris ? By what other name is he known ? Who were the Memphian chivalry ? "

Here is material for exhaustive research in geography, ancient and modern, history, botany, astronomy, meteorology, chronology, and archæology. The industrious student may get almost as much information out of *Paradise Lost* as from one of those handy compilations of useful knowledge which are sold on the railway cars for twenty-five cents. As for the poetry of Milton, that is another matter.

AMBIGUITY

People who like this sort of thing will find this the sort of thing they like.

(PRESIDENT LINCOLN'S criticism of a book.)

A statement is ambiguous when it may be interpreted by the hearer or the reader in more than one way. The ambiguity may be intended, as in President Lincoln's sentence. It may be, usually is, unintended, and result from carelessness or want of skill : such was the cricket reporter's " Then they tried Parker with his three short legs ".

" Equivocation " was Macbeth's word for ambiguity :

> I pull in resolution, and begin
> To doubt the equivocation of the fiend
> That lies like truth.

And later he exclaims,

> Be these juggling fiends no more believed
> That palter with us in a double sense
> That kept the word of promise to our ear
> And break it to our hope.

AMERICAN ENGLISH

Most people in the United States of America and in Canada speak English ; nearly all of them understand English. We may, perhaps rightly, speak of the American version of the English language ; we are not justified in using the term " American language ". The sounds may differ as when our *futile, fertile, agile* come to be pronounced with the short *i,* when our *temporarily* and *primarily* have the accent on *ar* instead of on the first syllable, when *leisure* rhymes with *seizure* not *pleasure,* and when we make the first syllable of *schedule* into *shed,* while in America it is *sked.* And, while we listened to the broadcast of the assumption by President Roosevelt of a fourth term of office, we were ever and again startled by *ceremónies* ; with a long-drawn-out and accented *mon.* But the language of the United States is still English, we have little difficulty in understanding it when we read American magazines or when we listen to the talk in American films. We and the Americans are alike " subjects of King Shakespeare ". Some divergences there are, however, between the English on this side of the Atlantic and the English on the other side.

We may be, temporarily at any rate, in a difficulty. The " candy store " does not immediately call into mind " sweet shop ". But we know the comparison " as sweet as sugar candy ".

Perhaps, too, we know that Shakespeare used " candied " with the sense of " sweet ", " flattering " : Hamlet says to his friend Horatio—

> Nay do not think I flatter. . . .
> No, let the candied tongue lick absurd pomp,
> And crook the pregnant hinges of the knee,
> Where thrift may follow fawning.

" Candy " with us, however, is the piece of crystallised sugar, made by several boilings and slow evaporation. In America the word extends over the whole range of confectionery containing sugar, and is used in the plural as often as in the singular : " The simple candies of yore—peppermint sticks, gum drops, candy hearts inscribed with sentimental mottoes—are supplemented by bread confectionery."

So with other words there may be a passing doubt : " Phonograph " for our " gramophone ", " fruit pie " for our " fruit tart ", " collar button " for our " collar stud ", " cookies " or " crackers " for our " biscuit ", " muffin " for our " scone " or " tea-cake ", " suspenders " for our " braces ", " bill " (" A dime makes as much noise on a collection plate as a quarter, and both make more noise than a bill. If you don't want your left hand to know what your right hand doeth, put in a bill ") for our " bank-note ", " automobile " for our " motor-car ", and " commuters " for our " season-ticket holders ". Being in New York you ask for " christmas snappers ". Ask for " crackers " and you get our " biscuits ", for " biscuits " and you get " muffins ", for " muffins " and you get " scones ". And if you should wish to have " punctures mended ", you must find a garage that announces " flats fixed ".

During the war years many British girls married American soldiers ; and the United States War Department thought it desirable to issue a delightful little book called *A Bride's Guide to the U.S.A.* Here is a little from *The Times*' comment on the guide :

Two pages of this booklet are devoted to a glossary of English words and phrases and their American equivalents— a useful item, which, in the reverse direction, was a feature of the previous pamphlet. Careful study may now save the British bride in America from receiving scones when she asks

for biscuits, and from being startled by a pair of " cloth over-
shoes " when she expects galoshes. Biscuits, she is told, will
henceforth be " cookies " or " crackers ", and galoshes will be
" rubbers ". More surprising still, boots become shoes, the
ground floor becomes the first floor, and a face flannel is con-
jured into a wash rag or wash cloth. All this suggests alarm
and despondency, but, as any American in Britain will tell
you, is not nearly so bad as it sounds. At first the bride will
doubtless prefer her accustomed margarine to oleomargarine,
pram to baby carriage, and chips to French fried potatoes.
(This last is certainly a mouthful ; it is remarkable how often
the old world beats the new for brevity.)

On the question of pronunciation the pamphlet is wisely
cautious. " Change your pronunciation if it causes misunderstanding—otherwise don't." The British bride may supplement this, if she desires, by studying HORWILL's " Modern
American Usage ", which will tell her such necessary things
as that the " ch " in " schedule " is hard, and that many
Americans pronounce the first syllable of " tutor " as " too ".
It will even give her CAROLYN WELLS's limerick :

> A tutor who tooted the flute
> Tried to tutor two tooters to toot.
>   Said the two to the tutor,
>   " Is it harder to toot or
> To tutor two tooters to toot ? "

No doubt after a year or so in the bosom of the " gigantic
daughter of the West " she will be tooting harmoniously with
the best of them. All these differences, when examined, seem
so small and superficial that they almost melt away entirely
under the sun of common sympathies. And the prevalence
of American films in British cinemas has given most British
brides such a thorough grounding in the American idiom that
they receive the equivalent of a flying start. They really have
little to worry about.

ANAGRAM

(a) How well her name an " Army " doth present,
    In whom the " Lord of Hosts " did pitch His tent.
    (GEORGE HERBERT.)

(b) This Gustavus (whose anagram is Augustus) was a great
    captain.
    (HOWELL.)

The Greek prefix *ana-* implies change, the Greek verb *graphein* is " to write " ; an anagram is a writing anew. It is a changing about of the letters in a word so as to produce a new word : *wed* is an anagram of *dew ; star* is an anagram of *tars ;* and, with no justification, some make an anagram of *Eva*, " the mother of mankind ", into *vae*, she being (they say) the source of all our woe ; *send ark* is an anagram of *darkens*.

The anagram is a frequent visitor to the cross-word puzzle. The clue, for instance, is " An insistent person—seen in trickles ", and you are expected to find in *trickles* an anagram of *stickler*.

Army in example (*a*) is an anagram of *Mary*. Regarding example (*b*) it will be recalled that in Middle English the two symbols *u* and *v* were used without distinction except that *v* was preferred when the letter began a word and *u* in the interior of a word : thus *vnder* and *euer* for *under* and *ever*.

ANALOGY

(*a*) Analogy is not proof but only illustration.

(*b*) " Can you apply a parable ? " he added, laying his hand upon Will's shoulder, " It is not the same thing as a reason, but usually vastly more convincing."

(Stevenson, Will o' the Mill.)

(*c*) As for the possibility of the House of Lords preventing ere long a reform of Parliament, I hold it to be the most absurd notion that ever entered into human imagination. I do not mean to be disrespectful. But the attempt of the Lords to stop the progress of reform reminds me of the great storm at Sidmouth, and of the conduct of the excellent Mrs. Partington on that occasion. In the winter of 1824, there set in a great flood upon the town—the tide rose to an incredible height—the waves rushed in upon the houses and everything was threatened with destruction. In the midst of this sublime and terrible storm, Dame Partington, who lived upon the Beach, was seen at the door of her house with mop and pattens, pushing away the Atlantic Ocean. The Atlantic was roused, Mrs. Partington's spirit was up ; but I need not tell you that the contest was unequal. The Atlantic Ocean beat Mrs. Partington. She was excellent at a slop, or a puddle, but she should not have meddled with a tempest. Gentlemen, be at your ease—be quiet and steady. You will beat Mrs. Partington.

(SYDNEY SMITH, during the controversy on
the First Reform Bill.)

Analogy is a comparison for the purpose of persuading. We show that two things are alike in some respects; and we ask our audience to think the things alike in other respects too. The analogy may help to convince though it does fall short of proving the point at issue. It may, indeed, mislead—as it did Lord Abinger when he started the legal doctrine of " common employment " on its chequered career. A butcher's workman was injured through the carelessness of a fellow-worker; the injured worker sued the butcher for damages; but in the result he failed.

If [said Lord Abinger] the master be liable to the servant in this action, the principle of that liability will be found to carry us to an alarming extent. If the owner of a carriage is responsible for the sufficiency of his carriage to his servant, he is responsible for the negligence of his coach-maker, or his harness-maker, or his coachman. The footman, therefore, who rides behind the carriage, may have an action against his master for a defect in the carriage owing to the negligence of the coach-maker, or for a defect in the harness arising from the negligence of the harness-maker, or for drunkenness, neglect, or want of skill in the coachman. Nor is there any reason why the principle should not extend to other classes of cases. The master, for example, would be liable to the servant for the negligence of the chambermaid for putting him into a damp bed; for that of the upholsterer for sending in a crazy bedstead, whereby he was made to fall down while asleep and injure himself; for the negligence of the cook in not properly cleaning the copper vessels used in the kitchen; or of the butcher in supplying the family with meat of a quality injurious to the health; of the builder for a defect in the foundation of the house, whereby it fell, and injured both the master and the servant by the ruins.

The effective analogy does add liveliness to writing. Look at Macaulay's comparison:

The effect of historical reading is analogous, in many respects, to that produced by foreign travel. The student, like the tourist, is transported into a new state of society. He sees new fashions. He hears new modes of expression. His mind is enlarged by contemplating the wide diversities of laws, of morals, and of manners. But men may travel far, and return with minds as contracted as if they had never stirred from their own market-town. In the same manner, men may know the dates of many battles and the genealogies of many royal houses, and yet be no wiser.

ANALYSIS

(*a*) *The mirage misleads the traveller in the Arabian desert.*

("The mirage" is the SUBJECT of this Simple Sentence. The rest is the PREDICATE, consisting of Transitive Verb, "misleads", Object, "the traveller", and what is called EXTENSION OF THE PREDICATE, "in the Arabian desert".)

(*b*) *Beneath the caravan all is dry and bare ; | but | far in advance, | and | far in the rear, is the semblance of refreshing waters.*

(Here we have two Simple Sentences placed in contrast to one another by the conjunction "but". Each part of the Compound Sentence has its own SUBJECT—"all" in the first, "*the semblance of refreshing waters*" in the second—and its own PREDICATE—"*is dry and bare*" in the first, "*is far in advance and far in the rear*" in the second.)

(*c*) *The pilgrims hasten forward | and | find nothing but sand where, an hour before, they had seen a lake.*

(Here we have a Compound of two sentences, the first a Simple Sentence, the second a Complex Sentence, joined by the Conjunction "and". In the Complex Sentence we have a clause, "*Where, an hour before, they had seen a lake*", doing duty in place of an Adverb. We may call this clause an Adverbial Clause : it extends the assertion —the Predicate—made by the Verb "*find*".)

(*d*) *They turn their eyes and see a lake where, an hour before, they were toiling through sand.*

(Here we have a Compound Sentence, similar in structure to (*c*).)

(The four sentences together constitute a paragraph of Macaulay's prose.)

You ANALYSE when you separate a sentence into its elements : you are then able to see the more clearly the relation of the

elements towards one another.   This breaking up of the structure
is more than an interesting mental exercise.   It helps to make
us appreciate the merit of good composition : we see plainly
the skill displayed, and we are induced to take greater pains
with our own composition.   ANALYSIS will not of itself make us
good composers.   It must help, though, provided we exercise
our analytical power upon examples of good composition—such
examples, for instance, as those four sentences making up one
of Macaulay's paragraphs.

Look, for instance, at this paragraph : it opens Stevenson's
delightful little story, " Will o' the Mill ".   Notice how both
the structure and the length of the sentences are varied.   Analyse
the sentences : pick out first the two chief elements, Subject
and Predicate ; then range around these the words and phrases
that develop their meaning.   Here is the paragraph :

The Mill where Will lived with his adopted parents stood
in a falling valley between pinewoods and great mountains.
Above, hill after hill soared upwards until they soared out of
the depth of the hardiest timber, and stood naked against the
sky.   Some way up, a long grey village lay like a seam or a
rag of vapour on a wooded hillside ; and, when the wind was
favourable, the sound of the church bells would drop down,
thin and silvery, to Will.   Below, the valley grew ever steeper
and steeper, and at the same time widened out on either hand ;
and from an eminence beside the mill it was possible to see
its whole length, and away beyond it over a wide plain, where
the river turned and shone, and moved on from city to city
on its voyage towards the sea.   It chanced that over this
valley there lay a pass into a neighbouring kingdom, so that,
quiet and rural as it was, the road that ran along beside the
river was a high thoroughfare between two splendid and
powerful societies.

Nor is this all we get from the practice of analysis ; for we can
hardly hope to understand fully the more complicated sentences
in great writings unless we analyse them into their elements.   We
cannot perhaps grasp the full import of this, the conclusion of a
much longer sentence of Milton's, at first reading :

I began thus far to assent both to them and divers of my
friends here at home, and not less to an inward prompting
which now grew daily upon me, that by labour and intent

31

study, which I take to be my portion in this life, joined with the strong propensity of nature, I might perhaps leave something so written to aftertimes, as they should not willingly let it die.

By sorting out the elements, however, by looking at them separately and making clear to ourselves how they stand towards one another, we get the full meaning. The core is this:

I began . . . to assent . . . that . . . I might . . . leave something so written.

ANTI-CLIMAX. (See " Climax ")

(a) And thou Dalhoussy the Great God of War,
Lieutenant-Colonel to the Earl of Mar.

(b) *Magnus :* You are lovely : you are divine (*she cannot restrain a gesture of triumph*). And you are enormously amusing.
  (*This anti-climax is too much for Orinthia's exaltation ; but she is too clever not to appreciate it.*)
(G. B. SHAW, The Apple Cart.)

(c) John Stuart Mill,
By a mighty effort of will,
Overcame his natural bonhomie,
And wrote " Principles of Political Economy ".
(EDMUND CLERIHEW BENTLEY.)

(d) But thousands die, without or this or that,
Die and endow a college—or a cat.
(POPE.)

The ANTI-CLIMAX—the descent, in contrast to the height before—may be purposed as in the examples ; and we laugh with the author. The effect of the impressive opening is cancelled, in an unexpected way, by a triviality. The anti-climax may, however, be unconscious and be, as a result, a little ludicrous. Then it is that we laugh at the author. Perhaps, for instance, you will consider that a little re-arrangement would improve this : " Our hills and dales, our hearths and homes, our wives and daughters, our flocks and herds, lie at the mercy of the invader." And the Chronicles might with advantage have left out the concluding sentence, in the account : " The rest of the acts of Asa, and all his might, and the cities which he built, are they not written in the chronicles of the kings of

Judah ? Nevertheless in the time of his old age he was diseased in his feet."

Perhaps you may think that Shakespeare's comment on his art is spoiled by the anti-climax of the last two lines :

> The poet's eye, in a fine frenzy rolling,
> Doth glance from heaven to earth, from earth to heaven ;
> And as imagination bodies forth
> The form of things unknown, the poet's pen
> Turns them to shapes, and gives to airy nothing
> A local habitation, and a name.
> Such tricks hath strong imagination
> That, if it would but apprehend some joy
> It comprehends some bringer of that joy :
> Or in the night, imagining some fear,
> How easy is a bush supposed a bear ?
>
> (*A Midsummer Night's Dream*, V, I.)

ANTITHESIS

(*a*) Thou shalt wax, and he shall dwindle.

(*b*) Oh, could I flow like thee, and make thy stream
My great example, as it is my theme !
Though deep, yet clear ; though gentle, yet not dull ;
Strong, without rage ; without o'erflowing, full.

> (DENHAM, writing of the Thames.)

(*c*) People who saw nothing of the godly but their uncouth visages and heard nothing from them but their groans and their whining hymns, might laugh at them. But those had little reason to laugh who encountered them in the hall of debate or in the field of battle.

> (LORD MACAULAY, writing of the Puritans.)

(*d*) Now, since these dead bones have already outlasted the living ones of Methuselah, and in a yard under ground and thin walls of clay outworn all the strong and specious buildings above it, and quietly rested under the drums and tramplings of three conquests, what prince can promise such diuturnity unto his relics ?

> (SIR THOMAS BROWNE, *Urn Burial*.)

(*e*) They that sow in tears shall reap in joy ; and he that goeth forth and weepeth, shall doubtless come home again with rejoicing, bringing his sheaves with him. (Psalms.)

(*f*) Slaves fight for what were better cast away—
The chain that binds them, and a tyrant's sway ;
But they that fight for freedom undertake
The noblest cause mankind can have at stake.

(COWPER, *Table Talk.*)

When you place two ideas in contrast to one another, you compose an ANTITHESIS (the plural of which is ANTITHESES). " But " and " yet " are the usual ushers of the contrasted idea. A well-devised antithesis quickens the attention and impresses the idea conveyed. See how effectively Bacon in his *Essays* contrasts Prosperity with Adversity—

The virtue of Prosperity is temperance, the virtue of Adversity is fortitude ; which in morals is the more heroical virtue. Prosperity is the blessing of the Old Testament ; Adversity is the blessing of the New : which carrieth the greater benediction, and the clearer revelation of God's favour. Yet, even in the Old Testament, if you listen to David's harp, you shall hear as many hearse-like airs as carols ; and the pencil of the Holy Ghost hath laboured more in describing the afflictions of Job than the felicities of Solomon. Prosperity is not without many fears and distastes ; and Adversity is not without comfort and hope. We see in needleworks and embroideries it is more pleasing to have a lively work upon a sad and solemn ground than to have a dark and melancholy work upon a lightsome ground ; judge therefore of the pleasure of the heart by the pleasure of the eye. Certainly virtue is like precious odours, most fragrant when they are incensed or crushed : for Prosperity doth best discover vice, but Adversity doth best discover virtue.

Macaulay was very fond of the stamping emphasis that is given by antithesis. Thus, he writes of Lord Byron : " He had a head which statuaries loved to copy, and a foot the deformity of which the beggars in the street mimicked."

APHESIS

Modern *squire* is older *esquire*, *rise* and *wake* and *round* are doublets of *arise* and *awake* and *around*. *Aggrieve* and *grieve*, *account* and *count* have much the same meanings. *Prentice* is a beheaded form of *apprentice*, *spy* of *espy*, *state* of *estate*, *cute* of *acute*, *'gainst* of *against*, *lone* of *alone*, *peal* of *appeal*, *sample* of *example*, *special* of *especial*, *story* of *history*, *venture* of *adven-*

ture. A like beheading has resulted in the surnames *Tolly* from *Saint Bartholomew*, *Tedman* from *Saint Edmund*, *Tobin* from *Saint Aubyn*.

This gradual and unintended loss of a weak syllable at the beginning of a word is sometimes called APHESIS. Thus, *casement* is aphetic for *encasement*, that which holds a thing together. The sergeant-major's *'shun* for *attention* and the child's *'cept* for *except* and *coz* for *because* are similar cuttings.

APOSTROPHE (POSSESSIVE CASE)

(*a*) There is not wind enough to twirl
The one red leaf, the last of its clan
That dances as often as dance it can,
Hanging so light, and hanging so high,
On the topmost twig that looks up at the sky.
    Hush beating heart of Christabel!
    Jesu, Marie, shield her well!
She folded her arms beneath her cloak,
And stole to the other side of the oak.

(COLERIDGE, *Christabel.*)

(*b*) The Atlantic was roused, Mrs. Partington's spirit was up; but I need not tell you that the contest was unequal.

Strōphē, a word of two syllables, is the Greek word meaning *aside* or *away*. The word of four syllables (*ăpŏstrŏfē*) is properly applied to an exclamatory address to a particular person. The speaker interrupts the course of the speech in order to invoke a dead or absent person. Note the apostrophe in Coleridge's lines above. The word when used of the sign that indicates omission of letters is properly one of three syllables (*ăpŏstrŏf*). Perhaps, however, we had better conform to custom and make of both words four syllables.

The old termination to mark the possessive was "es": the modern representative of this is *'s*.

The apostrophe is a printer's device, its purpose being to show the omission of a letter: it still does this in expressions like "I'll see" and "You can't". The sign was once used in plurals; it is still used in instances like the following, where its omission might lead to misunderstanding—

There are too many *and*'s in the sentence.
Dot your *i*'s and cross your *t*'s.

35

The mark denotes omission also in words like *can't* (for *cannot*) and *don't* (for *do not*).

The rules for the possessive apostrophe that emerge from the practice of good writers are these :

(a) *Always* add the apostrophe for the possessive, and *whenever you can*, the *s* also.

(b) Do not add the *s* when its addition would result in a disagreeable sound.

Thus : *the writer's words* (where we mean *one* writer) ; but *the writers' words* (where we mean *several* writers : the addition of another *s* sound to *writers'* would produce an ill-sounding hiss). We have *the men's service* (the *s* is attached to the plural) ; *the ladies' department* (the noun is made plural *before* being made possessive. Notice that the possessive *s* is like the *s* in *this*, whereas the plural *s* is like the *s* in *was*. The plural *s* often modifies a preceding consonant ; but the possessive *s* leaves the preceding consonant unaffected. Compare *wives*—" Husbands, love your wives, and be not bitter against them "—with *wife's*— " Such was the wife's dowry."

The use of the apostrophe with proper nouns varies. Three Londoners will have three ways of writing the name of the park of Saint James : there will be the full " Saint James's Park " ; the curtailed " St. James' Park " ; and the more curtailed " St. James Park ". Nor can we say with any assurance which of these three is most prevalent. *The Times* prefers the full, even though this does result in a superfluity of sibilants. " If ", runs its leader, " St. James's Square keeps on going gay in its present reckless fashion, there will scarcely be even a memory left of the old London House." Now and then indeed, we get a formal ruling upon the matters. Thus we are enjoined by the whole august Board of Directors of Lloyds Bank to omit the apostrophe and to call the bank " Lloyds ". (We get, indeed, there a useful distinction from the great insurance institution which still calls itself " Lloyd's ". But to get the distinction was not the impelling motive for the omission : for we have a similar simplifying in " Barclays Bank ".) Insistence on the possessive sign is quite modern. In the first presentation to the world of Milton's *l'Allegro* there are, for instance, only two signs of the possessive. They occur in

36

> Nods, and Becks, and Wreathed Smiles
> Such as hang on Hebe's cheek.

and in

> Then lies him down the Lubbar Fend,
> And stretched out all the chimney's length
> Basks at the fire his hairy strength.

other possessives are without distinctive sign. Thus

> Then to the well-trod stage anon,
> If Jonsons learned Sock be on
> Or sweetest Shakespeare fancies childe,
> Warble his native wood-notes wilde.

APOTHEGM (or APOPHTHEGM)

(*a*) Diogenes said of a young man that danced daintily, and was much commended : " The better, the worse."

(LORD BACON, Apothegms.)

(*b*) He that hath wife and children hath given hostages to fortune ; for they are impediments to great enterprises, either of virtue or mischief.

(LORD BACON, Essays.)

The apothegm is a statement in a few words intended to startle the hearers and make them attend to what the speaker considers —or pretends to consider—an important truth. Usually the apothegm for the purpose of emphasis exaggerates, or it discards all qualifications, or it asserts as general what is true only of some instances (perhaps even of a minority of the instances). Thus when Johnson suddenly uttered an apothegm at which many will start : " Patriotism is the last refuge of a scoundrel ", he was talking to triumph rather than for truth. And his comment on Goldsmith was not intended to be taken as strict truth : " No man was more foolish when he had not a pen in his hand, or more wise when he had."

APPROPRIATE PREPOSITIONS

(*a*) The money *in* your possession is money *at* your disposal.

(*b*) Being unconscious *of* the need he was insensible *to* the proposal.

(*c*) You acquiesce *in* a proposal when you agree *to* it.

Is there a difference between " a taste of the pleasures of life " and " a taste for the pleasures of life " ? Yes. " Taste of " is equivalent to a " sample ", it is something of a test. " A taste of the pleasures of life " is a participation in them. " Taste for " implies a liking, a propensity towards : " A taste for the pleasures of life " is a desire to enjoy them.

The appropriate preposition is often a matter of custom— an idiom—for which no very convincing reason can be given. We say " *agree with him* " and " *agree to his proposal* ", but " *disagree with both him and his proposal* "; we say " *confidence in him* ", " *an objection to your writing* ", " *conduct offending against good manners* ", and so on.

Look, too, at the manner in which a preposition modifies meaning. You consult a solicitor when you seek his advice : you consult with your friends when you consider a matter in their company and with their help. You attend school when you make attendances ; you attend to your lesson when you give your attention to it. You lecture to an appreciative audience, and your words are welcome ; you lecture a lazy student and your words may not be so welcome. You witness an accident when you see it ; you witness to a man's honesty when you testify to it. You own a book ; it is your property. You own to a fault ; you acknowledge it. You swear fidelity, when you make a promise for the future ; you swear to an occurrence that you have seen in the past. You have finished your paper, when you have done what you can with it in the time allotted to you ; you have finished with the paper, when you have read all you want to read in it.

Here is a selection of words followed by suitable prepositions :

abhorrence of (" a right abhorrence of such conduct ")
access to (" He importunes access to you ")
access of (" an access of fever ")
accommodate to (" accommodate the eye to different dis-
    tances ")
accommodate with (" accommodate a person with lodgings ")
accompanied by (" accompanied by his wife ")
accompanied with (" a word accompanied with a blow ")
accord with (" a firm and lasting accord with France ")
accuse of (" to accuse him of felony ")
acquiesce in (" not to protest against is to acquiesce
    in ")
adapted to (" measures adapted to the needs ")

adept in (" adept in the secrets of the art ")

adverse to (" a vote adverse to the proposal ")

affinity to *or* between (" related by affinity ")

blame for (" he is to blame for it ")

coincide with (" his interest coincided with his duty ")

compare with *or* to (" shall I compare thee to a summer's day ? ")

compatible with (" heat is compatible with moisture ")

conformable to (" this is conformable to reason ")

conversant with (" conversant with questions of finance ")

correspond with (" silver penny supposed to correspond with a pennyweight ")

correspond to (" the body corresponds to external conditions ")

destitute of (" a barren waste destitute of trees ")

differ from (" one star differeth from another star in glory "). But the preposition *with* is found with persons : " We'll never differ with a crowded pit."

different from (but *to* is quite usual and is probably encroaching)

disappointed of (" Miserably disappointed of his expectations ")

disappointed in (" I am disappointed in him ")

divide between (" Divide with reason between self-love and society ")

divide among (" He divided Canaan among the Israelites ")

emerge from (" to emerge from the crowd ")

enjoin upon (" enjoin upon them strict obedience ")

foreign to *or* from (" foreign to people's thoughts ", " foreign from his purpose ")

healed of (" healed of my infatuation ")

impose upon (" a burden imposed upon the people ")

independent of, *but* dependent on *or* upon

militate against *or* for (" all the facts militate for and not against this conclusion ")

necessary to (" Light so necessary is to life ")

prevail against (" The gates of hell shall not prevail against it ")

reconcile to *or* with (" Custom reconciles us to everything ", " Reconcile thyself with thy God ")

reflect upon (" the charge reflects upon his employer ")

rely upon (" rely upon thy virtue ")

replete with (" gardens replete with flowers ")

sensible *or* to (" sensible to feeling as to sight ")
thirst after *or* for (" hunger and thirst after righteousness ",
" thirst for revenge ").

ARGUMENT (DEDUCTION : INDUCTION)

(*a*) In arguing, too, the parson owned his skill ;
For, e'en though vanquished, he could argue still ;
While words of learned length and thundering sound
Amazed the gazing rustics ranged around.

(GOLDSMITH'S Village Schoolmaster in *The Deserted Village*.)

(*b*) All argument, but most his plays, persuade
That for anointed dullness he was made.

(DRYDEN, writing of his rival, Shadwell.)

(*c*) Myself when young did eagerly frequent
Doctor and Saint, and heard great argument
About it and about ; but evermore
Came out by the same door as in I went.

(*Omar Khayyám.*)

You argue when you use language for the purpose of reasoning ; you argue effectively when you succeed in persuading yourself or others. In the English language you have an admirable means of argument. For by its use you can do these three things : you can put ideas into words ; you can thereby make a record of the ideas and ponder over them ; from these recorded ideas you can reach out to farther and ever farther fields of knowledge.

You reason by DEDUCTION (*a posteriori*) when you proceed from effects to causes, from particular statements to a general rule. It is deductive argument when from a number of observed facts—" A man does not give twopence for a thing he can get as easily for a penny " and the like—you evolve the economic law " Men scheme to achieve their aims by the easiest means."

You reason by INDUCTION (*a priori*) when you proceed from causes to effects, from an abstract statement to its particular application. It is inductive reasoning when you assert : " People resent being under compulsion ; we may expect them, therefore, to evade a law when they can do so with impunity."

The modes by which through argument you may influence men's minds are many. Some of these modes have distinctive names. There is *argumentum ad hominem*, based upon the supposed wants and wishes of those addressed, the *argument ad crumenam*, addressed to the purse of those addressed rather than to their reason, the *argumentum ad baculinam*, the threat of force rather than the appeal to reason, and so on.

ARTICLE ("A" or "THE")

> I promised, if you'd watch a dinner out,
> We'd see truth dawn together—truth that peeps
> Over the glass's edge when dinner's done.

In "a dinner" *a* is sometimes called the INDEFINITE ARTICLE : in "the glass's edge" *the* is sometimes called the DEFINITE ARTICLE. Of one politician it was said that he was never in want of a word ; he always had something or other at his command. Of his rival it was said that he was never in want of the word ; he had at command the exact word wanted for his purpose. *A* or *an* is "one of a number", the old meaning of "one" being clearly seen in phrases like, "A penny a mile ", "If two ride on a horse, one must ride behind."

The is connected with *this* and *that* ("Demonstrative Adjectives" we call them). *The* marks out the individual. In such phrases as "the more the merrier ", "the less said the sooner mended ", *the* is more an adverb of degree than an adjective. The expansion of the second phrase is "to-the-extent that we say less, to-that-extent mending will be speeded up ". So in Shakespeare's line "The fewer men, the greater share of honour." *The* is in such a phrase *by so much*. In sentences like

> How sleep the brave who sink to rest
> By all their country's wishes blest !

the is again the Article, turning the adjective "brave" into a noun. So in the lines,

> To each his suffering : all are men
>   Condemned alike to groan ;
> The tender for another's pain
>   Th' unfeeling for his own.

ASSIMILATION

Latin *tempus* is English *tense*, Latin *amita* is English *aunt*, Latin *comitem* is English *count*, the *n* sound being closer to the *t* and the *k* sound than the *m* sound is.

The sounds in a word—more particularly the sounds of *l* and *n* and *r*—have a tendency to imitate, to slip into one another, as we say the words. The changed form may, indeed, become the recognised form of the word. This tendency of a sound to imitate its neighbours is ASSIMILATION. Instances in addition to those given above are these. In many of our English words the *v* or *f* sound has become merged into the sound of a following consonant. The Old English for *lady* was *hlæfdige* (the loaf-kneader); our word *poor* once, like the French word *pauvre* and like the English word *poverty*, had the *v* sound. Our *curfew* is *cover-fire* (*couvrefeu*), our *kerchief* is *cover-head* (*couvrechef*).

ASSONANCE. (See "**Echoes**")

(*a*) In Xanadu did Kubla Khan
    A stately pleasure-dome decree,
    Where Alph the sacred river ran
    Through caverns measureless to man.

(COLERIDGE.)

(*b*) Make me thy lyre, even as the forest is :
    What if my leaves are falling like its own ?
    The tumult of thy mighty harmonies
    Will take from both a deep autumnal tone.

(SHELLEY.)

Note in (*b*) the prevailing *m* sound, the *l* (of *lyre, leaves, falling, like*), the *f* and *v* (of *forest, falling, even, leaves*), and so on.

Here are four lines from a poem of Robert Bridges. Read the lines aloud and notice the quite striking repetition of sounds, repetition that adds greatly to the delight of the lines :

Wanton with long delay the gay spring leaping cometh,
    The blackthorn starreth now his bough on the eve of May,
All day in the sweet box tree the bee for pleasure hummeth,
    The cuckoo sends afloat his note on the air all day.

You have, besides the end-rhymes—*cometh, hummeth ; May-day*—the internal rhymes—*delay, gay ; now, bough ; tree, bee ; afloat, note*. You have the pleasing repetition of the *l* sound in *long, delay, leaping* and of the *b* sound in *blackthorn, bough*. And the last two words, *all day*, leave you with the echo of the preceding *a* sounds : *delay, gay, May, all day*. This echoing of sounds in syllables or words is sometimes called ASSONANCE.

AUXILIARY VERBS

(a) " *The Danes,* an' please your honour," quoth the corporal,
" who were on the left at the siege of Limerick, were all
auxiliaries."—" And very good ones," said my uncle *Toby.*
—" But the auxiliaries, *Trim,* my brother is talking about,
—I conceive to be different things."

(Tristram Shandy.)

(b) Alice could see, as well as if she were looking over their
shoulders, that all the jurors were writing down " stupid
things " on their slates, and she could even make out that
one of them didn't know how to spell " stupid ", and that he
had to ask his neighbour to tell him.   " A nice muddle their
slates will be in before the trial's over," thought Alice.

(Alice in Wonderland.)

In English we have a great number of verbs that are used
to form tenses, moods, voices, and so on, of other verbs. These
are AUXILIARY VERBS. In the Alice extract the words *could,
were, did, had, will,* are auxiliaries. These auxiliaries are not
easily mastered by foreigners ; and some who are not foreigners
at times use the wrong auxiliary.

The English language differs from Latin (and in a less degree
from French) in having additional words rather than modifications in the words themselves to indicate modifications in
meaning. We have auxiliaries of Tense. " I talk " is a statement in the Present Tense ; " I shall talk " and " he will talk "
are statements in the Future Tense. We have auxiliaries of
Voice : " I saw the race " is in the Active Voice ; " The race
was seen by me " is in the Passive Voice.

B

BALLAD

(a) The king sits in Dunfermline town
     Drinking the blood-red wine.

(Beginning of the Ballad of Sir Patrick Spens.)

(b) There was a youth, and a well-beloved youth,
     And he was an esquire's son,
He loved the bailiff's daughter dear,
     That lived in Islington.

(The Bailiff's Daughter of Islington.)

(*c*) A wandering minstrel I—
  A thing of shreds and patches,
Of ballads, songs and snatches
  And dreamy lullaby.

(W. S. GILBERT, The Mikado.)

The ballad was at the first a song to dance to. *Ballet* is a word kin to *ballade*. We now use the name to signify a simple story in verse, usually in the form above. The " melancholy Jacques " speaks of such sentimental song—" And then the lover, sighing like furnace, with a woful ballad made to his mistress' eyebrow." Many are like Sir Philip Sidney in their delight in the old ballads. Of *Chevy Chase* he wrote : " Certainly I must confess mine own barbarousness, I never hear the old tale of Percy and Douglas, that I found not my heart moved more than with a trumpet." Others despise them, or pretend to do so : and, indeed, it is easy to make fun of them. Thus, Calverly has :

  The farmer's daughter hath soft brown hair,
    (*Butter and eggs and a pound of cheese*)
  And I met with a ballad, I can't say where,
    Which wholly consisted of lines like these.

And Doctor Johnson, too, mimicked the simple language of the ballad :

    As with my hat upon my head,
      I walked along the Strand,
    I there did meet another man,
      With his hat in his hand.

Perhaps, too, you remember how vigorously the Host interrupted Chaucer's ballad : " For Heaven's sake, no more of this ", he said, " My ears ache with your silly doggerel." Yet he was accounted a wise man who said, " If I were permitted to make all the ballads, I need not care who should make the laws of a nation."

BATHOS. (See "**Climax**")
    Mark him of shoulders curved, of stature tall,
    Black hair and vivid eye and meagre cheek,
    His prominent features like an eagle's beak.

Bathos is the Greek word for *depth*. When there is a descent from the elevated to the commonplace, we may speak of

" BATHOS ": " Bathos, the art of sinking in poetry ", is one of Pope's titles. Often enough the descent is unintended by its author ; and his hearers laugh at him instead of with him : the speaker, called upon to praise Oxford, speaks of its glories ; and he continues, " And when I speak of Oxford, I do not think of this college or that college but of Oxford as a whole. And, gentlemen, what a whole Oxford is ! "

BLANK VERSE

(a) The night was winter in his roughest mood,
The morning sharp and clear. But now at noon,
Upon the southern side of the slant hills,
And where the woods fence off the northern blast,
The season smiles, resigning all its rage,
And has the warmth of May. The vault is blue
Without a cloud, and white without a speck
The dazzling splendour of the scene below.

(WILLIAM COWPER, *The Task.*)

(b) English heroic verse without rhyme . . . which consists in apt numbers, fit quantity of syllables, and the sense variously drawn out from one verse into another, not in the jingling sound of like endings.

(MILTON's definition of " Blank Verse ".)

BLANK VERSE is verse without end-rhyme. Usually, as in this example from *The Task*, the term is applied to the lines of five iambics (iambic pentameter). The normal line in the plays of the great dramatists is this iambic pentameter, of five feet consisting of an unaccented followed by an accented syllable. Thus, here are two lines from Marlowe,

O, thou art fairer than the evening air,
Clad in the beauty of a thousand stars ;

here are two from Shakespeare,

But, look, the morn, in russet mantle clad,
Walks o'er the dew of yon high eastward hill,

and here two from Milton,

High on a throne of royal state which far
Outshone the wealth of Ormus and of Ind.

You note that the writers, to the advantage of their writings, now and again diverge from the normal iambic foot (unaccented

45

followed by accented syllable). Thus the first foot (" Clad in ") of Marlowe's second line, the first foot (" Walks o'er ") of Shakespeare's second line, and the first foot (" High on ") of Milton's first line are all trochees (accented syllable followed by unaccented). That is, the usual structure of English blank verse is iambic pentameters with variations on them.

BOMBAST. (See also " Hyperbole ")

(*a*) The frantic hero's wild delirium past,
Now insipidity succeeds bombast.

(SHERIDAN, The Critic.)

(*b*) And, if thou prate of mountains, let them throw
Millions of acres on us, till our ground,
Singeing his pate against the burning zone,
Make Ossa like a wart ! Nay, an thou'lt mouth,
I'll rant as well as thou.

(Hamlet.)

(*c*) He is many times flat, insipid ; his comic wit degenerating into clenches, his serious swelling into bombast. But he is always great, when some great occasion is presented to him.

(DRYDEN of Shakespeare in *An Essay of Dramatic Poesy*.)

Lovers and advertisers and others often say more than the truth ; and they usually are understood to say more. Even lovers take the bombast with a grain of salt : thus, poor Medea puts a period to Jason's protestations by :

> " Ah, sweet," she said, " let be,
> Wert thou more fickle than the restless sea,
> Still should I love thee, knowing thee for such."

The law imposes some curb on the extravagant promises of advertisement : but the puff, which is bombast in a minor key, is countenanced and goes unscathed. Mr. Puff, who was an adept at " the puff direct, the puff preliminary, the puff collateral, the puff collusive, and the puff oblique or puff by implication ", explains his method in *The Critic*. He also explains to one who demurs " and do you think there are many who are influenced by this ? " his faith in his prescription " O lud, yes, sir ! the number of those who undergo the fatigue of judging for themselves is very small indeed."

C

CÆSURA

(a) The busy sylphs   surround their darling care,
These set the head,   and those divide the hair,
Some fold the sleeve,   whilst others plait the gown;
And Betty's praised   for labours not her own.
         (POPE, *The Rape of the Lock.*)

(b) Now came still Evening on, and Twilight gray
Had in her sober livery   all things clad;
Silence accompanied;   for beast and bird,
They to their grassy couch,   these to their nest
Were slunk: all but the wakeful nightingale,
She all night long her amorous descant sang.
Silence was pleased;   now glowed the firmament.
         (MILTON, *Paradise Lost.*)

In longer English verses there is usually a break (a cutting or CÆSURA) about the middle of the line. In " To be or not to be—that is the question "; the Cæsura comes after the third foot. In the lines from Pope given above, the Cæsura comes almost uniformly after the second foot. Poets like Milton give variety to their verse by moving the Cæsura, or by omitting it: in example (b) the effect of the smooth flow " She all night long her amorous descant sang " gains by contrasts with the broken lines before and after.

CAPITAL LETTERS AS MEANS OF EMPHASIS

(a) When the KING AND QUEEN were seen in their Coronation Coach near Hyde Park Corner not only by their subjects lining the route, but also by an army of viewers scattered through the Home Counties, it was clear that television was here at last.

         (*The Times.*)

(b) A few days ago the Secretary of the Zoological Society challenged the word " rhinoceri " which appeared in these columns as a plural of " rhinoceros ".

         (*The Times.*)

(c) If there is another European War it will differ from the Great War at least as terribly as the Great War differed from the lesser operations of Napoleon.

         (G. M. TREVELYAN.)

(*d*) Early in 1918, while the war was still raging, the Fourth
Reform Bill was passed by universal consent, giving what
was practically Manhood Suffrage and a large instalment
of the new principle of Woman Suffrage.

(G. M. Trevelyan.)

(*e*) He saw the dark wainscot and timbered roof,
    The long tables, and the faces merry and keen,
The College eight and their trainer dining aloof,
    The Dons on their dais serene.

(H. Newbolt.)

In English there is ample space for the exercise of individual
taste. Consistency is not to be looked for ; nor is consistency
greatly desirable. Here is a firm making it a rule of the house
that the name of its particular goods shall always have the
initial capital. You are not obliged to call the writing with a
capital incorrect, even though writing with a small letter is
quite correct. By the use of the capital the firm declares that
its goods are worth emphasis, they stand out from the generality.
They are *the* goods.

The use of *capitals*—like the use of decorative type or of
italics—is a mechanical device for giving to an important idea
important treatment. It is often quite effective.

Former writers (or printers) made much use of the initial
capital. In Milton's *l'Allegro* as first printed you have, for
instance :

> Haste thee nymph, and bring with Thee
> Jest and youthful Jollity,
> Quips and cranks and wanton Wiles,
> Nods, and Becks, and wreathed Smiles.

The modern printer seems to have the rule, " When in doubt
use lower case ", use the smaller rather than the capital letter.

CAPITALS

(*a*) THE TIMES, MONDAY, MAY 6, 1940.

(*b*) The crucial debate of the week in the House of Commons
will be concerned with the campaign in Norway.

(*c*) That Labour will be found in the Government before the
war is over is certain.

(*d*) You shall go home directly, Le Fever, said my uncle Toby, to my house,—and we'll send for a doctor to see what's the matter,—and we'll have an apothecary,—and the corporal shall be your nurse;—and I'll be your servant, Le Fever.

(*Tristram Shandy*.)

Letters of a special form and of a large size usually head a page, begin a line of poetry, introduce a new sentence. These are CAPITAL (or HEAD) LETTERS. "*Majuscule*" ("*somewhat larger*") as distinct from "*minuscule*" ("*somewhat less*") is at times used as the name.

There is a capital for each proper noun (of day, of month, of place, and of person). There is usually also a capital letter for the adjective corresponding to the noun: *British*, *French*, and so on. But, when the adjective no longer readily calls up its noun, we write the words with a small letter: *saturnine, jovial, stentorian*, and so on.

Thus, *The Times* comments upon certain " Procrustean regulations ", comparing them with " draconic laws ", and in the same breath blames some " tantalising offers ". The assumption seems to be that Procrustes, the fabulous robber that brought about uniformity among his victims by stretching or by mutilating them, is less known among us than the Grecian legislator, Draco, or the severely punished Tantalus.

When a common noun and a proper noun are together, the common noun also has the capital initial: the *River Thames*, *Herne Bay*, and the like: we may write " bishops, priests, and deacons ", but we write " the Bishop of London ".

There is a capital of special design £ to stand as the initial for *libræ* (pounds). The Americans imitate us in this, using the sign $ (pieces of eight) for their dollars, whereas the French are content with a small letter for their francs (fr.).

There is also a capital letter for common nouns that, being used in one special sense, partake of the nature of proper names: *Budget, Sinking Fund*, and the like. We find—" The North felt the depression more than the South " (*North* and *South* being here parts of the country), but " The compass points to the magnetic north." And here is a sentence of Macaulay's: " There were some Nonconformists in the number; for the

Bishops had wisely resolved not to show any distrust of the Protestant Dissenters."

Woolsack is in itself a common noun, but used as a variant of " the honour and power appertaining to the office of the Lord Chancellor " it is a proper noun. In " a man of middle age " the term *middle age* is used in the general sense and the noun *age* is a common noun ; in " the last enchantment of the Middle Age ", the term *Middle Age* is used with a particular significance, and *Age* is a proper noun. Used as a common noun the words begin with a small letter, used as a proper noun they begin with a capital.

The convention regarding capitals in the opening and closing of letters is this : for the opening capitalise each word, " My Dear Sir " ; for the close, capitalise the first and last words, " Your obedient Servant ".

For titles the custom is to give a capital to all the important words : " *Alice's Adventures in Wonderland* " ; " *The Taming of the Shrew* " ; " *The Decline and Fall of the Roman Empire* ", and so on.

There is a capital letter for the initial word of each sentence, and as a rule, for the beginning of lines of poetry.

We may speak of an abstraction as though it were a person. Then, too, the capital is usual—

> Let not Ambition mock their useful toil,
> Their homely joys, or destiny obscure,
> Nor Grandeur hear, with a disdainful smile,
> The short and simple annals of the poor.

Notice that, even after a comma or a colon, a capital is used to usher in a quotation. Thus : " Mr. Churchill said, ' We must respect the rights and opinion of others while holding firmly to our own faith and convictions.' "

CASE. (See " **Nominative** " and " **Objective Case** ")

(*a*) Sir Hugh, persuade me not : I will make a Star-chamber matter of it ; if he were twenty Sir John Falstaffs he shall not abuse Robert Shallow, Esquire.

(*b*) All his successors, gone before him, have done't, and all his ancestors, that come after him, may : they may give the dozen white luces in their coat.

(*c*) Pistol, did you pick Master Slender's purse?

The English language has retained separate forms for the " cases " of pronouns. Thus, in the extracts above (from *The Merry Wives of Windsor*), the pronoun *I* is in the Nominative Case ; the pronoun *me*, being the object of the Transitive Verb *persuade*, is in the Objective Case ; the pronoun *his*, denoting ownership of *successors*, is in the Possessive Case. The only remnant of the old inflexions for indicating the cases of nouns is the apostrophe and *s* for the possessive. Thus *Master Slender's* is, we know from its form quite apart from its work in the sentence, in the Possessive Case.

But, till we look at the relation of each to the other words in the sentence, we cannot tell that Sir John Falstaff is in the Nominative Case and Robert Shallow in the Objective Case. In Latin both *puer puellam amat* and *puellam puer amat* admit of one meaning, " The boy likes the girl." In English the statement " The boy the girl likes " would be hopelessly ambiguous. That is why the position of words in an English sentence is a matter of great importance. And we may define case as " The FORM or POSITION of a Noun or Pronoun that indicates its relation to the other parts of the Sentence." (See further under " *Nominative Case* ", " *Objective Case* ", and " *Apostrophe* ").

CAUSATIVE VERBS

(*a*) What God hath cleansed, that call not thou common.

(*Acts* x. 15.)

(*b*) Lo ! sweetened with the summer light,
The full-juiced apple, waxing over-mellow
Drops in a silent autumn night.

(TENNYSON, *The Lotus-Eaters*.)

Cleansed is *made clean*, *sweetened* is *made sweet*. A verb that thus expresses a cause is a CAUSATIVE VERB. Compare *blacken*, *startle*, *brighter*, and *darker*.

CIRCUMLOCUTION (PERIPHRASIS)

(*a*) In the case of both boys and girls there were many spelling mistakes. (Both boys and girls made many mistakes in spelling.)

51

(b) The climatic conditions were not conducive to the enjoyment of our picnic. (Bad weather spoiled our picnic.)

(c) The answer is in the negative. (The answer is No.)

(d) It cannot in the opinion of His Majesty's Government be classified as slavery in the extreme acceptance of the word without some risk of terminological inexactitude. (So Mr. Churchill in his very early days as a Minister dealt with the question of why the Government had lied in regard to native workers in the South African mines.)

(e) I may truly say with the hook-nosed fellow of Rome— " I came, saw, and overcame."

(Henry IV, II, III.)

CIRCUMLOCUTION is a roundabout way of saying a thing ; it is a using of more words than are needed to express the thought. It would at times seem that an author has made his resolve not to call a thing by its ordinary name—the name that springs to your mind when you think of that thing. He contrives a circumlocution for you ; and you interpret it as you interpret the clues in a crossword puzzle. Wordsworth's robin is " The pensive warbler of the ruddy breast " ; his skylark is the " Ethereal minstrel ! pilgrim of the skies " ; his cuckoo is the " Blithe new comer, darling of the Spring ". He entitles his sonnet " Within King's College Chapel " : the title is requisite ; for you have in the sonnet only " this immense and glorious work of fine intelligence " to denote the subject of the sonnet.

Nearly always, no doubt, the single word is preferable to its expanded substitute : it is far better to say, and to write, *Cheshire Cheese* than *That which Cestria sends*, *Tenacious paste of solid milk* ; better to say *Eggs* than *ovarious food*, which is what the poet Thomson does as he speaks of the cragsman in the Hebrides who

to the rocks
Dire-clinging gathers his ovarious food.

On the statue of Mr. Pitt in the London Guildhall the ending words of the inscription are " He died poor ". Beyond question these words are better than the substitute proposed by an alderman, " He expired in necessitous circumstances ".

Yet the roundabout way of saying a thing, the circumlocution, has its uses. Politeness may dictate it. In *The Times*, for instance, there is the tactful " This perversion of the truth can deceive no one " ; perhaps " This lie " would have been too blunt. The craving after variety may well justify it. Every one of us has the irresistible temptation to expand now and then in our talk. The bare facts make so poor a display that we are well-nigh bound to elaborate.

Besides, these expansions—these ingenious ways of giving freshness to an old idea—give ever so much delight, to their author and to those to whom he speaks. We do, very soon, get a little weary of hearing them—of hearing " The Bard of Avon " for " Shakespeare " or " his prominent feature " for " nose ". At first hearing even these may give pleasure ; and, when a master writer devises fresh ways of saying a thing, the pleasure does not wane. Look, for instance, at Fitzgerald's circumlocution for " savers and spenders "—" those who husbanded the golden grain, And those who flung it to the winds like Rain ". Or see how ingeniously the poet avoids the humdrum name " pair of scissors ". Now it is " a two-edged weapon " :

Clarissa drew with tempting grace
A two-edged weapon from her shining case.

Now it is " the glittering forfex " :

The peer now spreads the glittering forfex wide,
To inclose the lock ; now joins it, to divide.

" The lock of the lady's hair ", that is. Then the scissors becomes " the fatal engine ", and " unresisted steel ". And isn't this a gay expansion of " they drank coffee " ?—

For lo ! the board with cups and spoons is crowned,
The berries crackle, and the mill turns round ;
On shining altars of Japan they raise
The silver lamp ; the fiery spirits blaze :
From silver spouts the grateful liquors glide
While China's earth receives the smoking tide ;
At once they gratify their scent and taste,
And frequent cups prolong the rich repast.

But which of these two versions do you prefer ? The first is that of *The Times* :

The Cabinet have exhaustively examined the procedures for transferring power which may fall to be adopted if the original plan of May 16th, 1946, has finally to be abandoned as unworkable, and precautions have been taken to obviate any delay which might result from further references to London in the course of the approaching conversations by providing in advance so far as possible for any issue that may emerge.

The second is that of Mr. Harold Nicolson in *The Spectator* :

Lord Mountbatten has now received instructions what to do if the 1946 plan fails.

CLICHÉ. (See " **Hackneyed Phrases** ")

(*a*) Watch whether he begins any of his answers with " the fact is ", because that is usually the beginning of a lie.
    (Lady Brocklehurst before beginning the cross-examination of " The Admirable Crichton ".)

(*b*) Whene'er you find " the cooling western breeze ",
    In the next line, it " whispers through the trees " :
    If crystal streams " with pleasing murmurs creep ",
    The reader's threatened, not in vain, with sleep :
    Then, at the last and only couplet fraught
    With some unmeaning thing they call a thought,
    A needless Alexandrine ends the song,
    That, like a wounded snake, drags its slow length along.
                                    (POPE, *Essay on Criticism*.)

[An " Alexandrine " is a line of six feet—twelve syllables —sometimes introduced to give variety in a poem of five-feet lines. The last line of the extract is an instance. The name may have come from twelve-syllabled line poems praising Alexander the Great.]

The literal meaning of the French word CLICHÉ, is " a metal type of wood-engraving, from which prints are made ". It is an easy transfer to the phrase used with annoying frequency, at times indeed not very aptly. " There comes a time in the life of every man " is the preacher's cliché : it recurs in every sermon ; you wait for it and smile when it comes. Do you ever interpose in your talk, " You know " ? It is a curious expletive ; for if your auditor does know, why trouble yourself to tell him—or, usually, her ? Curious the expression is, yet how glibly it comes from our tongues. And what a number of times you have read—perhaps written—" Hoping this will find you as well as it leaves me ! "

Every class has its ever-recurring phrases. The literary

critic cannot get far without speaking of "valuable human document" or "the results of scholarly research" or "well worth reading" or "wealth of detail" or "faint tinge of irony pervades it" or "a genuine contribution to literature" or that "it augurs well for the future of the author". The business man in his letters can hardly help saying "beg to acknowledge", "yours to hand", "of even date", and the like. And some speakers seem to use "as a matter of fact" in lieu of a pause or of "eh-eh", when they would like time to think.

And some phrases seem common to all classes :

"And how does your mistress ?" cried my father, taking the same steps over again from the landing and calling to Susannah, whom he saw passing by the foot of the stairs with a huge pin-cushion in her hand—" How does your mistress ?" "As well," said Susannah, tripping by but without looking up, "as can be expected." "What a fool am I !" said my father, drawing his leg back again—" let things be as they will, brother Toby, 'tis ever the precise answer."

CLIMAX

(a) We have come to dedicate a portion of that field as a final resting-place for those who here gave their lives that the nation might live. It is altogether fit and proper that we should do this. But in a larger sense we cannot dedicate, we cannot consecrate, we cannot hallow this ground.

(From ABRAHAM LINCOLN's Dedicatory Address
at Gettysburg.)

(b) I impeach him in the name of the Commons of Great Britain in Parliament assembled, whose parliamentary trust he has betrayed. I impeach him in the name of all the Commons of Great Britain, whose national character he has dishonoured. I impeach him in the name of the people of India, whose laws, rights, and liberties he has subverted, whose properties he has destroyed, whose country he has laid waste and desolate. I impeach him in the name and by the virtue of those eternal laws of justice which he has violated. I impeach him in the name of human nature itself, which he has cruelly outraged, injured and oppressed in both sexes, in every age, rank, situation, and condition of life.

(Peroration of BURKE's Impeachment of
Warren Hastings.)

(*c*) And now abideth Faith, Hope, Charity—these three: but the greatest of these is Charity.

(1 Corinthians xiii.)

(*d*) Our revels now are ended : these our actors,
As I foretold you, were all spirits and
Are melted into air, into thin air :
And, like the baseless fabric of this vision,
The cloud-capped towers, the gorgeous palaces,
The solemn temples, the great globe itself,
Yea, all which it inherit, shall dissolve ;
And, like this insubstantial pageant faded,
Leave not a rack behind.

(The Tempest.)

(*e*) *Abiit, excessit, evasit, erupit* (Cicero) : " He departed, he withdrew, he went out, he broke forth."

" Climax " is the Greek word for a ladder : when you express ideas of gathering intensity you compose a climax. Consider the three verbs in the last sentence of the Lincoln extract. They all express the setting aside for a special purpose ; but they express this ever more forcibly. The three constitute a climbing up the ladder of feeling.

" To dedicate " is the general term, meaning to make over formally by words spoken or written ; we say, for instance, that the king's highway is dedicated to the use of the public. " To consecrate " is to dedicate for a sacred purpose, to do this by something greater than mere words : " The brave men, living and dead, who struggled here, have consecrated it, far above our poor power to add or detract." " Consecrate " is the learned Latin term. " Hallow " is the term that has always been in the English tongue, that arouses the deeper feeling : " hallowed be Thy name ", is the prayer.

You often find the English word more expressive than the foreign importation. The English " hearty " is more fraught with feeling than the Latin " cordial ", the English " fatherly " than the Latin " paternal ".

To set forth an idea with growing force is a device favoured by a skilled orator. You remember how, in the play, Antony points first to the wounds made by the less important conspirators till, when he comes to the wound made by the " well-

beloved Brutus "—" This was the most unkindest cut of all "—
the hearers are carried away with the intensity of their feelings.
And, very likely, you have noticed how an orator, as he expands
not so much what he thinks as what he wishes you to think he
thinks, keeps the more impressive thought to the end. That
is why a prudent speaker carefully prepares and industriously
commits to memory what he calls his peroration, the close of
his speech. For this peroration is to be the final blow crushing
his opponents, or the final call to which his supporters will
give eager response.

CLIMAX is a climbing up from weak to strong, from what is
negligible to what is weighty. ANTI-CLIMAX is a climbing down
from strong to weak, from weighty to negligible. Those seeking
to amuse us make good use of the anti-climax:

> One speaks of the glory of the British Queen,
> And one describes a charming Indian screen.

This is from Pope's *Rape of the Lock*; and one of his contemporaries wrote of a great lawyer:

> Persuasion tips his tongue whene'er he talks,
> And he has Chambers in the King's Bench Walks.

When the descent is unintended, it may make us amused though
the speaker intended us to be gravely impressed. BATHOS is
the name at times applied to this descent from the elevated to
the commonplace. The bathos is, you will realise, meant to
amuse when Pope writes about the lady from whose head the
curls had been cut:

> Then flashed the living lightning from her eyes,
> And screams of horror rend the affrighted skies,
> Not louder shrieks to judging Heaven are cast,
> When husbands, or when lapdogs breathe their last
> Or when rich China vessels, fallen from high,
> In glittering dust and painted fragments lie!

COGNATE OBJECT

(*a*) I have fought a good fight.

(*b* He carries weight! he rides a race!
   'Tis for a thousand pounds!

(COWPER, John Gilpin.)

(c) I heard thee speak me a speech once, but it was never acted.

(*Hamlet.*)

(d) The sun is coming down to earth, and the fields and the waters shout to him golden shouts.

(MEREDITH, *Ordeal of Richard Feverel.*)

When the verb and its Object are—like *fought* and *fight*, *rides* and *race*—akin to one another in sense, the Object is sometimes called the Cognate Object (or Cognate Accusative). An Intransitive Verb, having this Cognate Object, is used like a Transitive Verb : thus " He lived a hard life." The use of the pronoun *it* is such a cognate : as when Pepys writes in his diary " I to my office and hard at it till noon " or when Browning has " ' Dust and ashes ', so you creak it and I lack the heart to scold ", or when Shakespeare has " Foot it featly here and there ".

COGNATE WORDS

ransom, redemption ; eve, even, evening ; fancy, phantasy.

Words that have a common ancestor are COGNATE WORDS—*potion* and *poison*, *diamond* and *adamant*, *benison* and *benediction*, are instances. Usually they occur as a result of introduction into English at two different times and, very likely, in two different ways. The simpler of the cognates has come into the language at an early date and by way of speech—the cognate that is longer and nearer to the original has come at a late period of the history of the language and by way of writing. *Ransom* is an instance of the first, *redemption* of the second.

COHERENCE. (See also " Conjunction ")

But in a larger sense we cannot dedicate, we cannot consecrate, we cannot hallow this ground. The brave men, living and dead, who struggled here, have consecrated it far above our power to add or detract. The world will little note nor long remember what we say here, but it can never forget what they did here. It is for us, the living, rather, to be dedicated here to the unfinished work which they who fought here have thus far so nobly advanced. It is rather for us to be here dedicated to the great task remaining before us ; that from these honoured dead we take increased devotion to that cause for which they gave the last full measure of devotion ; that we here highly resolve that these dead shall not have died in vain ; that this nation, under God, shall have a new birth of freedom, and that government of the people, by the people, and for the people, shall not perish from the earth.

(ABRAHAM LINCOLN, Address at Gettysburg.)

When there is a harmonious connection of the parts of your speech or your writing, you have achieved COHERENCE IN COMPOSITION. No abrupt break in the train of thought occurs. There is orderly arrangement so that the reader is able to follow without great effort the working of the writer's mind. In one way or other you have composed a unit ; you have not placed together a number of fragments unconnected.

The example above is a coherent paragraph. See how it develops in orderly manner. The introductory conjunction " but " links the paragraph to the preceding one, referring back especially to " We have come to dedicate a portion of that field ". The second sentence gives the reason for the first statement. The third amplifies the reason. Then, in a natural transition, the call to a following of the example comes ; and the final sentence emphasises the call.

COLLECTIVE NOUNS

(a) No mob attacked by regular soldiers was ever more completely routed. The little band of Frenchmen, who ventured to confront the English, were swept down the stream of fugitives.

(MACAULAY, Essay on Clive.)

(b) The Government appointed a strong Committee to make recommendations.

A COLLECTIVE NOUN is the name of many individuals grouped together : a library is a gathering of books, a forest of trees, a crew of sailors. In strictness the name of the group is a singular noun. The speaker or writer, however, may have prominent in his mind the constituent individuals of the group ; and he slides into the plural when he uses the corresponding verb or pronoun. In modern English, indeed, the plural comes more often than the logical singular : we have " The Committee are agreed upon their findings " rather than " is agreed upon its findings ".

Note, however, that certain collectives in the singular form, like plenty or library or train, do not take the plural : you

59

have, for instance, " A plenty of candles lights up this chapel, and this scene of age and youth, and early memories and pompous death." The verb you note is *lights*, not *light* (the singular, not the plural). The plural comes only with collectives denoting living beings : " The vast majority had never known a time when Queen Victoria had not been reigning over them." (The collective noun *majority* is replaced by the pronoun *them*, not by *it*.) Look too, at these lines :

> Now came still Evening on, and Twilight grey
> Had in her sober livery all things clad ;
> Silence accompanied ; for beast and bird,
> They to their grassy couch, these to their nests,
> Were slunk : all, but the wakeful nightingale.

Milton uses *beast* and *bird* as collective nouns ; and you have the corresponding plurals, *they* and *their*.

The fact that the collective noun can, quite in accordance with good usage, be treated either as a singular or as a plural noun prompts us to have a care. We should be consistent in the matter. Look at these two sentences : they come from Matthew Arnold's *Essays in Criticism* :

> In our race are thousands of readers, presently there will be millions, who know not a word of Greek and Latin, and will never learn these languages. If this host of readers are ever to gain any sense of the power and charm of the great poets of antiquity, their way to gain it, is through the original power of Milton.

" This host of readers " treats *host* as a singular ; " are ever to gain ", however, treats *host* as a plural.

Look, too, at this B.B.C. statement : " What's left of the Japanese garrison are thought to have taken refuge in the hills." The phrase " What's left of the Japanese garrison " is equal to " the remnant " ; and " What is left " looks on this as a singular. But then comes " are thought " ; and this looks on " the remnant ", or " what is left ", as a plural. Perhaps we should change either " What's left " to " What are left " or " are thought " to " is thought ".

COLLOQUIALISM

(*a*) " ' Lovely Creetur '," repeated Sam.
 " 'Tain't in poetry, is it ? " interposed his father.

"No, no," replied Sam.

"Werry glad to hear it," said Mr. Weller, "Poetry's unnat'ral; no man ever talked poetry 'cept a beadle on boxin' day, or Warren's blackin', or Rowland's oil, or some o' them low fellows; never you let yourself down to talk poetry, my boy. Begin agin, Sammy."

(Pickwick Papers.)

(b) "Who did you pass on the road?" the King went on, holding his hand to the Messenger for some more hay.

"Nobody," said the Messenger.

"Quite right," said the King, "this young lady saw him, too. So of course Nobody walks slower than you."

"I do my best," the Messenger said in a sulky tone; "I'm sure nobody walks much faster than I do."

"He can't do that," said the King, "or else he'd have been there first."

(Alice in Wonderland.)

(c) It is to be observed, that Johnson's colloquial style was as blunt, direct and downright, as his style of studied compositions was involved and circuitous. As when Topham, Beauclerc, and Langton knocked him up at his chambers at three in the morning, and he came to the door with the poker in his hand, but seeing them, exclaimed, "What, is it you, my lads? Then I'll have a frisk with you!" and he afterwards reproaches Langton, who was a literary milksop, for leaving them to go to an engagement "with some *un-idead* girls". What words to come from the mouth of the great-moralist and lexicographer!

(WILLIAM HAZLITT.)

You use many an expression in familiar talk that you would not use in your formal writing, or your formal speech. Such expressions, perhaps diverging from strict grammar, are COLLOQUIALISMS; for there is, or ought to be, in colloquy among familiars, an agreeable easiness.

In that entertaining passage from *Alice in Wonderland*, for instance, the stickler for correctness would inform the King that *whom*, not *who*, is the objective case of the interrogative pronoun, that his question should therefore be couched "Whom did you pass on the road?" that *slower* is an adjective, the corresponding adverb being *more slowly*; and that *or else* is a colloquialism, better replaced by *for then*. Besides, if Alice or the Messenger had answered the question in formal manner and said, " I did not meet anyone on the road ", the King would not have been able to make play with " Nobody ". To be sure, this was a perverse misinterpretation of the King's. But, then, without this perversity we should not have had the fun ; and with the formal correctness much of the naturalness of the passage would have gone.

" Nobody " is, quite true, sometimes used in the sense of a person of little importance. " She vowed that it was a delightful ball : that there was everybody that everyone knew, and only a *very* few nobodies in the whole room." So Thackeray speaks of Becky at the Brussels ball, adding, however, for your guidance that this was " genteel jargon ". " It is a fact, that in a fortnight, and after three dinners in general society, this young woman had got up the genteel jargon so well, that a native could not speak it better." *Nobody* is, however, in familiar talk usually the equivalent of *no one* ; it is the negative of *somebody*. So we have the proverbial expression, " What's everybody's business is nobody's business."

Teachers of grammar do try to maintain in talk, no less than in writing, the distinction between *who* and *whom*. Their task is difficult indeed. Consider a little. *Who*, you will agree, is both correct and natural in sentences like, " Who is here so base that would be a bondman ? " or in " Be good, sweet maid, and let who can be clever." The objective *whom* could hardly be superseded by *who* in a prepositional phrase :

> I must have liberty
> Withal, as large a charter as the wind
> To blow on whom I please.

Whom is also in accordance with the grammar books in such sentences as " Whom the gods love die young " and " This is a fellow who has eluded me, but whom I now have tightly by the heels."

There is a tendency, however, to use *who* for the objective as well as for the nominative : " Who were you with last night ? " is the question in the music-hall song. The tendency is, as you might expect, much more noticeable in talk. Instances of the use in writing are not hard to find, however, especially where the pronoun, as in our passage, comes at the beginning of the sentence. Still, *who* for the objective does not conform to formal grammar.

The trouble is that in English—different in this respect from a highly-inflected language like ancient Latin or modern German—there are very few words having different forms for nominative and objective. With such forms as do occur, *who* and *whom* for instance, people are, as a result, apt to make mistakes; for they need to discriminate only rarely.

However, it is worth while to get clear ideas about the distinction. Look at these two sentences from *The Tempest*

(a)   he is drowned
Whom thus we stray to find; and the sea mocks
Our frustrate search on land.

(b) And in these fits I leave them, whilst I visit
Young Ferdinand,—whom they suppose is drowned—
And his and my loved darling.

In (a) *whom* is objective—" we stray to find whom "—and is therefore in accordance with our grammar books. In (b), however, the parenthesis might be re-arranged, and *whom* is not in accordance with grammar. Whether our knowledge of the distinction should impel us in our talk to say " Whom did you give it to ? " or " To whom did you give it ? " rather than the colloquial " Who did you give it to ? " is debatable. " He wore horn-rimmed spectacles and said ' whom '" is supposed to be an apt description of one over-pedantic.

COLON

(a) He is despised and rejected of men; a man of sorrows, and acquainted with grief: he hath no form nor comeliness; and when we shall see him, there is no beauty that we should desire him.

(*Isaiah* liii. 3.)

(b) No war, or battle's sound
Was heard the world around:
   The idle spear and shield were high uphung;
The hooked chariot stood
Unstained with hostile blood:
   The trumpet spake not to the armed throng;

And kings sat still with awful eye,
As if they surely knew their sovereign lord was by.
(MILTON, *Ode to the Nativity*.)

(c) This be the verse you grave for me :
Here he lies where he longed to be :
Home is the sailor, home from the sea,
And the hunter home from the hill.

(STEVENSON.)

(d) Here the desolation might have stopped : and the naked
edifices, which were no longer employed in the service of
idolatry, might have been protected from the destructive
rage of fanaticism.   Many of these temples were the most
splendid and beautiful monuments of Grecian architec-
ture : and the Emperor himself was interested not to
deface the splendour of his own cities, or to diminish the
value of his own possessions.   Those stately edifices might
be suffered to remain, as so many lasting trophies of the
victory of Christ.   In the decline of the arts, they might
be usefully converted into magazines, manufactures, or
places of public assembly : and perhaps when the walls
of the temple had been sufficiently purified by holy rites,
the worship of the true Deity might be allowed to expiate
the ancient guilt of idolatry.

(GIBBON.)

The COLON marks wider divisions in the sentence than the
COMMA and the SEMI-COLON. Frequent in older writing—
notably in the parallel sentences of the Bible, and in the balanced
sentences of writers like Gibbon—it is in modern writing almost
confined to a few odd jobs. It ushers in an enumeration or
a lengthy quotation (a dash sometimes doing duty for it here),
or an explanation.

COMMA

(a) *July 14th*, 1661—(Lord's Day) : Up, and my wife, a little
before four, and to make ready : and by and by Mrs.
Turner come to us by agreement, and she and I stayed
talking below while my wife dressed herself, which vexed
me that she was so long about it, keeping us till past
five o'clock before she was ready.

(SAMUEL PEPYS, in his *Diary*.)

(*b*) I have been long wakened from that dream of hope, in which I once boasted myself with so much exultation,

My Lord,

Your Lordship's most humble,

Most obedient servant,

SAM JOHNSON.

The COMMA is the punctuation mark used to mark off the smallest member of a sentence. Thus it marks off phrases in apposition. " Died at his house in Burbage Street, St. Giles's, John Cavanagh, the famous hand-fives player." So with our small insertions into a sentence. Here are a few instances from Scott's *Guy Mannering* :

It so happened, notwithstanding his precautions, that he could not avoid meeting his late tenants during their retreat from his property.

It was in a hollow way, near the top of a steep ascent, upon the verge of the Ellangowan estate, that Mr. Bertram met the gipsy procession. Four or five men formed the advanced guard, wrapped in long loose greatcoats that hid their tall slender figures, as the large slouched hats, drawn over their brows, concealed their wild features, dark eyes, and swarthy faces.

The race, it is true, which he had thus summarily dismissed from their ancient place of refuge, was idle and vicious.

(See also " *Parenthesis* ", " *Absolute Construction* ", " *Nominative of Address* ".)

COMMA (IN ENUMERATION)

(*a*) The letters show how the burden of men is made heavier by slovenly dates, illegible signatures, and forgetfulness that writing is something meant to be read.

(MORLEY, *Life of Gladstone.*)

(*b*) In the Middle Ages men thought and acted corporately. The status of every man was fixed by his place in some community—manor, borough, guild, learned University, or convent.

(TREVELYAN, *History of England.*)

(*c*) Then hey for croft and hop-yard, and hill, and field, and pond,

With Bredon Hill before me and Malvern Hill beyond :

The hawthorn white i' the hedgerow, and all the Spring's attire

In the comely land of Teme and Lugg, and Clent, and
Clee, and Wyre.

(JOHN MASEFIELD, *London Town*.)

(*d*) The sound of the cornet, flute, harp, sackbut, psaltery,
dulcimer, and all kinds of music.

(*Ezekiel*.)

In the second example (from Trevelyan's *History of England*),
there is in the original no comma after " University ". Perhaps
you agree, though, that the comma prevents possible mistake :
for " learned University " and " convent " are not alternatives.
The practice of *The Times* is to omit the comma before a
predicate, and to use it in enumerations even when *and* follows
the last item. Thus : speaking of the mounting guard by
the Dominion troops : " Today, tomorrow, and on Thursday,
Australian, New Zealand, and South African troops will continue the innovation begun yesterday by the Canadians."

Note how, after enumeration, Macaulay uses " these " as a
summary :

The circumstances which have most influence on the happiness of mankind—the changes of manners and morals, the
transition of communities from poverty to wealth, from
ignorance to knowledge, from ferocity to humanity—these
are, for the most part, noiseless revolutions.

Look at this sentence from *The Times* report of a Rugby
match between England and Wales : " A newcomer to international football, R. Peel, of Bedford, Longland and Bedford,
the Rugby League player were the best of the England pack."
Would it not be better to take away the comma after *Peel* and
to insert a comma after *Longland* ?

COMMON NOUNS BECOMING PROPER NOUNS

(*a*) The Bank is authorised to issue Treasury Notes.

(*b*) The Archbishop will preach next Sunday in the Abbey.

(*c*) Many men of less parts have made their way to the Woolsack or to the Episcopal Bench.

(MACAULAY, speaking of Goldsmith.)

The COMMON NOUN, having a meaning in itself, is applicable
to all individuals of the same class. We sometimes, however,
use a common noun—and we are understood so to use it—as

66

denoting one particular person or one particular thing of the class. We then make of it a kind of proper noun : " the Bank " (i.e. the Bank of England), " the Treasury " (i.e. the Treasury Department of the Government of Great Britain), " the Abbey " (i.e. the Cathedral Church of St. Peter at Westminster) are instances. When we use these names as individual labels, we write them with a capital : thus " the British Museum ", " the Aborigines ", " the Conservatives ", " the Far East ", " *The Taming of the Shrew* ".

COMPARISON (OF ADJECTIVES AND ADVERBS)

(*a*) Heard melodies are sweet, but those unheard
    Are sweeter : therefore, ye soft pipes, play on.

(KEATS.)

(*b*) The sweetest songs are those that tell of saddest thought.

(SHELLEY.)

(*c*) Clunton and Clunbury,
    Clungunford and Clun,
  Are the quietest places
    Under the sun.

(A. E. HOUSMAN, *A Shropshire Lad*.)

There can, strictly speaking, be no more or less of certain qualities. A thing is either *wooden* or *not wooden*. So with the adjectives *weekly, unique, circular, dead, Russian, real, impossible, excellent*. *Excellent*, for instance, means " surpassing in some good quality ", " superior " ; *excellent* is already a comparative. ' A most excellent dinner " is therefore, hardly a good substitute for " a very good dinner ". " Deader than a door-nail " may pass in colloquial speech ; it does not stand examination.

Other descriptive adjectives—like *sweet* and *quiet* in the examples—admit of more or less, admit of COMPARISON, that is. The adjective (or adverb) used when two persons or things are considered together is said to be in the COMPARATIVE DEGREE : *sweeter* in (*a*), the comparison being between " melodies heard " and " melodies unheard ", is in the Comparative Degree.

When more than two things enter into the comparison, the adjective (or adverb) is in the SUPERLATIVE DEGREE : *quietest*, in (*c*), the comparison between the Cluns and all other places, is in the Superlative Degree. The Superlative, however, is quite often used when the comparison is only latent, is used in fact as an emphatic word. The pedantic lady was not justified in finding fault with her husband's " My Dearest Maria ", her return letter opening with the request : " My Dear John, I beg that you will mind either your morals or your grammar. You call me your *dearest* Maria ; am I to understand that you have other Marias ? " But John had abundant authority for using " dearest " in the sense of " very dear " ; if you tell a mother that her baby is " the sweetest little fellow " she does not assume that you have made a critical examination of all other babies.

The usual way of forming, from the simple adjective or adverb, the Comparative and Superlative is by the addition (sometimes with slight spelling modification) of *er* and *est* ; but the adverbs *more* and *most*, *less* and *too*, also serve. Some of our older words have different words for the degrees ; *good*, *better*, *best* ; *bad* or *ill*, *worse*, *worst* ; *little*, *less*, *least*, and so on. Thus, in " 'Tis better to have loved and lost than never to have loved at all ", *better* is the Comparative degree of *good* ; in " A sorrow's crown of sorrow is remembering happier things ", *happier* is the Comparative Degree of *happy* ; in " a sadder and a wiser man ", the *sadder* is from *sad*, *wiser* from *wise*.

COMPARISON. (See also " Similes ")

(*a*) Shall I compare thee to a summer's day ?
　Thou art more lovely and more temperate ;
　Rough winds do shake the darling buds of May
　And summer's lease hath all too short a date :

Sometimes too hot the eye of heaven shines,
And often is his gold complexion dimmed ;
And every fair from fair sometimes declines,
By chance, or nature's changing course, untrimmed.

But thy eternal summer shall not fade,
Nor lose possession of that fair thou owest ;
Nor shall Death brag thou wander'st in his shade,
When in eternal lines to time thou growest.

So long as men can breathe, or eyes can see,
So long lives this, and this gives life to thee.
　　　　　　　　　　　　　　　　(SHAKESPEARE.)

(b) Soft as silk : sound as a top : lighter than a feather :
brown as a berry : sharp as a needle : happy as a king.
—These are from John Gay's *A New Song of New
Similes*.

It is well, when deciding upon our comparisons, that we make
distinct in our minds both the idea we wish to illustrate and
also the illustration itself. The important question is this :
" Does this in fact resemble—in that particular point that I
wish to impress—the first idea ? " You don't wish to expose
yourself to unsparing criticism such as Macaulay wrote of a
contemporary poet, popular in his day but now long forgotten.
Here is the poet's comparison :

> The soul, aspiring, pants its source to mount,
> As streams meander level with their fount.

And here is the critic's comment :

> We take this to be, on the whole, the worst similitude in
> the world. In the first place, no stream meanders, or can
> possibly meander, level with its fount. In the next place, if
> streams did meander level with their founts, no two notions
> can be less like each other than that of meandering level and
> that of mounting upwards.

COMPLEMENT. (See " Copulative Verbs ")

The COMPLEMENT of a verb is that which fills up—completes
—the statement made by the verb. Thus " He became " is
incomplete until we add " *king* "; " *king* " is, we say, the
COMPLEMENT of " *became* ". Grammar asks that a pronoun in
a complement should be in the same case as that of the noun or
pronoun preceding the verb. Thus, in " Sing me a song of a
lad that is gone, Say could that lad be I ", you have *I* in the
Nominative Case, as *lad* is ; and in this vaunt of Cæsar you have
I am he (not *him*) : " I do know but one That unassailable holds
on his rank Unshaked of motion : and that I am he Let me a
little show even in this."

As often, however, there is a conflict between strict grammar and colloquial speech—and much besides colloquial speech.
" It's me " is current enough, and " Heedless of grammar they
all cried, ' That's him.' " But then we have also Shelley's
prayer to the West Wind, " Be thou me, impetuous one ! "

COMPOUND WORDS : HYPHENS

(*a*) The ploughman homeward plods his weary way.

(*b*) The breezy call of incense-breathing morn,
The swallow twittering from the straw-built shed,
The cock's shrill clarion, or the echoing horn,
No more shall rouse them from their lowly bed.

(*c*) We are met on a great battle-field of that war. We have
come to dedicate a portion of that field as a final resting-
place for those who here gave their lives that that nation
might live.

COMPOUND WORDS go through three stages. Two or more
separate words are used together : *public house, tobacco pouch.*
Through constant association they become joined by a hyphen :
*battle-field ; lift-man ; wrist-watch ; to-day ; brother-in-law ;
man-of-war.* Finally, as the two words merge into one, the
hyphen disappears : *playmate, handkerchief, notwithstanding.*
For a time usage fluctuates. Tennyson, for instance, writes of :

> Jewels five-words long
> That on the stretched fore-finger of all Time
> Sparkle for ever :

Probably you will now find *forefinger* without the hyphen.

Are we to write a solid word, *diningroom*, or a hyphenated,
dining-room, or two words, *dining room* ? There is a question
upon which our printers have not yet reached—are not likely
to reach—agreement with one another, or with writers.

Perhaps these rules will, at all events, keep us consistent in
our own usage :

(1) The hyphen is a means whereby, for a particular purpose,
two words are made into one : *apple-tree* (the first word indicating a particular kind), *grass-green* (green like the grass), *penny-
wise* (wise in relation to pennies) and *pound-foolish, father-in-law,
man-of-war.*

(2) When the novelty of the compound has gone, we may well
omit the hyphen, unless as *father-in-law*, the resulting word
would be too cumbrous. Write *blackbird, downfall, whitewash,
overcome, barefoot, scarecrow, spendthrift, outlive.*

So, too, where there is no present consciousness that the word
is a compound we shall not find the hyphen. Thus, a hyphen

is usually uncalled for in *gospel* (*good-tidings*), *daisy* (*day's-eye*), *holiday* (*holy-day*), *Christmas* (*Christ's mass*).

(3) Omit the hyphen when the words may stand independently. Write " *The Major General* " but " *Major-General Dawkins* ". Write " *The Solicitor General* ", but " *The Solicitor-General's contentions* " ; for we could hardly place the *'s* at the end of the separated adjective. Write " *The Court Martial was convened* ", but " *The Court-Martial's decision will be promulgated* ".

(4) Write *waterpot* (where there is a single strong accent and on the first syllable), *downfall, breakfast, whitewash, spendthrift, barefoot, makeshift, masterpiece, spellbound*. Contrast these with *grass-grown, purse-proud, penny-wise, long-haired, kill-joy, man-of-war, half-an-hour, coach-house.*

Note how useful the hyphen may be in preventing possible misunderstanding. " *A superfluous-hair remover* " is what a lady welcomes, " *A superfluous hair-remover* " is one that nobody wants. " *Irish bacon-tax* " would be " *a tax imposed in Ireland on bacon* " *;* " *Irish-bacon tax* " is the proper name for " *a tax on Irish bacon* ". " *A violent anti-trade-unionist* " is the right name for one bitterly antagonistic to trade-unions ; " *a violent anti-trade unionist* " would describe a unionist much opposed to trade. " *A waste-paper basket* " is a receptacle for papers you do not want ; " *a waste paper basket* " would seem to be a basket made of paper and unwanted. In " She was a light house-keeper's daughter " it would prevent misinterpretation if you linked " light " and " house ". So it would if you wrote of the cricket match not as " a low scoring game ", but as " a low-scoring game " ; and if you linked " rain " and " swept " in " The scene in rain swept Downing Street ".

CONCISENESS (BREVITY)

(*a*) Therefore, since brevity is the soul of wit
And tediousness the limbs and outward flourishes,
I will be brief.

(Polonius in *Hamlet*.)

(*b*) Words are like leaves ; and, where they most abound,
Much fruit of sense beneath is rarely found.

(Pope.)

(*c*) The translation of the Greek original is : " One told me of thy fate, Heraclitus, and wrung me to tears, and I

71

remembered how often both of us, let the sun sink as we talked ; but thou methinks, O friend from Helicarnassus, art ashes long and long ago ; yet thy nightingale-notes live, whereon Hades the ravisher of all things shall not lay his hand." [57 words.]

The verse expansion of W. J. Cory is :

They told me, Heraclitus, they told me you were dead,
They brought me bitter news to hear and bitter tears to
    shed,
I wept as I remembered how often you and I
Had tired the sun with talking and sent him down the sky.

And now that you are lying, my dear old Carian guest,
A handful of grey ashes, long, long ago at rest,
Still are thy pleasant voices, thy nightingales, awake ;
For Death, he taketh all away, but them he cannot take.
    [85 words.]

(d) Let thy speech be short, comprehending much in few words.

(Apocrypha.)

The aim of writers in other days was to be copious. We now seek to be concise rather than copious ; we say things effectively, and then stop. The short way of putting a thing probably conforms to the great guiding rule, that so far as in us lies we should economise the attention of our hearers or (when fortune gives us any) of our readers. We should give access speedily to such meaning as we have. Cut off excrescences ; then there is a greater chance of getting attention paid to the essentials.

There is fun at times in the copious way, as when Dickens expands " Then we sang together ' Auld Lang Syne ' " into " Then Mrs. Micawber and myself had the honour of uniting our voices to yours in the well-known strain of the immortal bard nurtured beyond the Tweed."

And perhaps it was in fun that Doctor Johnson paraphrased his first emphatic judgment :

Talking of the Comedy of " The Rehearsal " [relates Boswell], he said, " It has not wit enough to keep it sweet." This was easy ;—he therefore caught himself, and pronounced a more rounded sentence ; "It has not vitality enough to preserve it from putrefaction."

"Be *concise* in your speech and writing " is the sound general rule ; you do not wish to be blamed for " a barren superfluity of words ". Still, you must not be so brief as to be obscure. *Brevis esse laboro, obscurus fio* : "It is ", wrote Horace, " when I try to be concise that I become unintelligible." That is, you may carry conciseness too far. For when you speak or write you have not communicated your thoughts unless another has the ability to interpret your words in the manner you intended. Language is a matter of co-operation ; you need the help of your hearers or your readers.

Yet it is unwise to expect a great deal of help. That is why you try to make your meaning easy of access. You use words that can be readily understood : you also give adequate indication of your meaning. To be very sparing of words is to invite an erroneous or an incomplete interpretation of your thoughts. Not many, for instance, will understand from a shaking of the head what Puff, in *The Critic*, intended them to understand. Lord Burleigh comes in, dolefully shakes his head and exits.

"Now, pray what did he mean by that ? " asks Sneer. "You don't take it ? " says Puff. "No, I don't, upon my soul." "Why, by that shake of the head, he gave you to understand that, even though they had more justice in their cause and wisdom in their measures—yet, if there was not a greater spirit shown on the part of the people, the country would at last fall a sacrifice to the hostile ambition of the Spanish monarchy."

To be sure, that is a humorous exaggeration. But it does carry a lesson : dumb show and expression of face may convey something to some minds. We usually deceive ourselves in expecting them to convey much.

CONJUNCTION
(a) We will unite the White Rose and the Red ;
Smile Heaven upon this fair Conjunction.
(Henry VIII.)

(b) It was impossible to live a month at Cranford and not know the daily habits of each resident ; and long before my visit was ended I knew much concerning the whole

Brown trio. There was nothing new to be discovered respecting their poverty; for they had spoken simply and openly about that from the very first. They made no mystery of the necessity for their being economical. All that remained to be discovered was the captain's infinite kindness of heart, and the varied modes in which, unconsciously to himself, he manifested it.

(Mrs. Gaskell, Cranford.)

So far as English composition is concerned, a CONJUNCTION is a word used to connect, to join words or phrases or sentences together. In the passage from *Cranford* the words *and, before, for*, are conjunctions. The conjunction may, however, do more than merely join. It may (like *for* in the extract) introduce a reason; it may (like *before* in the extract) define time, or space; it may (like *but* in " The waves beside them danced, but they Outdid the sparkling waves in glee ") introduce a contrast; it may give an alternative (like *or* in " Bless your honour! cried *Trim*, advancing three steps as he spoke, does a man think of his christian name when he goes upon the attack?—Or when he stands in the trench, *Trim*? cried my uncle *Toby*, looking firm. —Or when he enters a breach? said *Trim*, pushing in between two chairs.—Or forces the lines? cried my uncle, rising up, and pushing his crutch like a pike.—Or faces a platoon? cried *Trim*, presenting his stick like a fire-lock.—Or when he marches up the glacis? cried my uncle *Toby*, looking warm and setting his foot upon his stool ").

Words other than conjunctions act as joining words too. (See the note on " *Coherence* ".)

Some consider it a blemish to begin a sentence with a conjunction; they object to a conjunction immediately after a full stop. The practice of good writers, and of good speakers, gives no countenance to the objection. After all, if your speech or your writing is to be a connected whole, there must be some way or other of carrying on the thought from one sentence to the next; and it might be argued that the beginning of a sentence is quite a natural place for the conjunction. You will find examples in plenty. Look at this passage of Macaulay's. He is writing of Addison:

As an observer of life, of manners, of all the shades of

human character, he stands in the first class. And what he observed he had the art of communicating in two widely different ways. He could describe virtues, vices, habits, whims, as well as Clarendon. But he could do something better. He could call human beings into existence, and make them exhibit themselves. If we wish to find anything more vivid than Addison's best portraits, we must go either to Shakespeare or to Cervantes.

But what shall we say of Addison's humour, of his sense of the ludicrous, of his power of awakening that sense in others, and of drawing mirth from incidents which occur every day and from little peculiarities of temper and manner, such as may be found in every man ? We feel the charm : we give ourselves up to it ; but we strive in vain to analyse

Macaulay, you notice, begins sentences with *And*, *But* and *If* in the one paragraph ; he even links a following paragraph by the conjunction *But*.

CONNOTATION : DENOTATION

(a) Time hath brought the word " knave " to a connotation of ill qualities. (In Old English the word meant simply a " boy " ; then it was " a boy employed as a servant " ; now the denotation is " a base, crafty rogue ".)

(b) It was late in November 1456. The snow fell over Paris with rigorous, relentless persistence ; sometimes the wind made a sally and scattered it in flying vortices ; sometimes there was a lull, and flake after flake descended out of black night air, silent, circuitous, interminable. To poor people, looking up under moist eyebrows, it seemed a wonder where it all came from.

(R. L. STEVENSON, *A Lodging for the Night*.)

The CONNOTATION of a term is what that term implies ; the DENOTATION of a term is what the term can be applied to. As we enlarge the connotation (by way of adjectives or adjective-substitutes) so we limit the denotation. Consider Falstaff's, " Three misbegotten rogues in Kendal green came at my back and let drive at me." The term " rogues " already expresses in summary form a number of attributes, we may look upon it as a portmanteau term for dishonest-dishonourable-mischievous-knavish-men. It can be applied, one hopes, to few

75

among us; and, when we add the attributes "misbegotten" and "in Kendal green", we limit its application—its denotation—still further; and "three" makes the denotation quite precise.

The names that have connotation are called COMMON NAMES. When a name—like *November* or *Paris* in the extract above—is tacked as a label to a thing, this name has no connotation. Appropriated as it is to a single individual we call the term a PROPER NOUN. To be sure, the same name may be the index of many individuals. *Sydney* is such a term. It is applicable to many persons and to many places. But, when we use the term, we have in mind one thing only.

Perhaps every PROPER NOUN was once connotative: it was more than an index like the number on a house or the letters denoting motor-car districts. *Armstrong* meant at its first application what it said: it is not likely that it was used ironically. The modern "Armstrong" may be a weakling. Many of the surnames among us were nicknames, convenient or comic labels given by our ancestors when, in the twelfth and thirteenth centuries, surnames became customary. *Grace* was, we are told, *gras*, or fat; *Cameron* is "crooked nose" and the answering epithet is *Campbell* or "wry-mouth". Occupational names—the ubiquitous *Smith*, the *Chapman*, or dealer, the *Faulkner*, or falconer—are now applied without any idea of denoting occupation. And when we say "Margaret", the pearl, or "Esther" the star, or "Susanna", the lily, we rarely call into mind the first meaning. The word in our minds has a denotation; it has no connotation.

Whenever we are not sure—or, possibly, when we suspect our hearers not to be sure—about the full implication of a term, we are prone to add attributes already implied. We make explicit what is implicit. The British Ambassador to Washington died suddenly of "toxic poisoning" says the certificate. This is to say "poisonous poisoning"; it is the verbiage exemplified in "lone substitute". True, there is something to be said for this kind of expansion when we wish to emphasise an implied attribute, to make it more prominent than when involved in the term. Look again at the Stevenson quotation. "The snow", he writes, "fell over Paris with rigorous, relentless persistence." Perhaps the attributes "rigorous" and "relentless" are latent in "persistence"; they are none the less effective. So, too, a "vortex" is a whirling mass; "flying" dots the i's, makes explicit what is already implicit.

CONSONANT

(a) The sounds of speech are classified into consonants and vowels.

(b) The opinion is consonant with law. (COKE.)

In our speech we have sounds that we can easily utter by themselves and sounds that go together with others. The first are VOWELS; and Sweet's definition of vowel is this, "A vowel may be defined as voice (forced breath) modified by some definite configuration of the super-glottal passages, but without audible friction (which would make it into a consonant)." One good way of arranging the consonants into classes is the nearness of their approach to vowels. Thus:

Semi-vowels: *y* and *w*.
Liquids: *l* and *r*.
Nasals: *m*, *n*, and *ng*.
Fricatives (Spirants): (1) Voice: *v*, *th* (as in *with*), *a*.
    (2) Breath: *f*, *th* (as in *writhe*), *s*.
Mutes: *b*, *d*, *g*; *p*. *t*, *k*.

CONTEXT OF A WORD

(a) After him, then, and bring him back.

(b) After he came all went wrong.

(c) You go first, I'll follow after.

In (a) "after" must be regarded as a verb; in (b) as a conjunction; in (c) as an adverb. You can determine the function of an English word (what "part of speech" it is), and its meaning also, only by considering its work in the sentence. Consider this: Your old Latin friend *mensa* is a noun. That is quite certain: you could not mistake *mensa* for a verb or an adjective. In English, however, there is an astonishing freedom in the use of words. From some of Shakespeare's bold usages we might almost be tempted to say that a word may, by reason of its use, be any part of speech the writer pleases. "Word" itself is, for instance, usually a noun, a name: it is a noun in

77

that preceding sentence. It becomes a verb in Cleopatra's comment after listening to her conqueror's honeyed speech,

> He words me, girls, he words me, that I should not
> Be noble to myself.

So with the word " after ". In these sentences, where it signifies " behind in place or order ", it is an ADVERB : " Jack fell down and broke his crown, and Jill came tumbling after " ; " They lived happily ever after." It is a PREPOSITION, taking a noun or a pronoun in the objective case, in sentences like : " After me cometh a man that is preferred before me " ; " Wolsey was greedy after power " ; " Make an enquiry after his health."

" After " is a CONJUNCTION, joining as it does a dependent clause to its principal clause, in sentences like : " We had a pleasant evening after that wretched fellow went away ", " Make your decision after you have heard both sides of this argument."

These three usages do not exhaust the changes. Literary usage may make of " after " a descriptive word, an ADJECTIVE, that is. " After " is clearly an adjective in such expressions as : " the after deck ", " in after life " " such a scene as no after events have been able to efface ", and in Shakespeare's

> So smile the heavens upon this holy act,
> That after hours with sorrow chide us not.

We must even admit that " after " may be used as a VERB, as in our first example. If you are asked to define a word in isolation, you should perhaps—so far as concerns our older words, at any rate—ask for its context, its setting. For when a word has been current in the mouths of many generations, it is apt to take on meanings other than the first meaning. At times the later meanings may diverge greatly, both from one another and from the earlier ones. Look at the word " fast ", for instance, in these two sentences : " Stand fast in the faith ", " Is this a slow or a fast train ? " You interpret " fast " in the first sentence as " fixed, firm, constant ". It is this meaning that the word has in the Navy's " Make fast ", in phrases like " Fast aground ", and in the sentence " England must be the fast friend of France."

In the second sentence, however, you interpret " fast " not as " fixed, stationary ", but as " rapidly moving "—contrasted,

that is, with " slow ".   How has this curious development come
about ?   Clearly, it calls for strength, for resolution, to stand
fast in a position from which others are striving to oust you ;
a post fast in the ground is not easy to move.   But the strength
enabling one to stand firm implies the strength to move—to
move, moreover, with rapidity.   So, if you are a fast bowler
you can make the ball travel down the pitch at great pace.

The adjective " fine " exhibits similar developments.   " A
fine needle ", is a thin sharp-pointed one ; " a fine bullock "
is a fat one.   " Fine " is, in fact, akin to the word " finish " :
a thing well-finished has the qualities that are desirable for that
particular thing, though not maybe for another thing.   " A fine
child " is plump and strong ; " fine lace " is delicate in its
structure ; " a fine day " is one in which it is a delight to be
abroad ; " pure gold is twenty-four carats fine " ; and so on.

An ordinary English word is not a rigid thing.   It takes on
different shades of meaning from the differing contexts in which
it is found.   When, therefore, you are asked for the meaning
of a word you seek first to note the word in its setting.   Look,
for example, at this adjective " brave ".   Of course, it has its
usual meaning of " courageous, stout-hearted " in sentences like
" None but the brave deserve the fair."   But you must modify
that meaning in order to interpret Miranda's exclamation " O
brave new world ! "   There it is " splendid, showy " ; it is the
Scottish " braw ".

(See also " *Development of Meaning* ".)

COPULATIVE VERBS

(*a*) I know you are my eldest brother.

(*b*) I am the youngest son of Sir Rowland de Bois.

(*c*) The spirit of my father grows strong in me.

(*d*) When I break that oath, let me turn monster.

(*e*) The dullness of the fool is the whetstone of the wits.

(*f*) Were you made the messenger ?

The verb " to be " and other verbs often join nouns and
pronouns referring to the same person or thing.   So doing,
these are COPULATIVE VERBS, coupling the same cases.   Thus,
note the distinction between " Elizabeth became Queen " (where
queen is in the Nominative Case after the Copulative Verb

became) and " The bonnet became her " (where *her* is in the Objective Case, governed by the Transitive Verb *became*).

CORRELATIVE

(*a*) As cold waters to a thirsty soul, so is good news from a far country.

(Proverbs.)

(*b*) Though deep, yet clear : though gentle, yet not dull.

(*c*) Father and son, husband and wife, and other such correlative terms.

When one word brings into mind another, the two words are CORRELATIVE. *As* and *so*, *though* and *yet*, in (*a*) and (*b*) are correlatives. *Either* and *or*, *parent* and *child*, *then* and *when*, *cause* and *effect* are other pairs. One of the two implies the other, even though the other may not be expressed.

COURTESY IN SPEECH

The true gentleman in like manner carefully avoids whatever may cause a jar or a jolt in the minds of those with whom he is cast :—all clashing of opinion, or collision of feeling, all restraint, or suspicion, or gloom, or resentment ; his great concern being to make every one at their ease and at home. He has his eyes on all his company ; he is tender towards the bashful, gentle towards the distant, and merciful towards the absurd ; he can recollect to whom he is speaking ; he guards against unseasonable allusion, or topics which may irritate ; he is seldom prominent in conversation, and never wearisome. He makes light of favours while he does them, and seems to be receiving when he is conferring.

He never speaks of himself except when compelled, never defends himself by a mere retort, he has no ears for slander or gossip, is scrupulous in imputing motives to those who interfere with him, and interprets everything for the best. He is never mean or little in his disputes, never takes unfair advantage, never mistakes personalities or sharp sayings for arguments, or insinuates evil which he dare not say out. From a longsighted prudence, he observes the maxim of the ancient sage, that we should ever conduct ourselves towards our enemy as if he were one day to be our friend.

(CARDINAL NEWMAN.)

We can nearly always say clearly what we mean and not be rude or offensive.

Blunt speech—when you call a spade a spade, not an agricultural implement—is good on occasions. In all probability, the occasions are rare. During the critical debate between Cæsar and Antony in the play, one of Cæsar's counsellors puts forward a plea for reconciliation, temporary at all events—

> If it might please you to enforce no further
> The griefs between ye : to forget them quite
> Were to remember that the present need
> Speaks to atone you.

And the blunt-spoken Enorbarbus translates the euphemisms into plainer terms : " Or, if you borrow one another's love for the instant, you may, when you hear no more words of Pompey, return it again : when you shall have nothing else to do." Perhaps Enorbarbus deserved the rebuke of Antony—" Thou art a soldier only : speak no more " ; but he still permits himself the answer, " That truth should be silent I had almost forgot."

We are not, to be sure, obliged to be for ever earnestly seeking after pleasing expressions in our speech and writing. Still, there is no need to give gratuitous offence ; and, when people expect to be addressed in one way, it appears foolish deliberately to disappoint their expectations. The various Departments of Government, for instance, have devised for themselves set forms. You may think that other forms would be shorter and just as effective ; but your opinion is not an adequate reason for diverging from them.

Thus, the Treasury—the august Department that guards the nation's money—has its whimsical preferences. In the ordinary business letter you would say something like " The matter is urgent and we ask for a speedy reply " ; to the Treasury you say " It would be much appreciated if my Lords of the Treasury could be moved to give an early reply." In the ordinary business letter you might say : " The disability is due to military service. Before serving he was in good health." " Attributable to " is preferred by the Treasury to " due to " and " prior to " to " before ".

Our correspondent—our hearer, too—may, indeed, ask us to be blunt in our expressions : " Speak to me home, mince not the general tongue ", says Antony to the Messenger. " Taint my faults with such full licence as both truth and malice have power to utter." We need not, however, be precipitate in accepting the invitation.

CUSTOM IN LANGUAGE. (See also "Idiom")

" Take some more tea," said the March Hare to Alice, very earnestly.

" I've had nothing yet," Alice replied in an offended tone, " so I can't take more."

" You mean you can't take less," said the Hatter; " It's very easy to take *more* than nothing."

If we are to be rigidly accurate in our talk—if we are always " to speak by the card "—the Mad Hatter was justified in his rude criticism of Alice's speech. But then we are not rigidly accurate. Language is not a matter of mathematics; it is a matter of what custom dictates; and the words that are current run about the streets and market places, at times without carrying a precise meaning. Custom declares that " more " implies addition to " something "; and addition to " nothing " is " some ". " Take some tea ", is the interpretation Alice put upon the invitation.

We all use words, in our writing as well as in our talk, with no acute sense of the strict meaning that should be attached to them; and, like Alice in the story, we are surprised and a little confused when we are challenged about them. We ought not to be greatly distressed by the challenge. Our answer to it is that our use conforms to the practice of our fellows, and that the sense in which they will interpret the word is the correct sense. The word may have had a different sense at its first entry into this language. Yet, for many of our words, to use the word in the old sense would lead to confusion.

In some old phrases, recognised by us as old, we are prepared to accept a modified meaning. This word, " prevent ", for instance, bears its primary meaning in the words of the prayer, " Prevent us, O Lord, in all our doings with Thy most gracious favour ", and in " Thy grace may always prevent and follow us." There it means " to go before "—go before to prepare the way and make it plain. We invite misunderstanding, however, when we use the word in that sense now: you are, for example, pulled up short when Milton, speaking of the kings

82

on the way to Bethlehem says, " O run ! prevent them with thy humble ode "—that is, make your gift before they make theirs. We should err to copy in our ordinary talk those old-fashioned uses.

Or look at this curious collocation, " permanent wave ". Now the very essence of a wave is that it is for ever altering :

> When you do dance I wish you
> A wave o' the sea that you might ever do
> Nothing but that.

And " permanent " means " remaining "—remaining through all changes and chances. " Permanent " is opposed to " temporary ". A " permanent wave " is, therefore, neither permanent nor a wave. Yet, since those who say the words and those who hear them attach the one meaning to them, they must be regarded as the correct way of naming a setting of the hair into temporary curls. The hairdresser who attracts customers by advertising " Double Life Perms " is using the correct language —correct because the readers of the advertisement interpret the words in the sense intended by him : he is offering to produce curls that have a rigidity more lasting than the ordinary.

Where custom speaks it is unwise to go counter because of an assumed greater correctness. Better go with the crowd and pronounce *cinema* as *sĭn-em-a*, even though we still retain the *k* sound and the long *i* in the less-used word, the adjective *kĭnetic*. *The Oxford Dictionary* asserts that to pronounce *cocaine* as *kōkain* instead of *kŏkain* is " vulgar ". Vulgar it may be ; but it is general, and therefore correct for the purpose of transmitting thought from one mind to another.

Knowledge of the original of a word is no infallible guide to its present pronunciation, or indeed its present use. Thus *deficit* (*dĕfisit*), with the short *e*, is probably more frequently heard, though the Latin would suggest long *e*. This long *e* many retain, pronouncing the word *dē-fis-it*. The original sound may actually mislead : we say *āgent* and *ālien* where the Latin *a* is short ; we say *ĕditor* where the Latin is *ēditor* ; we say *cŏmic* (contrast Milton's *Cōmus*), *ĕcho* and *ĕthics*, where the Greek *o* and *e* are long ; we call the ancient questioner *Sŏcrates*, though he called himself *Sōcrates* ; most people speak of the *Ĭdylls of the King*, with a short initial vowel, though *Ĭdyll* is consistent with the original Greek; in his Latin lesson the schoolboy will say *mĭnor*, he will say *mīnor* when he speaks English. *Pătriot* will, no doubt, persist long beside *pātriot*, because of the Latin; but it is probably better to fall in with the tendency and say *pātriot*. *Demēsne* (*dimēn*) will probably conquer and so preserve the rhyme in Keats' sonnet, " Much have I travelled in the realms of gold ", where he makes it rhyme with *seen, been, serene*; though *dĭmān* is the lawyer's pronunciation, and since the word is connected with *domain*, is more " correct ".

D

DASH

Here are some instances of the use of the Dash:

(*a*)　Who would fardels bear,
To grunt and sweat under a weary life,
But that the dread of something after death,—
The undiscovered country from whose bourn
No traveller returns,—puzzles the will ?

(Hamlet.)

(*b*) If my friend and I eat your cakes—for which we have neither of us natural inclination—we shall expect you to join us at supper by way of recompense.

(R. L. STEVENSON, *The Suicide Club*.)

(*c*) As soon as we two were alone—" What," said Prince Florizel, " is the use of this confabulation, Geraldine ? I see you are flurried, whereas my mind is very tranquilly made up. I will see the end of this."

(R. L. STEVENSON, *The Suicide Club*.)

(*d*) You all did love him once,—not without cause :
What cause withholds you, then, to mourn for him ?

(Julius Cæsar.)

The DASH as a mark of punctuation, may serve as in (*a*) and (*b*) to mark off a parenthesis : in this function it serves as a substitute for brackets. Or it may indicate—as in (*c*) and (*d*) —an abrupt pause in the sentence. In (*d*), as you will notice, it adds weight to the comma. Other instances when the dash acts as reinforcement are these from Froude's *Words about Oxford* :

(i) Many long years had passed since I visited Oxford,—some twenty-eight or more.

(ii) I sat and sipped my wine, thinking of the fate of cities,—of Nineveh the renowned, of the marbles lately recovered from thence with the mysterious arrow-headed characters.

(iii) Numerous skiffs of the university-men were alive on the water, realizing the lines,—

> Some lightly o'er the current swim,
> Some show their gaily gilded trim
> Quick glancing to the sun.

DATIVE

(*a*) Give me some sack.

(*b*) Good sir, this my ring was given me by my wife.

(*c*) What prince can promise such diuturnity unto his relics ?

The type of the Indirect Object is *me* in " You give it to me " and in (*a*) and (*b*) above. That is why the Indirect Object is at times called the DATIVE CASE, " dative " being connected with " donation ", " donor ", " condone ", from the Latin verb meaning " give ". You notice that, quite often, the preposition *to* does not appear before the noun or pronoun. It is to be understood by the hearer or the reader ; and the need to do so may cause a moment of hesitation in reaching the intended meaning. Thus *The Times* comments on the appointment of a seventy-seven-year-old admiral as the Japanese Prime Minister : " The newcomer is a hardy veteran and offers public confidence the support of an older tradition." You read this twice before you realise that *to* is to be understood before *public*.

DENOTATION. (See " Connotation ")

DETACHED PHRASE (THE) : NOMINATIVE ABSOLUTE

(*a*) She was wrapped in a white morning dress, her hair falling on her shoulders and her large eyes fixed and without light.

(THACKERAY, Vanity Fair.)

(*b*) Here with a Loaf of Bread beneath the Bough,
A Flask of Wine, a Book of Verse—and thou
  Beside me singing in the Wilderness—
And Wilderness is Paradise enow.

(FITZGERALD, Omar Khayyám.)

The use of language calls for co-operation. The speaker puts his thoughts into words, the hearer is called upon to turn the sounds into thought again. The writer makes some black marks upon white paper, the reader's part is to interpret these marks in the intended sense. On occasion you need to give a deal of help, of good-natured complacency, to the writer. To reach the real meaning of an absolute clause for example, is not always easy. There is no difficulty in that fine sentence of Thackeray's : the two phrases detached from the usual construction of the sentence—the phrases " her hair falling on her shoulders " and " her large eyes fixed and without light "—admirably complete the picture. The picture would be far less effective if we turned those descriptive phrases into sentences, " Her hair fell on her shoulders. Her large eyes were fixed and without light." You would have instead of one picture, three separate pictures.

These short hurried sentences may be quite fitting. Look at a little of Froude's account of the capture of the treasure ship—

> The *Pelican* sailed two feet to the *Cacafuego's* one. Drake filled his empty wine-skins with water and trailed them astern to stop his way. The chase supposed that she was followed by some heavy-loaded trader, and, wishing for company on a lonely voyage, she slackened sail and waited for him to come up.

Where the quiet scene, not the bustle of movement, is the writer's thought, the detached phrase is at times highly effective. The phrase in parenthesis in the lines from *Omar Khayyám* is a good example. Here are others :

> In the stalls, still in her black widow's hood, sat Esmond's dear mistress, her son by her side.

(" Son ", you would say, is in the Nominative Absolute Case.) For, when it is a pronoun in the absolute phrase, we feel it necessary to use the Nominative form. Thus, " I being a poor man and he being a millionaire, which of us will she choose ? " It is not, you note, " me being " or " him being ".

Pepys, in his breathless way, often uses the construction—

> Twenty pieces of new gold, a pleasant sight. It cheered my heart ; and, the boy gone, I home to supper, and showed them my wife.

And here are illustrations from Hardy's *Far from the Madding Crowd* :

> Supper being ended, Coggan began his lyric.
>
> Here the shearers knelt, the sun slanting in upon their bleached shirts, tanned arms, and the polished shears they flourished.
>
> It was still the beaming time of evening, though night was stealthily making itself visible low down upon the ground, the western lines of light raking the earth without alighting upon it to any extent, or illuminating the dead levels at all.

Supper in the first Hardy sentence, *sun* in the second, and *lines* in the third are instances of nouns in the Nominative Absolute Case.

DEVELOPMENT OF MEANING

(*a*) A word is a sign made by the vocal organs ; and the sign may be represented by other and visible signs called letters.

(*b*) To speak no slander, no, nor listen to it,
To honour his own word as if his God's.

(TENNYSON, Guinevere.)

(*c*) Be not too tame neither, but let your own discretion be your tutor ; suit the action to the word, the word to the action ; with this special observance, that you o'erstep not the modesty of nature.

(Hamlet.)

(*d*) But yesterday the word of Cæsar might have stood against the world.

(Julius Cæsar.)

In a living language new means of expression come not so much by the introduction or the making of new words but by the adaptation of old words to new uses. You will agree that (*a*) above gives the primary meaning of *word*. In (*b*) *word* has developed into promise ; in (*c*) into sense or meaning ; in (*d*) into command. There is a development of meaning, to so great an extent at times that the original sense of the word retires far into the background. Consider " word " itself, for instance. In Cleopatra's exclamation, " He words me, girls, he words me ", the simple meaning has developed into " seeks to deceive me by words in which I am foolish to put faith ". The one sound plays many parts : your happiness is " beyond words " when you cannot express it in language; you "speak a word in season" when you say what is right at the right time; you "have words" when you enter into contention. And other good English idioms are "bring word swiftly", "pledge your word", "say the word only", "at a word", "on your word", "as good as your word".

So with the word "have": it is used, and understood, in senses removed from the primary sense. "Have some marmalade" is more English nowadays than "Eat some marmalade"; "Have another cup of tea" than "Drink another cup of tea". And the foreigner, learning our language, will think strange the varied interpretations of "have" in such phrases as : "Let me have men about me that are fat" (see and hear, be accompanied by); "They have a car" (own); "You have me, have you not?" (understand); "I have to be there by nine" (am obliged); "They have it that Rhodes has been captured" (report); "The master let him have it soundly" ("let him have it soundly"—thrashed him well); "You have me there" (puzzle); "Bargain with him, and he'll have you" (get the better of you); "Have at them!" (attack).

This paragraph from W. S. Landor deals with the topic in a very interesting way :

> There is a fastidiousness in the use of language that indicates an atrophy of mind. We must take words as the world presents them to us, without looking at the root. If we grubbed under this and laid it bare, we should leave no room for our thoughts to lie evenly, and every expression would be constrained and cramped. We should scarcely find a metaphor in the purest author that is not fake or imperfect, nor could we imagine one ourselves that would not be stiff and frigid. Take, for instance, a phrase in common use, *You are rather late*. Can anything seem plainer? Yet *rather*, as you know, meant originally *earlier*, being the comparative of *rathe* ; the "rathe primrose" of the poet recalls it. We cannot say, *You are sooner late*; but who is so troublesome and silly as to question the propriety of saying *You are rather late*? We likewise say *bad orthography* and *false orthography*; how can there be false or bad *right-spelling*?

DIGRESSIONS

(*a*) Vanity of vanities, saith the preacher; all is vanity.

(*b*) When I came to my castle, for so I think I called it ever after this, I fled into it like one pursued.

(Robinson Crusoe.)

(*c*) " I have sworn," said King Richard—and his voice was heard above all the tumult, which now waxed wild and loud—" never to strike one whose shoulder bears the cross."

(The Talisman.)

(*d*) Here, under leave of Brutus and the rest,
(For Brutus is an honourable man,
So are they all, all honourable men),
Come I to speak in Cæsar's funeral.

(Julius Cæsar.)

The insertions into the sentences, marked off by commas or dashes or brackets, are illustrations of the PARENTHESIS (plural PARENTHESES). The speaker has turned aside to make an explanation or to supply information throwing light upon the main statement : he has digressed a little ; and we may call the little insertions DIGRESSIONS.

See how Browning makes his Bishop turn aside from argument to a genial offer of refreshment :

You peep up from your utterly naked boards
Into some snug and well-appointed berth,
Like mine, for instance (try the cooler jug—
Put back the other, but don't jog the ice)
And mortified you mutter " Well and good—
He sits enjoying his sea-furniture—
'Tis stout and proper and there's store of it,
Though I've the better notion, all agree,
Of fitting rooms up ! "

The term is usually applied, however, to a more substantial insertion into narrative or speech or exposition or other composition.

Thus, Milton laments in *Lycidas* the loss of his friend " dead ere his prime " ; and he turns aside from his lamentation to the fine episode :

Alas ! what boots it with uncessant care
To tend the homely, slighted, shepherd's trade
And strictly meditate the thankless Muse ?
Were it not better done, as others use,

To sport with Amaryllis in the shade,
Or with the tangles of Neæra's hair ?
Fame is the spur that the clear spirit doth raise
(That last infirmity of noble mind)
To scorn delights, and live laborious days ;
But the fair guerdon when we hope to find,
And think to burst out into sudden blaze,
Comes the blind Fury with the abhorred shears
And slits the thin-spun life. " But not the praise,"
Phœbus replied, and touch'd my trembling ears ;
" Fame is no plant that grows on mortal soil,
Nor in the glistering foil
Set off to the world, nor in broad rumour lies :
But lives and spreads aloft by those pure eyes
And perfect witness of all-judging Jove ;
As he pronounces lastly on each deed,
Of so much fame in heaven expect thy need ! "

Perhaps no writer digressed at such a rate as Sterne did : he
ushers in one topic and before he is fairly started, he is launched
upon another, then another ; and you must read many pages—
delightful pages they are—before you find that he has wrenched
himself back to the first topic. He admonishes himself upon
his propensity : " I danced myself into *Pedrillo's* pavilion, where
pulling out a paper of black lines, that I might go on straight
forwards, without digression or parenthesis, in my uncle Toby's
amours . . ." But he paid as little heed to his self-admonish-
ings as any of us do.

DILEMMA ("HORNS" OF A DILEMMA)

(a) The Commissioners for raising the benevolence were told
by Bishop Morton to use this dilemma : if they met with
any that were sparing, they should tell the sparers that
they must needs have, because they laid up ; and, if they
were spenders, they must needs have, because it was in
their port and manner of living.

(BACON, *History of Henry VII.*)

(b) *Yorick* was cutting the manuscript of his sermon into slips
so that the company might light their pipes. This annoyed
Didius :

" If the sermon is of no better worth than to light pipes
with—'twas certainly, Sir, not good enough to be preached
before so learned a body ; and if 'twas good enough to be

preached before so learned a body—'twas certainly, Sir, too good to light their pipes with afterwards."

" I have got him fast hung up," quoth *Didius* to himself, " upon one of the two horns of my dilemma—let him get off as he can."

" I have undergone such unspeakable torments, in bringing forth this sermon," quoth *Yorick* upon this occasion—" that I declare, *Didius*, I would suffer martyrdom, before I would sit down and make such another : it came from my head instead of my heart—and it is for the pain it gave me, both in the preaching and writing of it, that I revenge myself of it in this manner.—To preach, to show the extent of our reading, or the subtleties of our wit—to parade in the eyes of the vulgar with the beggarly accounts of a little learning, tinselled over with a few words that glitter, but convey little light and less warmth—is a dishonest use of the poor single half-hour in a week which is put into our hands."

(STERNE, *Tristram Shandy.*)

Strictly speaking, a DILEMMA is a forced choice between two courses of action. Both courses are disagreeable or dangerous or unprofitable ; but one may be more so than the other. The suggestion is that the less disagreeable or dangerous or unprofitable should be adopted. Perhaps, however, the use of " dilemma " as a variant of " perplexity " (" I lost the train and was in a dilemma ") is so common that we are foolish to insist upon the strict application of the term.

" We must hang together, or hang separately " says the ruffian : we must either stick to the gang, much as some of us dislike their ways, or we shall be taken by the police and deservedly hanged. The disagreeable alternatives are the two " horns of the dilemma ". Pope, pestered by a crowd of suitors, protested that he must needs be impaled :

A dire dilemma ! either way I'm sped,
If foes, they write ; if friends they read me dead.

DIMINUTIVES

hillock, mannikin, cockerel, chicken, damsel, turret, brooklet, asterisk.

DIMINUTIVE is a name denoting a little one of its kind : a

hillock is a *little hill*; a *damsel* is a *little dame*; an *asterisk* is a *little star*. The suffixes that form these diminutives are:

- (*a*) Old English *el* (*satchel*, a *little sack*); *en* (*chicken*); *ie* (*lassie*); *ling* (*darling*, a *little dear*); *ock* (*hillock*); *kin* (*mannikin*);
- (*b*) Latin *sel* (*damsel*); *et* (*turret*, a *little tower*); *let* (*streamlet*); *ette* (*cigarette*); *ule* (*globule*, a *little globe*);
- (*c*) Greek *isk* (*asterisk*).

DIRECT OBJECT. (See " Object ")

DIRECT SPEECH, ORATIO RECTA. (See also **"Reported Speech "**)

- (*a*) After dinner we went to the Green Dragon on Lambeth Hill, and there we sang of all sorts of things, and I ventured with good success upon things at first sight, and after that I played upon my flageolet, and staid there till nine o'clock, very merry and drawn on with one song after another till it came to be so late. So parted and thence home, where I found my wife and maid a-washing. I staid up till the bellman came by with his bell just under my window as I was writing of this very line, and cried, " Past one of the clock, and a cold, frosty, windy morning." I then went to bed, and left my wife and the maid a-washing still.

  (SAMUEL PEPYS.)

- (*b*) " It was kind of you to come back to us, Henry," Lady Esmond said, " I thought you might come."

  " We read of the fleet coming to Portsmouth. Why did you not come from Portsmouth ? " Frank asked.

  (THACKERAY, *Henry Esmond*.)

- (*c*) Indeed, my good Scholar, we may say of Angling, as Dr. Boteler said of strawberries : " Doubtless God could have made a better berry, but doubtless God never did " : and so, if I might be judge, God never did make a more calm, quiet, innocent recreation, than Angling.

  (IZAAK WALTON, *The Compleat Angler*.)

The words actually used by a speaker—such quotations as are in the extracts above enclosed by inverted commas—are called " direct speech ". We turn the direct speech into reported speech by changing the tense of the verbs to the past and by changing the persons of the pronouns. Thus, we turn (*b*) into the report : *Lady Esmond said that it was kind of him to come back to them ; she had thought he might come. And Frank said that they had read of the fleet coming to Portsmouth, and asked why he had not come from Portsmouth.* Note that the mark of interrogation is *not* placed after a reported question.

DOUBLED CONSONANTS

accommodation, business, committee.

An unlucky decision to write a single consonant where fashion dictates a double consonant, a double consonant where fashion dictates a single one, is productive of many spelling errors. Here are a few words liable to error from that cause : *abbreviation, all right* (in America this is telescoped into *alright*) (notice the distinction too, between " They came all together " and " It is altogether wrong to do this "), *battalion, believe, disappear, unparalleled, accommodate, committee, camelia, desiccated* (dried for preservation), *moccasins, exaggerate, woollen* (note the American *woolen*), *skilful, fulfil, businesses, until, disappoint.*

Here again careful observation is our safeguard ; for sound gives little guidance. You have *committee* and *comity* (the comity of nations implies a courteous recognition among the nations of each other's laws) ; you have *levelling* and *paralleled* ; *Britain* and *Brittany* ; *harass* and *embarrass.*

Subject to its many exceptions we may give this rule : where you add an inflexion, like *ed* or *est*, you double the final consonant in these events :

(*a*) When the original is a single syllable : *pot* becomes *potted*, *knot* becomes *knotted*.

(*b*) When the final syllable is accented : *regret* becomes *regretted*, *demur* becomes *demurred* and *demurrage*.

(*c*) When the final letter is *l*, preceded by a single vowel : *level* becomes *levelled*, *control* becomes *controllable*, *travel* becomes *travelling*, *jewel* becomes *jewellery*.

The consonant remains single in *failure* when the *l* is preceded by a double vowel, and in *boiling*. American usage, we may note, sweeps away this distinction, *travel* becomes *traveler*, and so on ; and our usage is approaching that of our cousins. We already drop the second *l* in *almighty, almost, already, always, wilful.*

DOUBLE PLURALS

(*a*) (i) " Indexes " are alphabetical lists, placed as a rule at the end of a book, of the topics dealt with in the book, with indicators of where those topics are to be found.

(ii) " Indices " are figures (like the 3 in 4^3) indicating how many times the accompanying figure is to be a factor : 4^3 is $4 \times 4 \times 4$ or 64.

(*b*) (i) " Geniuses " are people having extraordinary capacity.

(ii) The " genii " of Arabian tales are wonder-working spirits.

(*c*) (i) We few, we happy few, we band of brothers ;
For he to-day that sheds his blood with me
Shall be my brother.

(*Henry V.*)

(ii) No uncle, I'll none ; Adam's sons are my brethren ;
and, truly, I hold it a sin to match in my kindred.
(Beatrice in *Much Ado About Nothing.*)

(*d*) (i) Take care of the pence and the pounds will take care of themselves.

(ii) Silver pennies constituted the chief money for a long period of our history.

Some names retain a foreign or an obsolete plural but, at the same time, are used with the ordinary plural ending. The economising instinct in our language brings it about that we use the different plurals with different shades of meaning. Thus, *brothers* is the ordinary plural ; *brethren* is for the pulpit or the platform. *Pence* is the plural when we have in mind a collective value ; *pennies* is the plural when we have in mind the separate coins.

DOUBLE POSSESSIVE

(*a*) It was that fatal and perfidious bark
That sunk so low that sacred head of thine.

(MILTON, *Lycidas.*)

(*b*) That tongue of his that bade the
Romans mark him.

(*Julius Cæsar.*)

There is apparently a double possessive in such a sentence as " He's always poking that nose of his into other people's business " and in the opening sentence of *Antony and Cleopatra,*

94

" Nay, but this dotage of our general's o'erflows the measure."
What is the explanation ?

This particular idiom is both well authorised and is useful
in enabling us to discriminate between allied ideas. The phrase
" an impartial judgment of his " signifies a judgment *by* him ;
" an impartial judgment of him " signifies a judgment *concerning*
him. " A friend of Tom's " would be one whom Tom likes ;
" a friend of Tom " would be one who likes Tom, whether or
not Tom felt friendliness in return. " A picture of the King "
is his likeness ; " a picture of the King's " is one belonging to
him. And we should note that the picture may be the only
one he has.

The popular explanation of the construction, that it is an
ellipsis for " a picture of the King's pictures ", that is, one
from among several pictures, is hardly correct. The explanation
might apply to such a phrase as " a play of Shakespeare's " ;
it could hardly apply to " that tongue of his ". *Of* cannot be
here used as denoting a part ; for he has but one tongue. A
similar comment applies to " of thine " in Milton's lines.

Nor can the explanation apply to a phrase like " an enemy
of ours ". This certainly cannot be construed " an enemy of
our enemies " ; *he* presumably would be a friend of ours. The
fact is that *of* in such phrases introduces a parallel expression,
a noun or pronoun in apposition. " The Island of Cyprus "
is " The island, Cyprus ". " The City of York " is " The
City, named York ". " This son of mine " is an effective way
of saying " This, my son ".

DOUBLETS AND TRIPLETS

(*a*) New Presbyter is but old Priest writ large.

(MILTON.)

(*b*) The *cloak* is in shape like the bell (*cloch*) that tells the
clock.

In our language are many pairs of words of the one origin,
but introduced at different times, and divergent in form and
meaning. These pairs are DOUBLETS. One word has perhaps
been brought by way of speech, another by way of writing.
Words brought by the first method tend to vary greatly from
the original ; words brought by the second method keep close

to the original. In many instances the word in English has only shed its foreign inflections. The original Latin, for example, is *abbreviatum* ; the importation through writing gives us *abbreviate*, the importation through speech gives us *abridge*. From the original Latin *redemptionem* we have the written *redemption* and the spoken *ransom*. *Pauper(em)* gives *pauper* and *poor*, the one transferred by learned writers from book to book, the other among the donations of the Normans to our language. In the example from Milton's sonnet, *Presbyter* is the original Greek stripped of inflection ; *priest* is the later, not (as Milton suggests) the earlier, modification.

Other pairs are *amiable* and *amicable*, *antique* and *antic*, *compute* and *count*, *major* and *mayor*, *pallid* and *pale*, *separate* and *sever*, *triumph* and *trump*, *captive* and *caitiff*, *diurnal* and *journal*, *secure* and *sure*, *fragile* and *frail*, *insulate* and *isolate*, *hotel* and *hospital*. Similar pairs from a Greek original are *adamant* and *diamond*, *scandal* and *slander*, *blaspheme* and *blame*, *phantasy* and *fancy*, *balsam* and *balm*, *iota* and *jot*, the first very near the original, the second modified in the course of passage.

Instances exist where more than two words from the common original persist side by side. The Greek *diskos* (the picture you call " The Discobolos " is of the quoit-thrower) has given us the learned *disc* (a round plate), *dais* (the raised floor in a hall), *desk* (a sloping table) and *dish* (a platter)—the various things resembling one another in little more than having a flat surface. *Dame*, *dam*, *donna* and *duenna* all diverge from the Latin *domina*, as *sir*, *sire*, *senior*, *señor* and *signor* do from the Latin *senior*. *Leal*, *loyal*, *legal* ; *card*, *chart*, *carte* ; *ration*, *ratio*, *reason* ; *plan*, *plane*, *plain*, are other groups from a common original.

E

" E " (SILENT or MUTE)

1. wine, paste, cake, bite, rode.
2. live, have, love, gave, brave.
3. nice, defence, twice.
4. drudge, bridge, age.
5. pulse, furze, horse, curse.
6. choice, grimace, caprice, police, foible.
7. are, were, come, one, none.

SILENT OR MUTE " E " is still retained in English spelling :

1. to indicate that the preceding vowel is long (contrast, *wĭn* and *păst* with *wine* and *pāste*) ;
2. to indicate that *v* is the consonant, not the vowel. (In early printing *live* was *liue*. That is why no English word ends in *v*. For, of course, such a word as *Slav* is not really English) ;
3. to indicate that *c* has the soft *s* sound (not the hard *k* sound as in *tic-tac*) ;
4. to indicate that *g* has the soft *j* sound (not the hard *g* sound as in *drug*, *bag*) ;
5. In words where *s* or *z* is preceded by a consonant.
6. In many words adopted from the French.
7. In many words from the caprice of printers.

But many spellings, in which silent *e* may or may not occur, hardly come under rule. We have " *Magdalen* College " at Oxford, " *Magdalene* College " at Cambridge, and both are sounded the same. We have *judgement* and *judgment* ; *moveable* and *movable* ; *loveable* and *lovable*. Usually, however,

(*a*) when a syllable is added, the silent *e* is dropped before a vowel : *changing*, *loving*, *drudging*, *braving*.

(*b*) when a syllable is added, the silent *e* is retained before a consonant : *forceful*, *nicely*, *changeling*.

But note : *gaugeable*, *noticeable*, *enforceable*, *singeing* (i.e. slightly burning), where the *e* is retained to indicate the soft sound of *c* or *g* (compare " Singing a song ").

"ECHOES" (ASSONANCE)

(*a*) The barge she sat in like a burnished throne
Burned on the water ; the poop was beaten gold,
Purple the sails, and so perfumed that
The winds were love-sick with them.
(*Antony and Cleopatra.*)

(*b*) No growth of moor or coppice,
No heather flower or vine,
But bloomless buds of poppies,
Green grapes of Proserpine,

> Pale beds of flowering rushes
> Where no leaf blooms or blushes
> Save this whereout she crushes
> For dead men deadly wine.

(SWINBURNE, Garden of Proserpine.)

There is assonance (or echo) when you have effective correspondence of sounds. See how, among other echoes, the vowels of " Xanadu " are repeated in a different order in *Kubla Khan*.

> In Xanadu did Kubla Khan
> A stately pleasure-dome decree.

In studying sounds you are studying an aspect of language in which from the earliest times men have rejoiced. You know how, as you listen to a Beethoven symphony, the one glorious theme comes recurrent in varied settings; your ear craves to hear it again, and the composer contents you. The recurrent sounds in spoken words please the ear, too.

Read aloud this line, " Sonorous metal blowing martial sounds." For the moment, don't bother about the meaning. Listen to the sounds; notice how cunningly the sounds of " sonorous metal " are echoed in " martial sounds ". Some phrases almost sing themselves, phrases like " Hark, hark, the lark at heaven's gate sings." You feel inclined to repeat the line in order to catch the harmony again.

Stevenson writes about " The House Beautiful "—

> A naked house, a naked moor,
> A shivering pool before the door,
> A garden bare of flowers and fruit,
> And poplars at the garden foot;
> Such is the place that I live in,
> Bleak without and bare within.

Delightful echoes are here in plenty; but now comes the outburst,

> Yet shall your ragged moor receive
> The incomparable pomp of eve.

You can't resist the repetition, " the incomparable pomp of eve ". You roll it round the tongue as you would a delicious chocolate cream.

The meaning of the words used matters. Of course it does,

—matters very much. Yet there is no reason why, because we are intent upon the meaning, we should not rejoice in the music of the sounds. At times in fact we do so delight in the sounds that we pay little attention to meaning. We read from this Chorus in *Atlanta*:

> When the hounds of spring are on winter's traces,
> The mother of months in meadow or plain
> Fills the shadows and windy places
> With lisp of leaves and ripple of rain;

and we get something of the meaning. The meaning, though, is of less interest to us than the music: " lisp of leaves " we say " and ripple of rain "; " mother of months in meadow and plain ". The passages in prose and poetry that cling to our memory do so far more by reason of sound than by reason of sense: the lines of Shakespeare that spontaneously came to mind are lines like, " In maiden meditation, fancy free "; " After life's fitful fever he sleeps well "; " A young man married is a man that's marred."

One further instance will delight you: it is in those wonderful lines where Milton speaks of Lethé, the river that brings forgetfulness:

> Far off from these a slow and silent stream,
> Lethé, the river of oblivion, rolls
> Her watery labyrinth, whereof who drinks
> Forthwith his former state and being forgets—
> Forgets both joy and grief, pleasure and pain.

EMPHASIS. (See also " Repetition ")

(*a*) Crispin Crispian shall ne'er go by,
  From this day to the ending of the world,
  But we in it shall be remembered,
  We few, we happy few, we band of brothers.

  (*Henry V.*)

(*b*) Now abideth faith, hope, charity, these three; but the greatest of these is charity.

  (1 *Corinthians* xiii.)

(*c*) A book is written, not to multiply the voice merely, not to carry it merely, but to preserve it.

  (RUSKIN, *Sesame and Lilies.*)

99

We emphasise a word or a phrase when we give that word or phrase treatment that makes it prominent. In (*a*) the pronoun *we* is emphasised by being repeated in varied connections. In (*b*) *these three* emphasises *faith*, *hope*, *charity*. In (*c*) the adverb *merely* emphasises the verbs *multiply* and *carry*. Writers employ all manner of devices in order to ask for our special attention to one or other of their ideas.

Thus, the Exclamation Mark—the Note of Admiration it is called at times—may ask you to believe something or other to be worthy of your delighted astonishment. Lady Mary Montagu describes Fair Fatima :

> That surprising harmony of features, that charming result of the whole ! that exact proportion of body ! that lovely bloom of complexion unsullied by art ! the unutterable enchantment of her smile. But her eyes !—large and black, with all the soft languishment of the blue.

Inversion, the placing of the words in an unexpected part of the sentence, also serves to draw extra attention. (See " *Inversion* ".)

EPENTHESIS

Chamber, with an inserted *b* to make the pronunciation easier, comes from the earlier *camera* ; *thunder*, with an inserted *d* between *n* and *r*, comes from the earlier *thunor* ; *tender* has a *d* inserted, the Latin origin of the word being *tener*(*um*). To-day the pronunciation of *Henry* as *Henery* is not unknown ; the inserted *e* seems to help the speaker.

Such an insertion is at times called EPENTHESIS.

EPIGRAMS. (See also " Antithesis ")

(*a*) When I said that I would die a bachelor, I did not think I should live till I were married.

> (Benedick in *Much Ado About Nothing*.)

(*b*) Here lies our Sovereign Lord, the King,
Whose word no man relies on,
Who never said a foolish thing
Nor never did a wise one.

> (LORD ROCHESTER, on Charles II.)

(*c*) What is an epigram ? a dwarfish whole,
Its body brevity, and wit its soul.

> (BRANDER MATTHEWS, *American Epigrams*.)

An EPIGRAM is a pointed saying, very often a contrast between what you might expect and the actual. " He went to Athens and—he wrote his name " : the preliminaries promised much, the achievement was negligible. " He that can, does ; he that cannot, teaches " : or, to paraphrase, " He that can make a fortune, makes it ; he that cannot, teaches economics."

Benedick had long inveighed against marriage. Yet he married. What matter ? " When I said that I would die a bachelor ", he declared, " I did not think I should live till I were married." Doctor Johnson, never unduly complimentary where women were concerned, declared on one occasion, " A woman's preaching is like a dog's walking on his hind legs. It is not well done ; but you are surprised to find it done at all."

Voltaire visited London when Londoners were less tolerant than they are now. A mob chased him in the street because his foreign garb annoyed them. He mounted a bench and addressed them, " Am I not luckless enough already, not to have been born one of yourselves ? " Whereupon, we are told, his assailants cheered him, three times three ; and those who had hooted him loudest carried him home in triumph. These crisp sayings, well devised to capture attention, are epigrams. Like the clever advertisement they have clarity and swiftness ; like that, too, they economise their words. A playwright, who still had much to learn, sent his play to a manager. The manager wrote :

> MY DEAR SIR,
> I have read your play.
> Oh ! my dear Sir.

From long ago comes to us in a Greek epitaph—which is also a good example of the epigram—an expression of weariness with the world : " I, Dionysius of Tarsus, lie here at sixty, having never married ; and I would that my father had not." The modern poet's version of this statement, that life hardly seems worth living, is L. A. G. Strong's—

> Bill Jupp lies 'ere, aged sixty year :
> From Tavistock 'e came.
> Single 'e bided, and 'e wished
> 'Is father done the same.

The short poem, ending in a witty and unanticipated thought, is a favourite vehicle of the epigram. Herrick, for example, was fond of quick transitions from gay to grave. He had a keen taste for the delights of life; he had also a keen sense of the inconstancy of those delights. " To Dianeme " he writes:

> Sweet, be not proud of those two eyes
> Which starlike sparkle in their skies;
> Nor be you proud, that you can see
> All hearts your captives; yours yet free;
> Be you not proud of that rich hair
> Which wantons with the lovesick air;
> Whenas that ruby which you wear,
> Sunk from the tip of your soft ear,
> Will last to be a precious stone,
> When all your world of beauty's gone.

The EPIGRAM is the method of the effective advertiser. He wants to shock you into attention to what he says; and he contrives a slogan with a sting in its tail. You will yourself be able to supply any number of instances. Indeed, one who would be a writer of really telling advertisements will give much thought to the neat, pithy sayings of great writers. For example, " The fear of every man that heard him was lest he should make an end ", wrote Ben Jonson in commendation of Lord Bacon's oratory.

> I know a thing that's most uncommon;
> (Envy be silent and attend!)
> I know a reasonable woman,
> Handsome and witty, yet a friend,

wrote Alexander Pope " On a certain Lady at Court ". Two very fine advertisements, you will agree.

Perhaps it does not say much for the natural propensity of men, and of women too, that the epigram is used to blame far more often than to praise. It is incident to the best of us that the faults of others, not their merits, arouse the more interest. In satire, therefore, where vice and folly are held up to ridicule, the epigram has ample scope. Addison was, it seems a little jealous of the rising fame of Pope; and Pope, a master of neat epigram, wrote some lines of which he said, " I sent the verses to Mr. Addison, and he used me very civilly ever after." It was, in fact, worth while not to court retaliation from one adept in shooting little poisoned arrows like those below. Addison would like to reign alone in letters; "Was there a writer", asks Pope, "who could

> Bear, like the Turk, no brother near the throne;
> View him with scornful yet with jealous eyes,
> And hate, for arts that caused himself to rise;
> Damn with faint praise, assent with civil leer,
> And without sneering, teach the rest to sneer;
> Willing to wound, and yet afraid to strike.
> Just hint a fault, and hesitate dislike."

EPILOGUE

(a) No epilogue, I pray you; for your play needs no excuse. Never excuse; for when the players are all dead, there need none to be blamed.

> (*A Midsummer Night's Dream.*)

(b) If it be true that "good wine needs no bush", 'tis true that a good play needs no epilogue.

> (*As You Like It.*)

The EPILOGUE is the concluding speech of a play, the last words (or peroration) of a speech, the good-bye of a novelist to his readers. It is at times called L'ENVOI, the parting message: look, for instance, at Kipling's poem "L'Envoi" beginning "There's a whisper down the field, where the year has shot her yield" and describing the leave-taking of the Eastward-bound.

EPONYM

The rewards of treachery are generally precarious, and the news from Stockholm that the eponymous traitor of the present war has been jettisoned by his Nazi masters will cause no surprise.

> (*The Times* of September 19th, 1940,
> speaking of Quisling.)

An EPONYM is one that gives his name to a people or a place or an institution, as Major Quisling did to the treachery that facilitated invasion.

Epicurus (denounced by his antagonists as a teacher extolling pleasure), gave us *epicure*. Duns Scotus, an able schoolman, bequeathed *dunce*; the gambling Earl of Sandwich, eager to find a meal that would not interfere with his avocation, left us *sandwich*; the great road-builder Macadam left his name to describe roads made in accordance with his plan. The Emperor Augustus is the eponym for our month *August*; Julius Cæsar for our month *July*.

ERRORS CONDONED BY CUSTOM

Errors, being condoned by custom, become good English. Custom in language is all-powerful. You may know, for instance, that *assets* was originally a singular noun : the French *assez* is " enough ", and *assets* meant " enough to discharge the burden of debts ". Yet you would be foolish to use *assets* as a noun of Singular Number (as Bacon does) and use *it* for the corresponding pronoun, and *is* for the verb. We must now look on *assets* as a plural and, when we do want a singular, use the word *asset*. And, as you will have noted, the original sense is absent when we speak of the *assets* of a bankrupt. The very meaning of " bankrupt " is not having enough to pay debts.

Riches was another of the foreign importations where the *s* was mistaken for the plural ending. The French *richesse*, one forerunner of the word, is singular ; and early writers used the word as a singular. Cassio says of Desdemona :

> O behold,
> The riches of the ship is come on shore

You will now, however, regard *riches* as a plural. But we have not yet—as we have with *assets*—coined a singular noun.

A perversion in the opposite direction is our regarding an original plural noun as a singular—sometimes, indeed, giving it a new plural. Such a word is *invoice*, meaning a list of goods sent with their prices and charges. This was once the French *envois* (the French verb, you remember, is *envoyer* " to send "). We must now look on *invoice* as a singular noun, its plural being *invoices*. The word " tweed "—" A roll of tweed from the Hebrides "—is another instance. It resulted from a mis-reading of " tweel ", the Scots form of " twill " (meaning " a woven fabric ". But we should be foolish to try to recall " tweel ".

In a good many of our words the spelling bears witness to a mistake. You come across the word *napery*, meaning house-hold linen. Well, our *apron* was part of this *napery* : it was a napkin at table to protect clothes from dirt or injury. But people got into the way of analysing *a napron* into *an apron*; and now we must not begin the noun with *n*. You know, too, the phrase " to eke out ", meaning " to supplement ", " make additions " to. Well, *an eke-name* was an added name; and now we make a new division and speak of *nick-name*. The word *newt* illustrates the opposite process: the *n* of the noun has been, by a mistake to which we must all bow, transferred to the article; *a newt* should really be *an ewt*.

This *n* does, in fact, seem to be a readily moved letter. *Ned* is a short form of the endearing address *mine Edward*, *Nan* of *Mine Ann*, *Nol* of *Mine Oliver*, and so on. (*See page* 8.)

ETHIC DATIVE

(*a*) See how this river comes me cranking in
And cuts me from the best of all my land
A huge half-moon, a monstrous cantle out.

               (Hotspur in *I Henry IV*.)

(*b*)   You shall mark
Many a duteous and knee-crooking knave,
That, doting on his own obsequious bondage,
Wears out his time, much like his master's ass,
For nought but provender, and when he's old, cashiered:
Whip me such honest knaves.

               (Iago in *Othello*.)

A peculiar use of the pronoun, in these days an affectation though common enough three hundred years ago, is its insertion into a sentence to signify an indirect interest in the matter. Such use—of the two *me's* in (*a*) and of *me* in (*b*)—is called the Ethic Dative: the dative of feeling. " So far as I am concerned " would be expansion of Hotspur's *me*; " on my behalf and for my pleasure " would be an expansion of Iago's.

ETYMOLOGY

Fact is usually less entertaining than fiction, and for this reason false etymologies are to most people more attractive than true ones.

               (A. C. BRADLEY.)

Etymology is a true account of the history of a word, its

origin and its successive modifications. Thus, Professor Bradley explains the name " Brighton ".

A thousand years ago or more, a man named Brihthelm lived on the coast of Sussex. When his neighbours spoke of his abode as Brihthelm's *tun*—this word, now pronounced " town ", having then the sense of " farm enclosure "—they were clearly not inventing a name for the place, but merely referring to it in the most obvious way possible. But long after Brihthelm was dead and forgotten, *Brihthelmstun* continued to be the name of the farm and of the village that had gathered round it. The village grew into a large town, which till quite lately was called Brighthelmstone, though the name is now contracted to Brighton.

EUPHEMISM. See also " Circumlocution ")

(*a*) The prince of the powers of darkness : the author of all evil. (*The devil.*)
  The light-fingered gentry. (*Pick-pockets.*)

(*b*) Annual income twenty pounds, annual expenditure nineteen nineteen six, result happiness. Annual income twenty pounds, annual expenditure twenty pounds ought and six, result misery. The blossom is blighted, the leaf is withered, the god of day goes down upon the dreary scene, and—and, in short you are for ever floored.
                    (Mr. Micawber in *David Copperfield.*)

The word descriptive of a disagreeable idea may be replaced by a word not in itself disagreeable, or by a roundabout phrase designed to veil a disagreeable reality : " to die " may be replaced by " to pass away ", " to fall asleep ". The substitute for the disagreeable word is a EUPHEMISM. Mr. Micawber probably felt less grief in regarding his position as being merely " the blossom is blighted " than in regarding it as " for ever floored ". In like manner the packer regards his act of appropriating a book or two while packing them as much less blameworthy when he speaks of " snooping " them than when he speaks of " stealing " them. Mr. Churchill's " terminological inexactitude " is less likely than " lie " to bring a blush, and his " innocuous desuetude " less likely than " dropping " to offend the colleague whose pet scheme had been shelved. Yet, " euphemism ", says one, " is more demoralising than coarseness ".

EUPHONY

O happy fair !
Your eyes are lode-stars ; and your tongue's sweet air
More tuneable than lark to shepherd's ear,
When wheat is green, when hawthorn buds appear.
(*A Midsummer Night's Dream.*)

There is EUPHONY in your writing when the reading of it
aloud produces a pleasant sound. There is CACOPHONY when
the reading aloud produces a disagreeable, an ugly sound.
Read aloud those lines above of Shakespeare and then these
two of Browning's :

Nokes hints blue, straight he turtle eats,
Stokes prints blue, claret crowns his cup.

The contrast there—between the smoothly flowing melody of
the first and the harsh, grating sounds of the congregated
consonants of the second—is a striking one. You will, however, find instances in abundance where some alterations in
the words or in the arrangement of them would result in a
more agreeable sound. To be sure you will not overlook the
fact that harshness of sound—" cacophony " you can call it in
distinction to " euphony "—is at times intended by the writer :
it was by Browning in the passage quoted.

EUPHUISM

(*a*) My good friend, I have read your new passions, and they
have renewed mine old pleasures, the which brought to
me no less delight than they have done to your self-
commendations. And certes had not one of mine eyes
about serious affairs been watchful, both by being too
busy, had been wanton : such is the nature of persuading
pleasure, that it melteth the marrow before it scorch the
skin and burneth before it warmeth. Not unlike unto
the oil of jet, which rotteth the bone and never rankleth
the flesh, or the scarab flies which enter into the root and
never touch the fruit.

And whereas you desire to have my opinion, you may
imagine that my stomach is rather cloyed than queasy,
and therefore mine appetite of less force than my affec-
tion, fearing rather a surfeit of sweetness than desiring a
satisfying. The repeating of love wrought in me a semblance of liking ; but searching the very veins of my heart

I could find nothing but a broad scar where I left a deep wound : and loose strings where I tied hard knots : and a table of steel where I framed a plot of wax.

Whereby I noted that young swans are grey, and the old white, young trees tender and the old tough, young men amorous, and growing in years, either wiser or warier. The coral plant in the water is a soft weed, on the land a hardstone : a sword frieth in the fire like a black eel ; but laid in earth like white snow : the heart in love is altogether passionate ; but free from desire altogether careless.

(JOHN LYLY, *Euphues.*)

(*b*) Harry, I do not only marvel where thou spendest thy time, but also how thou art accompanied ; for though the camomile, the more it is trodden on the faster it grows, yet youth, the more it is wasted the sooner it wears. There is a thing, Harry, which thou hast often heard of, and it is known to many in our land by the name of pitch : this pitch, as ancient writers do report, doth defile : so doth the company thou keepest : for, Harry, now I do not speak to thee in drink, but in tears ; not in pleasure, but in passion ; not in words only, but in woes also.

(*I Henry IV.*)

Two peculiar and very popular books at the time, *Euphues, The Anatomy of Wit*, and *Euphues and his England* were written by John Lyly towards the close of the sixteenth century : " Be valiant but not too venturous. Let your attire be comely, but not costly " are injunctions from *The Anatomy of Wit*.

The high-flown style of writing—full of antitheses and of strange similes derived usually from animals or vegetables or minerals—was for long eagerly copied. EUPHUISM is the name applied to the style. EUPHUISTIC is the adjective derived from the noun.

Example (*a*) gives an instance of Lyly's style ; example (*b*) is Falstaff's parody of it.

EXCLAMATION MARK (sometimes called MARK OF ADMIRATION)

(*a*) Might she sleep in peace—might she sleep in peace ; and we, too, when our struggles and pains are over ! But the earth is the Lord's, as the heaven is ; we are alike His creatures, here and yonder. I took a little flower off the hillock, and kissed it, and went my way, like the bird that had just lighted on the cross by me, back into the world again. Silent receptacle of death! tranquil depth of calm, out of reach of tempest an trouble! I felt as one who had been walking below the sea, and treading amidst the bones of shipwrecks.

(THACKERAY, Henry Esmond.)

(b) The year's at the spring,
    And day's at the morn;
    Morning's at seven;
The hillside's dew-pearled;
The lark's on the wing;
The snail's on the thorn:
God's in his heaven—
All's right with the world!

(ROBERT BROWNING.)

This mark is appropriate with genuine exclamations; it is hardly appropriate as a means of emphasising what is said. Look, for instance, at Matthew Arnold's address to Oxford. The mark is, you agree, quite appropriate after *city*, *serene*, *romantic*, *Philistine*, *loyalties*. But is it appropriate after *still* and *play*? Probably not.

No, we are all seekers still! seekers often make mistakes, and I wish mine to redound to my own discredit only, and not to touch Oxford. Beautiful city! so venerable, so lovely, so unravaged by the fierce intellectual life of our century, so serene!

There are our young barbarians, all at play! And yet, steeped in sentiment as she lies, spreading her gardens to the moonlight and whispering from her towers the last enchantments of the Middle Age, who will deny that Oxford, by her ineffable charm, keeps ever calling us nearer to the true goal of all of us, to the ideal, to perfection,—to beauty, in a word, which is only truth seen from another side?

Adorable dreamer, whose heart has been so romantic! who has given thyself so prodigally, given thyself to sides and to heroes not mine, only never to the Philistines! home of lost causes, and forsaken beliefs, and unpopular names, and impossible loyalties! What example could ever so inspire us to keep down the Philistine in ourselves? . . . She will forgive me, even if I have unwittingly drawn upon her a shot or two aimed at her unworthy son ; for she is generous, and the cause in which I fight is, after all, hers. Apparitions of a day, what is our puny warfare against the Philistines, compared with the warfare which this queen of romance has been waging against them for centuries, and will wage after we are gone ?

In Shelley's lines :

> O World ! O Life ! O Time !
> On whose last steps I climb,
> Trembling at that where I had stood
> When will return the glory of your prime
> No more,—Oh never more !

the *O* in *O World !* is a call for attention ; the *Oh* in *Oh never more !* is a cry of pain.

The example from Thackeray illustrates its use well. The mark indicates tone also. Thus, the words, *Jones has scored*, admits of three renderings :

> Jones has scored. (A matter-of-fact statement.)
> Jones has scored ? (A search for information.)
> Jones has scored ! (An exclamation of delight or of astonishment.)

EXPLETIVES

(a) And feeble expletives their aid do join
And ten dull words creep into one dull line.

(POPE.)

(b) Expletives he very early ejected from his verses ; but he now and then admits an epithet rather commodious than important. Each of the first six lines of the *Iliad* might lose two syllables with very little diminution of the meaning ; and sometimes, after all his art and labour, one verse seems to be made for the sake of another.

(DR. JOHNSON, on Pope.)

An EXPLETIVE—like " do " in the first example—is a filling-up word. The pronoun " they " in Wordsworth's lines is an expletive :

> What is't that ails young Henry Gill ?
> That evermore his teeth they chatter ?

and some people have such a poverty of words that they are

obliged to eke out their store by meaningless curses. The advice is proffered to cut out superfluities, to use no more words than are needed. Naturally we take the advice when we send a telegram. The most garrulous among us shrinks from the mounting cost of his dispatch. But we ignore the advice in our ordinary talk and our ordinary writing; and we probably do well to ignore it. What an exacting task we should have if we were compelled to give a strict account of every word we used. It would be like talking in mathematical symbols. Quite possibly a concentrated dinner cube would give us all the vitamins and other things needed. But some padding is agreeable; and the padding also conduces to digestion.

Every good writer—certainly every good speaker—knows that there must be a sprinkling of non-essential words that the essential words shall have their effect. Clumsy expansion we may condemn : better to say " own up " than " admit the soft impeachment ". But some expansions are delightful, even necessary. A speech in the bare manner of a statute would defy digestion. Some phrases—" depend upon it "; " Ladies and Gentlemen "; " I venture to observe "; " I would ask any member of this large and intelligent audience ", and the like—relieve the strain upon both speaker and hearers.

How natural, too, it is to use expletives ! Those interjections we use could, very likely, be omitted without affecting the sense of our statement. Thus, the only purpose of " Why man ! " in Shakespeare's " Why man ! he doth bestride the narrow world like a Colossus " is to emphasise and possibly to give a hint of the speaker's impatience. Still we all agree that our language would lack an agreeable ingredient if we rigorously excluded interjections.

Repetition itself, the saying in other words what has already been adequately said, often delights as well as impresses a particular thought. " The reaper was alone " is the bare statement. Does anyone cavil because Wordsworth brings along " single ", " solitary ", " by herself " and " alone " to express the one idea ?—

> Behold her, single in the field,
> Yon solitary Highland lass !

Reaping and singing by herself,
Stop here, or gently pass!
Alone she cuts and binds the grain
And sings a melancholy strain.

After all, we must not be exacting and expect to find, in every word we hear or see, a brilliant new idea.

F

FALLACY

(a) "Speaking of money," said the night-watchman thoughtfully, "the whole world would be different if we all had more of it. It would be a brighter world for everybody."

(b) *Cade :* He can speak French ; and therefore he is a traitor.
Suffolk : O gross and miserable ignorance!
Cade : Nay, answer, if you can : the Frenchmen are our enemies : go to, then, I ask but this : can he that speaks with the tongue of an enemy, be a good counsellor?
(SHAKESPEARE, *II Henry VI.*)

A FALLACY is an error in reasoning. In that delightful book, *Through the Looking Glass*, the Knight expounds his plan for getting over the gate :

"I'll tell you how I came to think of it," said the Knight. "You see, I said to myself, 'The only difficulty is with the feet : the head is high enough already.' Now, first I put my head on the top of the gate—then the head's high enough—then I stand on my head—then the feet are high enough you see—then I'm over, you see."

"Yes, I suppose you'd be over when that was done," Alice said thoughtfully ; "but don't you think it would be rather hard?"

"I haven't tried it yet," the Knight said gravely : "so I can't tell for certain—but I'm afraid it *would* be a little hard."

Don't you often meet, in political discussions more often than elsewhere, instances of the Knight's fallacy! The would-be reasoner fails because he neglects the proviso "other things being equal" : if the elevation of the feet did not entail the depression of the head, his argument would be valid. As it is, like so many we hear—read, too—it is invalid.

A man argues : " I was sick ; I took such a medicine ; I am well. Therefore the medicine cured my sickness." The conclusion may be true. But its truth is not established by the argument : the man may be well in spite of the medicine. We are told that, when an eclipse of the sun terrifies the women of China, they clatter with all their vigour upon whatever domestic utensil makes the most noise. The device is always successful in driving the black shadow away ; and belief is strengthened in the method of dealing effectively with eclipses. The fallacy is a natural one : because one thing happens after another, we often make the unjustified deduction that the first is the cause of the second. *Post hoc, ergo propter hoc* (" after that, therefore because of that ") is the Latin phrase.

Natural though the fallacy is, we do well to avoid it when we seek to convince another of the truth of our contention. He exposes the fallacy. He assumes—quite erroneously—that, because he has shown how unsound our argument is, he has also shown that what we contend for is false. But our contention may be true notwithstanding the ineptitude of its upholder. Better decline an argument than afford easy triumph to those who strive against the light. For, as a wary old philosopher tells us, " Every man is not a proper champion for truth nor fit to take up the gauntlet in the cause of verity."

Milton was a little hasty in his confident prediction :

" Though all the winds of doctrine were let loose to play upon the earth, so Truth be in the field, we do injuriously by licensing and prohibiting to misdoubt her strength. Let her and Falsehood grapple ; who ever knew Truth put to the worse in a free and open encounter ? "

Another fallacy, of which you must have noted lately many deplorable instances, is the one variously called " arguing in a circle ", " begging the question "—*petitio principii* is the Latin phrase. In the course of arguing a man assumes, quite unwittingly at times, the conclusion that he has set out to establish. He bases two conclusions one upon the other : " The policy of the Government is a good one. For we know that the Government is good. We know this because its policy is good." (" This beer is excellent because it was made of the very best malt and sugar and hops ; and we know how good these were from the excellent beer we have.") This mode of argument, or rather of evading an argument, is unjustly regarded as peculiarly incident to women. This is not so : the conscious or unconscious assumption of the point to be proved is as common among men. "You must vote conservative" : "Why?" you ask; "Because all sensible people will." "Foxhunting is not cruel"; "What reason have you for saying so?" "Because the fox enjoys the fun." It is only because a woman usually has tact enough to avoid an inconvenient discussion that she is supposed to resort readily to this "cheese-is-cheese-because-it-is-cheese" fallacy.

FALLING RHYTHM. (See "Metre")

Nobly, nobly Cape Saint Vincent to the North-west died away ;
Sunset ran, one glorious blood-red, reeking into Cadiz Bay ;
Bluish 'mid the burning water, full in face Trafalgar lay ;
In the dimmest North-east distance dawned Gibraltar grand and
    gray ;
"Here and here did England help me : how can I help Eng-
    land ?"—say,
Whose turns as I, this evening, turn to God to praise and pray,
While Jove's planet rises yonder, silent over Africa.
        (R. BROWNING, *Home-thoughts from the Sea*.)

When a strong accent is followed by a weak accent, or two weak accents, you have an instance of "falling rhythm". The single words, *youthful*, *dimple*, *wrinkled*, *jollity*, have such a falling rhythm ; and in verse the trochee (as in the instance above from Browning) and the dactyl (as in Hood's "Take her up tenderly") fall from strong to weak. Herrick's dainty lines *To Violets* is another good instance :

> Welcome, maids of honour !
>   You do bring
>   In the spring,
> And wait upon her.
>
> Yet though thus respected,
>   By-and-by
>   Ye do lie,
> Poor girls neglected.

Or again :

Here a solemn Fast we keep,
While all beauty lies asleep ;
Husht be all things (no noise here)
But the toning of a tear :
Or a sigh of such as bring
Cowslips for her covering.

(Epitaph.)

FIGURES OF SPEECH. (See "Simile, Metaphor", etc.)

(*a*) *All flesh is grass*, is not only metaphorically, but literally
true ; for all those creatures we behold are but the herbs
of the field, digested into flesh in them, or more remotely
carnified in ourselves.

(SIR THOMAS BROWNE.)

(*b*) You must speak upon the square with him. He stops a
metaphor like a suspected person in an enemy's country.
" A healthy book ! "—said one of his countrymen to me,
who had ventured to give that appellation to John Buncle
—" did I catch rightly what you said ? I have heard of
a man in health, and of a healthy state of body, but I do
not see how that epithet can be properly applied to a
book."

(CHARLES LAMB, of a Scotsman.)

We do not always " speak by the card ", and so speaking
keep to strict accuracy. We leave the literal, and we express
ourselves in figurative language. The varied ways in which we
give up precision for a greater impressiveness are FIGURES OF
SPEECH. (Simile and Metaphor are the type.) Those cards,
for instance, that take up so much time of so many of us may be
used as implied illustrations, as figures of speech, that is. Thus
we may describe an unsafe plan as " a house of cards "; we
state we are abandoning the project by declaring that " we are
throwing in our cards "; we " play our cards well " (or badly)
when we deserve to succeed (or to fail) ; we reveal our strength
when we " show our cards " or " put them on the table ", and
a " sure card " is a person or a project that is certain to bring
success.

The two paragraphs below show how effective the use of
figures of speech can be. The paragraphs are taken from
Burke's defence of his pension after an attack upon it by the
Duke of Bedford :

The grants to the House of Russell were so enormous as not only to outrage economy, but even to stagger credulity. The Duke of Bedford is the leviathan among all the creatures of the Crown. He tumbles about his unwieldy bulk; he plays and frolics in the ocean of the royal bounty. Huge as he is, and whilst " he lies floating many a rood ", he is still a creature. His ribs, his fins, his whalebone, his blubber, the very spiracles through which he spouts a torrent of brine against his origin and covers me all over with the spray, everything of him is from the throne. Is it for *him* to question the dispensation of the royal favour?

In private life I have not at all the honour of acquaintance with the noble Duke; but I ought to presume, and it costs me nothing to do so, that he abundantly deserves the esteem and love of all who live with him. But as to public service, why truly, it would not be more ridiculous for me to compare myself, in rank, in fortune, in splendid descent, in youth, in strength, or figure with the Duke of Bedford, than to make a parallel between his services and my attempts to be useful to my country. It would not be gross adulation, but uncivil irony to say that he has any public merit of his own to keep alive the idea of the services by which his vast landed pensions were obtained. My merits, whatever they are, are original and personal: his are derivative. It is his ancestor, the original pensioner, that has laid up this inexhaustible fund of merit which makes his Grace so very delicate and exceptious about the merit of all other grantees of the Crown. Had he permitted me to remain in quiet, I should have said, " 'Tis his estate: that's enough. It is his by law: what have I to do with it or its history? " He would naturally have said, on his side, " 'Tis this man's fortune. He is as good now as my ancestor was two hundred and fifty years ago. I am a young man with very old pensions; he is an old man with very young pensions: that's all."

And here is a note from Sterne:

Speaking of " the current of men and money to the metropolis ", Tristram Shandy says of his father:

a *current* was not the image he took most delight in,—a *distemper* was here his favourite metaphor, and he would run it down into a perfect allegory, by maintaining it was identically the same in the body national as in the body natural where the blood and spirits were drawn up into the head faster than they could find their ways down ;—a stoppage of circulation must come, which was death in both cases.

FOREIGN TERMS

(a) Out of his school he is no way pedantic in carriage or discourse ; contenting himself to be rich in Latin, though he doth not jingle it in every company wherein he comes.
(FULLER's " Good Schoolmaster ".)

(b) " Question two : ' Pabulum ', ' Cela va sans dire ', ' Par excellence ', ' Ne plus ultra '. What are these? Are there any more of them ? " " They are scholarship," replied Rob, " and there are two more, namely, ' tour de force ', and ' terra firma '."
(*A pretended examination upon a candidate for Fleet Street is proceeding.* See BARRIE'S *When a Man's Single.*)

The advice is sound : be sparing in the use of FOREIGN TERMS. Yet some are preferable to English-born substitutes. Though we write them in italics and though we pronounce them as we think they are pronounced abroad, they are part of the English Language. A *pied-à-terre* says more than *foot on the ground* ; a person's *bête noire* is more than his *black beast* ; to give *carte blanche* means more than to give him a *white card* : *dilettante* indicates one who toys with an art, perhaps with many arts, concentrating on none, and suggests more than the original *one that delights in.* " Evening dress is required by etiquette " is not so good as " Evening dress is *de rigeur* ". We should be at a loss without such importations as those.

If you do feel impelled to make a quotation, from Latin or other foreign language, it might be well to do as sensible old Burton did and supply a translation. Thus he apologises for the defects of his book in this way :

Our writings are so many dishes, our readers guests, our books like beauty, that which we admire another rejects ; so are we approved as men's fancies are inclined. (*Pro captu lectoris habent sua fata libelli.*) That which is most pleasing to one is *amaracum sui,* most harsh to another. *Quot homines, tot sententiae,* so many men, so many minds ; that which thou condemnest he commends.

117

" Gurth, I advise thee to call off Fangs, and leave the herd to their destiny, which, whether they meet with bands of travelling soldiers, or of outlaws, or of wandering pilgrims, can be little else than to be converted into Normans before morning, to thy no small ease and comfort."

" The swine turned Normans to my comfort ! " quoth Gurth ; " expound that to me, Wamba, for my brain is too dull and my mind too vexed to read riddles."

" Why, what call you those grunting brutes running about on their four legs ? " demanded Wamba.

" Swine, fool, swine," said the herd ; " every fool knows that."

" And swine is good Saxon," said the jester. " But how call you the sow when she is flayed and drawn and quartered and hung up by the heels like a traitor ? "

" Pork," answered the shepherd.

" I am very glad every fool knows that too," said Wamba, " and pork I think is good Norman-French, and so when the brute lives and is in the charge of a Saxon slave she goes by her Saxon name but becomes a Norman and is called ' pork ' when she is carried to the castle hall to feast among the nobles. What dost thou think of this, friend Gurth, ha ? "

" It is too true doctrine, friend Wamba, however it got into thy fool's pate."

" Nay I can tell you more," said Wamba in the same tone. " There is old Alderman Ox continues to hold his Saxon epithet while he is under the charge of serfs and bondsmen such as thou, but becomes Beef, a fiery French gallant when he arrives before the worshipful jaws that are destined to consume him. Mynheer Calf too, becomes Monsieur de Veau in the like manner ; he is Saxon when he required tendance, and takes a Norman name when he becomes matter of enjoyment."

(Gurth was the swineherd in SCOTT's *Ivanhoe*.)

At all periods our language has been hospitable to foreign elements ; and we now use an astonishing number of words, ultimately from other languages than English, without the least thought that we are going outside our native stock. Thus the lawyer's terms—*court, assize, judge, jury, justice, prison, gaol, chattel, money, rent, tax, council, parliament, bill, act*—are, like the words commented upon in the passage above, all of Old French origin.

There have been importations of words though we already had the home-produced word for the idea. Sometimes both words, the home product and the imported, survive. The English *whole* persists with the Danish *hale* ; but *hale*, as in the expression " hale and hearty " is restricted to one sense of " good ", " robust ", and " vigorous ", while *whole* remains the general term. The English *thatch*, the covering of a cottage or a stack, accompanies the Dutch *deck*, the covering of a ship. The passage from *Ivanhoe* is another illustration of how two words, once identical in meaning, have diverged in meaning.

English *ridge*, *bridge* and *church* are often replaced in northern dialects by Danish *rig*, *brig* and *kirk*. The English *east*, the quarter of the sunrise, is kin to the Latin *aurora*, the dawn ; English *hundred* to Latin *cent*. The Latin *maternal* lives along with English *motherly*, *cordial* with *hearty*, *beef* with *cow*, *rectitude* with *righteousness*, *juvenile* with *young*, *longitude* with *length*, *grain* with *corn* and a host of others.

A curious feature of our language is the frequency with which we prefer the foreigner when we need to use other than the simple noun, verb or adjective. Thus we use the English noun *ear*, but we go to the Latin for the adjective, *audible* (that can be heard), *auricular* (told in the ear, secret), and *aural* (belonging to the ear), and for the noun *aurist* (an ear specialist). The English verb *sit* is replaced by its Latin cognate in the adjective *sedentary* ; *two* has as its corresponding adjective *dual* and as its corresponding noun *duplicity*, in both of which words we have the Latin *duo* ; *foot* has *pedal* for " belonging to the foot ", and we say *pedestrian* rather than " *foot-goer* " ; the English pronoun *I* has the Latin *egotist* for the person always using *I*, and the Latin *egoist* for the person always thinking about himself. It is sometimes said that the Old English element in the vocabulary gives our language vigour and vividness and its appeal to the feelings ; and that the imported element, the Latin element in particular, gives our language stateliness and music and the capacity for expressing minute distinctions.

FREQUENTATIVE VERBS

(*a*) Lingering like an unloved guest.

(*b*) Hark ! hark ! the lark at Heaven's gate sings.

A FREQUENTATIVE VERB (like *linger* from *long* and *hark* from *hear*) expresses repetition of an action. Compare *nibble* from *nip*, *sparkle* from *spark*, *chatter* from *chat*, *dribble* from *drip*.

FULL STOP (PERIOD)

(*a*) One day when Will was about sixteen, a fat young man arrived at sunset to pass the night. He was a contented-looking fellow with a jolly eye and carried a knapsack. While dinner was preparing he sat in the arbour to read a book ; but as soon as he had begun to observe Will the book was laid aside ; he was plainly one of those who prefer living people to people made of ink and paper. Will, on his part, although he had not been much interested in the stranger at first sight, soon began to take a great deal of pleasure in his talk, which was full of good nature and good sense, and at last conceived a great respect for his character and wisdom. They sat far into the night and about two in the morning Will opened his heart to the young man, and told him how he longed to leave the valley and what bright hopes he had connected with the cities of the plain. The young man whistled and then broke into a smile.

(ROBERT LOUIS STEVENSON, Will o' the Mill.)

(*b*) " The name of those fabulous animals (pagan, I regret to say) who used to sing in the water, has quite escaped me." Mr. George Chuzzlewit suggested " Swans ". " No," said Mr. Pecksniff. " Not swans. Very like swans, too. Thank you." The nephew propounded " Oysters ". " No," said Mr. Pecksniff, " nor oysters. But by no means unlike oysters ; a very excellent idea ; thank you, my dear sir, very much. Wait. Sirens ! Dear me ! sirens, of course."

(CHARLES DICKENS, Martin Chuzzlewit.)

The FULL STOP (or PERIOD) indicates the close of a sentence It provides in a manner a resting-place for the reader before he embarks upon another sentence ; and the modern tendency, out of concern for the reader, provides these resting-places in plenty. It might, indeed, seem from the practice of many writers, that there is distrust of the power of readers. They are thought to be kin to the immortals described in *Gulliver's Travels* :

They never can amuse themselves with reading, because their memory will not serve to carry them from the beginning of the sentence to the end ; and by this defect they are deprived of the only entertainment whereof they might otherwise be capable.

The sentences in the Stevenson extract are considerably longer than those you find in your newspapers ; but you will surely not judge them to be too long The extract is a full paragraph so that you can note the variety in both the length and the structure of the sentences.

FUNCTION OF LANGUAGE

Papillia, wedded to her amorous spark,
Sighs for the shades,—" How charming is a park ! "
A park is purchased, but the fair he sees
All drowned in tears—" Oh odious, odious trees ! "

In these four lines Pope draws a picture of many a woman—many a man too—we all know. He has put what we vaguely thought into abiding words. The purpose of language is to express thought thus—to express thought more fully and more effectively than anything else can or does. Other modes of expression are faint, flickering lights. A well-developed language like English is the all-revealing sun. The words we use are vehicles of thought. If we choose well, they are good vehicles. They can be interpreted, by reader or readers, in the sense intended. Thereby they carry thought without substantial loss from mind to mind. If we choose not so well, our thought reaches the other mind impaired and distorted,—perhaps not at all.

It is this primary purpose of language, this carriage of thought, that is the matter of importance. You appreciate perhaps an explanation of what a metaphor is, what a simile. But only a little. You appreciate more some guidance concerning when to use a metaphor, when a simile, some guidance too, concerning what makes a metaphor or a simile appropriate or inappropriate. In short, the knowledge you seek—and ought to seek—is how to become an effective writer and speaker rather than the knowledge of terms in grammar and rhetoric. The terms are useful as means of reference. They are not the essential matter.

The essential matter is the effective carriage of thought; the "literature" we treasure consists of thoughts so admirably conveyed that the order of words is well worth preserving, well worth remembering. Consider for example, how far from the commonplace we are taken in Thackeray's account of Colonel Newcome's death. Thackeray's account is literature. Yours and mine might be quite successful records of what took place; in all likelihood, however, they would not be memorable speech. They would not be literature.

Some time afterwards Ethel came in with a scared face to our pale group. "He is calling for you again, dear lady," she said, going up to Madame de Florac who was still kneeling, "and just now he said he wanted Pendennis to take care of his boy. He will not know you." She hid her tears as she spoke.

She went into the room where Clive was at the bed's foot; the old man within it talked on rapidly for a while; then again he would sigh and be still; once more I heard him say hurriedly, "Take care of him when I'm in India," and then with a heartrending voice he called out "Léonore, Léonore!" She was kneeling at his side now. The patient's voice sank into faint murmurs; only a moan now and then announced that he was not asleep.

At the usual evening hour the chapel bell began to toll, and Thomas Newcome's hands outside the bed feebly beat time. And just as the last bell struck, a peculiar sweet smile shone over his face, and he lifted up his head a little, and quickly said "Adsum!" and fell back. It was the word we used at school, when names were called and lo! he, whose heart was as that of a little child had answered to his name and stood in the presence of the Master.

G

GENERAL AND SPECIFIC TERMS

(a) Necessaries in this section mean goods suitable to the condition of life of such infant and to his actual requirements at the time of the sale and delivery.

(This is the GENERAL STATEMENT, in the Sale of Goods Act.)

(*b*) Suppose the jury asks what is the meaning of necessaries. Does it mean in law, as in strictness, something indispensable ? The answer must be no. When they ask what is the meaning and it is expounded to them as being something reasonably required for the nourishment, clothing, lodging, education, and decent behaviour and appearance according to the station, how can such an explanation include these articles ? [The question was about a gold drinking-cup and a pair of solitaires, price £25.] But I may fairly be asked what is the rule ? It seems to me to be this. There are some things which cannot be necessaries—earrings for a male, a wild animal, and all things which are useless except for amusement or where utility is the subordinate consideration and the ornament the principal. On the other hand, there are also things which may or may not be, and which give rise to questions for a jury. For instance, an infant orders an expensive coat ; but it appears his trade or calling is of the nature that such a coat is necessary for his health ; or it is shown that a coat at half the price would not last half the time. Or if he ordered a broadcloth coat, and it is said he should have contented himself with fustian, evidence may be given as to his position and as to how people dress in that class in that neighbourhood, and then the question is for the jury.

(This is the concrete—the particular—the specific expansion in the judgment.)

We must have GENERAL terms. They are essential for accurate reasoning ; we need *animal* as well as *dog*, *horse*, and the rest ; we need *colour* as well as *blue* and *red*. The specific terms (those that bring one particular thing to mind) make, however, the deeper impression. That is why poet and orator and novelist are fond of them. One writer will say, " Now and again one should give himself up to profound thought " ; Emerson, using the specific terms, puts the idea more effectively : " It is wholesome to angle in those profound pools, though one be rewarded with nothing more than the leap of a fish that flashes his freckled side in the sun and as suddenly absconds in the dark waters again."

The hearer and the reader are, very likely, little moved by the GENERAL terms ; they may be greatly moved by the SPECIFIC.

For most purposes it is better to say " put a spoke in his wheel "
rather than " interfere with his projects ", better to say " throw
dust in the jurymen's eyes " rather than " obscure the issue
before the jury ".   Look at the outburst of Coriolanus :

> If you have writ your annals true, 'tis there
> That, like an eagle in a dovecot, I
> Fluttered your Volscians in Corioli.

Would " caused alarm " be nearly so effective as " fluttered " ?

Notice, too, the manner in which Shakespeare after he has
been moralising in general terms, drives home his thought by
a specific term familiar to everyone.   Here is Hamlet's question :

> For who would bear the whips and scorns of time,
> The oppressor's wrong, the proud man's contumely,
> The pangs of disprized love, the law's delay,
> The insolence of office and the spurns
> That patient merit of the unworthy takes
> When he himself might his quietus make
> With a bare bodkin ?

The attention had been a little drowsy over the abstract terms
wrong, contumely, pangs, merit.   The vivid, concrete term, " bare
bodkin ", jerks the attention wide-awake.

And look at these two parallel statements :

(*a*) When the manners, customs, and amusements of a nation
are cruel and barbarous, then the regulations of their penal
code will be severe.

(*b*) When men delight in battle, bull-fights, and combats of
gladiators, they will punish by hanging, burning, and the
rack.

You will agree that the specific terms of (*b*) make a deeper
impression than the general terms of (*a*).

GRAMMAR

> Heedless of grammar, they all cried, " That's him !—
> That's the scamp that had done this scandalous thing !
> That's the thief that has got my Lord Cardinal's ring."
>
> (BARHAM, *The Jackdaw of Rheims*.)

You study GRAMMAR when you look closely at the rules followed by good writers and speakers ; you write grammatical

English when you follow what is recognised to be good usage. And the usage is present usage. For custom is not more constant in language, the dress of thoughts, than it is in the dress of the body; and custom like fashion has its changes. In matters of language at any rate, *Quand tout le monde a tort, tout le monde a raison*; " When all make the same fault, the fault becomes good grammar." We can at times trace the changes in usage. The special form of the subjunctive for instance, now remains only in formal writings, and in a few isolated phrases like " If I were you ". We do say " If it were done " rather than " If it was done "; but that is very likely because Macbeth's exclamation, " If it were done when 'tis done, then 'twere well it were done quickly ", is a part of the language.

Apart from such expressions the use of the subjunctive now seems affectation. Hamlet says in relation to the gagging of the clowns, " Now this, though it make the unskilful laugh, cannot but make the judicious grieve." The modern version would be " though it makes the unskilful laugh ". Notice what an old-fashioned savour the subjunctives *take* and *be* lend to this passage of Jane Austen :

> I will not adopt that ungenerous and impolitic custom, so common with novel writers, of degrading by their contemptuous censure, the very performances to the number of which they are themselves adding; joining with their greatest enemies in bestowing the harshest epithets on such works, and scarcely ever permitting them to be read by their own heroine, who, if she accidentally take up a novel, is sure to turn over its insipid pages with disgust. Alas ! if the heroine of one novel be not patronised by the heroine of another, from whom can she expect protection and regard ?

Some among us are not greatly concerned about the rules of grammar. Others among us seem to get a deal of fun when we hear the flouting of grammar. Dickens raises many a good laugh out of what used to be called " breaking Priscian's head " : " Some people ", said Mrs. Gamp in *Martin Chuzzlewit*, " may be Rooshans, and others may be Prooshans; they are born so and will please themselves. Them which is of other natures thinks different."

H

" H "—UNSOUNDED, SILENT, MUTE

(a) An heir. An heiress. Wear it for an honour in thy cap. An honest man's the noblest work of God. He turns an honest penny. An hour they sat in Council.

(b) If the subject is worth studying at all, it is worth studying with an honest desire to arrive at the truth, even though the truth should turn out, as it sometimes will, to be disappointingly commonplace.

(A. G. BRADLEY.)

The letter *h* in these examples appears in the spelling but has no effect upon the sound of the words in which it occurs. It is not a crime to drop an aitch nor to sound an aitch that should be mute. Yet in some companies you had better commit the crime than falter in your dealing with the troublesome letter. There is even a difficulty about its name : we find the letter signified as *aitch, ache, h,* with plurals *aitches, aches, hs* and *h's*.

One difficulty about the sounding or not sounding arises from a quite recent tendency to pronounce words in accordance with the spelling. People see a letter in the written word, and they think (quite reasonably) that the letter should have some value. So it is that in several words, certainly without the *h* sound a while ago, the *h* now affects the pronunciation. " Humble " is now rarely heard without the aspirate, the *h* sound ; yet we are exhorted to confess our sins " with an humble, lowly, penitent, and obedient heart ". " Hospital " must now have its aspirate, though Sir Thomas Browne wrote, " For the world, I count it not an Inn but an Hospital, and a place not to live but to die in." So too, with " hotel ", and " hostler ", and " Hostel " : custom asks us to pronounce these with the *h* sounded. Till the nineteenth century the *h* in " herb " and its derivative was mute : " Ginger is the root of neither tree nor shrub but of an herbaceous plant." In " humour " and " humorous " the pronunciation of the *h* is quite a recent innovation : " I have an humour to knock you indifferently well ", says Fluellen in *Henry V.* Still, recent as the innovation is, we had better comply with custom and pronounce the *h*.

126

In fact there are to-day in English hardly half a dozen words with an initial *h* that we may say with assurance is not sounded. We still write " *an heir* " and " *an heiress* ". " Honour " ("Wear it for an honour in thy cap ") and its derivatives (Macaulay has " descended from an honourable family ") still has *h* mute. And we can still say, without incurring the condemnation of such as seem to watch for a dropped aitch, " An honest man's the noblest work of God ", or " He turns an honest penny ", or " An hour they sat in Council ". Moreover, when the syllable in which *h* occurs is unstressed better not obtrude the *h* sound. In a sentence like " Hunt has scored his third goal " neither *has* nor *his* asks for the sounded *h* ; and *forehead* still asks to be pronounced *forred*. In some dialects, Cockney in particular, strange pranks are played with the *h* : this, for instance, is given—given quite unjustly—as typical of Cockney speech, " It ain't the 'untin with the 'ounds that 'urts the 'orses 'ooves ; it's the 'ammer, 'ammer, 'ammer on the 'ard 'igh road."

HACKNEYED PHRASES (CLICHÉS)

Sweets to the sweet. 'Twas caviare to the general. Metal more attractive. Frailty, thy name is woman. Something rotten in the state of Denmark. A mote it is to trouble the mind's eye. Hoist with his own petard. Tear a passion to tatters. Split the ears of the groundlings. To out-herod Herod.

(All from SHAKESPEARE'S *Hamlet*.)

The hired horse—the hackney—loses much of its sprightliness by too frequent use. So with phrases. Those from *Hamlet* were not at all hackneyed when Shakespeare wrote them : they were fresh, vigorous offsprings of his wonderful power over words. In their context they are still phrases that delight you. But the most striking phrase, being lifted from its setting and used without tact, becomes trite and commonplace.

Yet we all use these ready-made phrases ; nor is there any compelling reason why we should not. You could not, for instance, better for their particular purpose, phrases like these from the Bible : " highways and hedges ", " smote him hip and thigh ", " lick the dust ", " a thorn in the flesh ", " a broken reed ", " the root of all evil ", " weighed in the balances and found wanting ", " a soft answer ", " a word in season ", " how are the mighty fallen ! " and any number of others that will spring to your mind.

As the example suggests, too, the plays of Shakespeare are full of phrases " familiar to our mouths as household words " ; they come pat ; and we utter them without having any sense of indebtedness.

Yet we should be sparing in our use of ready-made phrases. For, torn from its context, the phrase may lose its primary force ; and it may have become so battered and bruised with hard usage that it annoys our hearers or our readers. Much repetition may turn liking into loathing.

Very likely we all have some favourite form of expression, some hackneyed phrase that comes on the slightest pretext. Either of set purpose or quite unwittingly we become habituated to express a particular thought in the one way. In *The Apple Cart*, for instance, one of the characters declares : " I can spot his fist out of fifty columns." Apparently the trade-mark, the distinctive phrase, is " Singularly enough ". And the King retorts : " I have noticed that in a certain newspaper which loses no opportunity of disparaging the throne, the last sentence of the leading article invariably begins with the words ' Once for all '. Whose trade mark is that ? " " Every schoolboy knows " is Lord Macaulay's way of ushering in a piece of information far removed, we may be quite certain, from all but the very exceptional schoolboy. " And so to bed " is the diarist's conclusion of the day's entry. " But that's another story " is how Kipling teases you after whetting your curiosity.

This problem of the hackneyed phrase is, indeed, a curious one. What appears bright and vigorous to the readers who come upon it for the first time is tarnished and weak to one who has repeatedly met it. The phrase in its first use is a product of creative art ; it is adopted by others, loses its freshness, becomes commonplace, and may be irritating.

Thus Shakespeare speaks of " cool reason " ; and the adjective is apt. For he is contrasting the boiling imagination of the lunatic (and the lover) with the placid mental processes of men in their senses—

Lovers and madmen have such seething brains,
Such shaping fantasies, that apprehend
More than cool reason ever comprehends.

Now we have the adjunct *cool*—often *cold*—with *reason* whenever called for or not : " the verdict of cold reason " is in general no more than " the verdict of reason ". Again, the spectator of Cleopatra's triumphant progress to captivate Antony gave a lavish description of her environment. Gorgeous it was, yet he could find terms adequate. As for the great queen herself, however, his powers were bankrupt—

But for her person, it beggared all description.

How far the phrase " beggar description " has fallen from its first splendour !

HEROIC VERSE. (See " Metre ")

The English verse which we call Heroic, consists of no more than ten syllables.

(DRYDEN.)

Convention asks that the deeds of heroes shall be related in a stately form of verse, in English the iambic-pentameter line. Milton's *Paradise Lost*, a typical line of which is

So stretched out huge in length the Arch-fiend lay,

is in heroic verse ; and Pope, in his mock epic *The Rape of the Lock* also writes in heroic verse thus :

And beauty leads us with a single hair

HIS OR HER

(*a*) This ticket is not transferable : and the passenger's luggage is carried at his or her own risk.
(*b*) God send every one their heart's desire.
(SHAKESPEARE, *Much Ado about Nothing*.)

His or her is a stilted phrase that we are sometimes called upon to use because of the fact that in English we have no pronoun of the common gender, no single word to stand for *he-or-she*, *his-or-her*, unless we take " one " and " one's " as suitable for the purpose. The French, too, have nothing to represent *he-or-she*; but they have " son " to represent *his-or-her*, and " soi " to represent *him-or-her*.

When, therefore, as in Shakespeare's sentence, a pronoun of the common gender is called for, we are obliged to choose between a stilted correctness and an easy natural incorrectness. Faced with the choice, Shakespeare, as one might expect of a dramatist who knew his job thoroughly, says, by his practice, " Choose the easy and natural, even though it does give shock to a pedant here and there." This does not—you say, and rightly say—quite conclude the matter. For the dialogue of the play imitates, and ought to imitate, the language of the street and market-place; and such language stands on no ceremony. We should be disapp 'nted if we expected strict propriety of speech in the talk that goes on around us. We are very unusual people, too, if we are never included among the rule-breakers. We shall not depart wholly from convention; we shall not imitate the taxi-driver's idiom : " I'll find it, lady, right enough. I've never bin anywhere but wot I 'aven't bin able to find it." Still, our deference to convention need not be reverential.

In writing, however, not meant " to hold, as 'twere, the mirror up to nature ", are we not entitled to expect an adherence to grammar ? It is a matter of taste. We shall find " his or her " in the formal announcement; but not in writing that imitates talk.

When you are conscious that the correct is also the awkward, there is always the possibility of recasting your sentence. Here, for instance, is the sentence " If every one minded their own business, the world would be happier." Probably this colloquial expression is preferable to " If every one minded his or her own business ". Or, you could say " If every one minded his own business ".

For—we have statutory authority in the Interpretation Act—we are to take the masculine as including the feminine. It is at times forgotten that this rule exists. For example, the original version of the lines in a well-known hymn was " Soon will you and I be lying, Each within his narrow bed." *His* must be interpreted as *his-or-her*. But the editors of the modern version, whether resenting the cool assumption of the statute, or feeling that *his* cannot with propriety stand for *her*, have altered *his* to *our* : " each within our ", a singular with a plural.

HISTORIC PRESENT. (See "Idiom")

He through the arméd files
Darts his experienced eye, and soon traverse
The whole battalion views—their order due,
Their visages and stature as of gods ;
Their number last he sums. And now his heart
Distends with pride, and, hardening in his strength,
Glories.

(MILTON, *Paradise Lost.*)

The verbs, *darts, views, sums, distends, glories,* are instances of the Historic Present : the form of the Present Tense is used though the Past is spoken of.

When, wishing to make our narrative more vivid, we use the present tense where the past tense is intended, we are using the HISTORIC PRESENT. Carlyle in the *French Revolution* makes extensive use of the device :

We see Charlotte on Tuesday the ninth of July seated in the Caen Diligence, with a place for Paris. None takes farewell of her, wishes her Good-journey : her Father will find a line left, signifying that she is gone to England, that he must pardon her, and forget her. The drowsy Diligence lumbers along ; amid drowsy talk of Politics, in which she mingles not.

Using the Historic Present we seek to give the impression of actually being spectators of the events described. Here is a little from Lord Macnaghten's judgment in a well-known case (*Gluckstein* v. *Barnes*) :

These gentlemen set about forming a company to pay them a handsome sum for taking off their hands a property which they had contracted to buy with that end in view. They bring the company into existence by means of the usual machinery. They appoint themselves sole guardians and protectors of this creation of theirs, half-fledged and just struggling into life, bound hand and foot while yet unborn by contracts tending to their private advantage, and so fashioned by its makers that it could only act by their hands

131

and only see through their eyes. They issue a prospectus representing that they had agreed to purchase the property for a sum largely in excess of the amount which they had, in fact, to pay. On the faith of this prospectus they collect subscriptions from a confiding and credulous public. And then comes the last act. Secretly, and therefore dishonestly, they put into their own pockets the difference between the real and the pretended price. After a brief career the company is ordered to be wound up. In the course of the liquidation the trick is discovered.

HOMOGRAPHS

Words different in meaning—different in sound, too, it may be—are found with the same spelling. Such words are HOMO-GRAPHS. When the same sound accompanies the same spelling and the meaning only differs, the words are HOMONYMS. (See next article.)

Examples of homographs are : *bow* (to shoot with) rhyming with *so*, and *bow* (of a ship) rhyming with *now*; *gill* (of a fish), the *g* being as in *girl*, and *gill* (half a pint), the *g* being as in *Jill*; *lead* (the heavy metal) rhyming with *bed*, and *lead* (conduct) rhyming with *bead*; *lease* (of a house) rhyming with *fleece*, and *lease* (glean) rhyming with *please*; *lower* (let down) rhyming with *mower*, and *lower* (frown) rhyming with *power*; *sow* (the animal) rhyming with *now*, and *sow* (scatter seed) rhyming with *so*; *tear* (the noun) rhyming with *fear*, and *tear* (the verb) rhyming with *fair*; *éntrance* (opening into), with accent on *en*, and *entránce* (fill with delight), the accent on *trance*.

HOMONYMS and HOMOPHONES

(a) Canst thou not minister to a mind diseased,
  Pluck from the memory a rooted sorrow,
  Raze out the written troubles of the brain.
  (*Macbeth.*)

(b) I can raise no money by vile means.
  (*Julius Cæsar.*)

(c) The sun whose rays are all ablaze
  With ever-living glory
  Does not deny his majesty :
  He scorns to tell a story.
  (*The Mikado.*)

In these extracts, *raze*, *raise* and *rays* are similar sounds though they are different words. Such are HOMOPHONES. When the distinct words have not only the same sound but the same symbol they are sometimes called HOMONYMS : the word *bay* for instance, cannot be defined in isolation ; you need to know its context. " The bay horse ", " the Bay of Biscay ", " the bay windows ", " the bay tree "—in these the symbol " bay " stands for four distinct words. Look, too, at the word *sound* : in the phrase " safe and sound " it means *healthy* ; in " the sound of a trumpet " it means *noise* ; in " at anchor in the sound " it means *a channel of water*.

Here is what Fuller writes :

> Heralds new mould men's names—taking from them, adding to them, melting out all the liquid letters, torturing mutes to make them speak, and making vowels dumb—to bring it to a fallacious *homonym* at the last ; that their names may be the same with those noble houses they pretend to.

Consider the matter a little. Hear *seas* and *seize* : you cannot discriminate. See them in print or in writing : you can discriminate. Here are a few homophones upon which you can test your power to distinguish : *feign, fain, fane* (" He escaped death only by feigning it ", " I would fain die a dry death ", " Iona's holy fane "). *Bough, bow ; guilt, gilt ; skull, scull ; cent, scent, sent ; limb, limn* (" Appelles limned to life Loathed Vulcan's lovely wife ") ; *lesson, lessen ; pray, prey ; sword, soared ; mail, male ; yolk, yoke ; mien, mean ; tier, tear ; peak, pique ; knight, night ; need, knead ; dew, due ; bald, bawled ; cellar, seller ; ail, ale ; all, awl ; vain, vein, vane* (" What plume of feathers is he that indited this letter ? What vane ? What weather-cock ? ") ; *ware, wear* (" Let me taste your ware ", " Motley's the only wear ") ; *maid, made ; choler, collar ; wreck, reck ; write, rite, right ; through, threw ; plum, plumb ; heart, hart*.

Look at these examples :

guilt (" The guilt of blood is at your door ")
gilt (" Take the gilt off the gingerbread ")
cent (" Three per cent. is reasonable ")
scent (" He was upon a wrong scent ")

heart (" Lift up your heart ")
hart (" The hart doth lack a hind ")

throne (" A golden throne in the depths of the sea ")
thrown (" He has thrown good money after bad ")

told (" They went and told the sexton ")
tolled (" The sexton tolled the bell ")

two (" Two a penny, hot-cross buns ")
too (" This too solid flesh ")
to (" To bed, to bed, says sleepy head ")

sword (" He shall perish by the sword ")
soared (" The towering eagle soared aloft ")

climb (" The slow moon climbs ")
clime (" Men of every clime and country ")

cymbal (" Praise Him upon the well-tuned cymbals ")
symbol (" Salt was the symbol of friendship ")

cellar (" In cellar cool at ease I sit ")
seller (" He wrote the best seller of the year ")

choler (" Hollis, in choler, pulled him by the nose ")
collar (" Pull against the collar ")

miner (" The rugged miners poured to war ")
minor (" A minor has not yet reached twenty-one ")

stationary (" This stationary engine remains fixed ")
stationery (" Stationery includes paper, pen and ink ")

all (" All things that love the sun are out of doors ")
awl (" The cobbler kept him to his awl ")

hue (" Red with a violet hue ")
hew (" Hew down the bridge, Sir Consul ")

hole (" Round peg in a square hole ")
whole (" The whole night through ")

guest (" Our honoured guest ")
guessed (" I little guessed the end ")

hymn (" First hymn they the Father ")
him (" Let him depart, his passport shall be made ")

plumb (" Plumb down he drops ")
plum (" He put in his thumb and pulled out a plum ")

medal (" The reverse of the medal ")
meddle (" Neither make nor meddle ")

altar (" Lead a bride to the altar ")
alter (" Power to alter a decree ")

ball (" One black ball in three excludes ")
bawl (" Speak up, but do not bawl ")
birth (" Two children at one birth ")
berth (" A comfortable berth ")
mown (" The scent of new-mown hay ")
moan (" The moan of doves ")
yolk (" The yolk of an egg ")
yoke (" The savage bull doth bear the yoke ")
wall (" Grapes, long lingering on my only wall "
waul (" We waul and cry ")
waive (" I waive the objection ")
wave (" I wish you a wave of the sea ")
rowed (" They rowed across the stream ")
road (" On the road to Mandalay ")
rode (" He rode the horse well ")

Other languages have instances where the one sound (sometimes the one symbol) represents two quite distinct words. English has very many instances, largely owing to the progressive simplifying of forms. Thus in *dough* (flour made into a paste ready for baking) the now silent *gh* once stood for the *k* sound : the loss of that sound makes *dough* homophone with *doe* (the female of the deer). By a similar loss *weight* and *wait*, *might* and *mite*, *right* and *rite*, *bough* and *bow*, become homophones.

The presence of so many invitations to ambiguity in our language is something of a nuisance. Moreover, the nuisance is not wholly compensated by the fact that so many chances are offered of the mild form of humour called punning : " Archbishop Laud turned out Archy, the King's fool, for a pun, namely for saying at grace, ' Great praise be to God and little Laud to the devil '."

HYBRID

bicycle : amoral : cablegram : macadam

The words above contain elements that have come into English from more than one language : *bi* is the Latin prefix, *cycle* is from the Greek *kuklos*, a circle ; *a* is the Greek prefix, *moral* is from Latin ; *cable* is Middle English, *gram* is Greek.

Such words made up of elements from more than one language, are HYBRIDS : in the word *re-macadamise* is the Latin *re*, the Gaelic *mac*, the Hebrew *adam*, and the Greek *ise*.

There is no need to inveigh against the hybrid formation of a word ; but usually the result of putting together elements alien to one another results in an ugly product. The Stock Exchange term *backwardation* is an instance.

HYPERBOLE

(*a*) When in the chronicle of wasted time
    I see descriptions of the fairest wights,
And beauty making beautiful old rhyme
    In praise of ladies dead, and lovely knights ;

Then in the blazon of sweet beauty's best
    Of hand, of foot, of lip, of eye, of brow,
I see their antique pen would have expressed
    Ev'n such a beauty as you master now.

So all their praises are but prophecies
    Of this our time, all you prefiguring ;
And, for they looked but with divining eyes,
    They had not skill enough your worth to sing :

For we, which now behold these present days,
    Have eyes to wonder, but lack tongues to praise.
                      (SHAKESPEARE.)

(*b*) For that I have not washed my nose that bled,
    Or foiled some debile wretch, which, without note,
Here's many else have done, you shout me forth
    In acclamations hyperbolical.
            (SHAKESPEARE, *Coriolanus*.)

(*c*) The speaking in a perpetual hyperbole is comely in nothing but in love.
            (LORD BACON, *Essays*.)

It is a natural tendency, when you wish to emphasise, to exaggerate : you say more, and are understood to say more, than the strict truth. Macbeth's exclamation is a good example of such exaggeration :

What hands are here ? ha ! they pluck out mine eyes !
Will all great Neptune's ocean wash this blood

Clean from my hand ? No ; this my hand will rather
The multitudinous seas incarnadine,
Making the green one red.

Hȳpérbŏlē (a word of four syllables) was the name given by
the Greeks to the rhetorical device. The glorious piece of
hyperbole in Marlowe's *Doctor Faustus* is, very likely, well
known to you :

> Was this the face that launched a thousand ships,
> And burnt the topless towers of Ilium ?
> Sweet Helen, make me immortal with a kiss !
> Her lips suck forth my soul : see where it flies
> Come Helen, come, give me my soul again.
> Here will I dwell, for heaven be in these lips,
> And all is dross that is not Helena.
>   . . . .
>   . . . .
> O thou art fairer than the evening air,
> Clad in the beauty of a thousand stars.

The dividing line between hyperbole and bombast (rant) is
easy to cross. When Hamlet, emulating the extravagant talk
of Laertes, exclaims :

> let them throw
> Millions of acres on us, till our ground,
> Singeing his pate against the burning zone,
> Make Ossa like a wart !

he is quite aware that such talk is mere madness. " Nay," he
says, " An thou'lt mouth, I'll rant as well as thou." Intensely
disliking ostentation he met it with ostentation : " The bravery
of his grief ", he says, " did put me into a towering passion."
The contrast between the fancy-dress (" taffeta phrases ") and
the homespun (" kersey ") is that between

> Taffeta phrases, silken terms precise,
> Three-piled hyperboles, spruce affectation

and

> Russet yeas and honest kersey noes.
> > (*Love's Labour's Lost.*)

HYPHENS. (See **" Compound Words "**)

I

IAMBUS. (See "**Metre**")

(*a*) For poetry, he's past his prime,
  He takes an hour to find a rhyme:
  His fire is out, his wit decayed,
  His fancy sunk, his Muse a jade.
  I'd have him throw away his pen:
  But there's no talking to some men.
                    (DEAN SWIFT, *Verses on Himself*.)

(*b*) The actors in the old tragedies, as we read, piped their
iambics to a tune, speaking from under a mask, and wear-
ing stilts and a great head-dress. 'Twas thought the
dignity of the Tragic Muse required these appurtenances,
and that she was not to move except to a measure and
cadence. So Queen Medea slew her children to a slow
music: and King Agamemnon perished in a dying fall
(to use Mr. Dryden's words): the Chorus standing by
in a set attitude, and rhythmically and decorously bewailing
the fates of those great crowned persons. The Muse of
History hath encumbered herself with ceremony as well as
her Sister of the Theatre.
                    (THACKERAY, *Henry Esmond*.)

(*c*) Iambics march from short to long.
                    (COLERIDGE.)

IDIOM. (See also "**Custom**", "**Appropriate Prepositions**")

(*a*) I go to France next week.

(*b*) When I am dead, my dearest,
  Sing no sad songs for me.

(*c*) On the morrow after his instalment, he brings in a load
of moneybonds, all duly stamped, sealed with this or the
other Convent seal; frightful, unmanageable, a bottom-
less confusion of Convent finance. There they are—but
there at least they all are; all that shall be of them. Our
Lord Abbot demands that all the official seals in use among
us be now produced and delivered to him.
                    (CARLYLE.)

(*d*) "And I sez to 'er, I sez, 'You oughter be ashamed of
yerself,' I sez, 'wicked creature,' I sez, 'teachin' my boy
such things and 'im only a kid,' I sez; and wot do you

138

think she sez to me ? ' Teach 'im,' she sez, ' I couldn't teach 'im nothin',' she sez, ' and no more could no-one else.' "

(The mother on her encounter with the teacher.)

(e) He'll do no more than he can help.

An idiom is a peculiarity of the language. It may have a meaning different, and understood to be different, from the meaning in strict grammar : in (a) *go* is the grammatical form of the present tense, but the intended sense is the future ; in (b) *am*, the present form, also relates to the future ; in (c) *brings* and the other verbs are the present form, but the intended sense is the past ; in (e) *can* should logically be *cannot*. Yet, because custom dictates, these expressions are " correct ". Since usage approves of it, the idiom is " good English ".

None, for instance, is a telescoping of " no-one ", and is in strictness singular in number. Quite naturally, the word takes the singular verb in a sentence like Tennyson's " There is none like her, none." But then, the word has a sense of plurality ; and we find many instances of the plural verb. Thus, " And none serve with him but constrained things " (*Macbeth*) and " We shall meet again when there are none to separate us " (*Ivanhoe*). Modern usage indeed, prefers to treat " none " as a plural, reserving " no one " or " nobody " to do duty as the singular. Probably " were " would have been better than " was " in the broadcast announcement " None of the injured passengers was British " : we should not hesitate to write " No children were injured ".

The words *either* and *neither* when used as pronouns are, however, better regarded as singulars, even though there are many instances of their use as plurals : " Thersites' body is as good as Ajax ! When neither are alive " (*Cymbeline*). " Neither belong to his Saxon company " (*Ivanhoe*). For it is a waste of material when, having two words that could very well be relegated to different functions, we use them as though they are interchangeable. Thus, the *Queen Mary* speeded across the Atlantic to New York ; she speeded back to Southampton. She accomplished both passages in less time than that taken by any other vessel. And the broadcast announcer's voice was resonant with pride as he said : " This means that she has beaten the record in either direction." Now, being properly applied, " either " means " one of a pair ", either Southampton to New York or New York to Southampton. To be sure the announcer may say " Well, what's the trouble ? you pay your money and you take your choice ; if both passages are record passages, then either is." He may, too, advance Tennyson's precedent :

> On either side of the river lie
> Long fields of barley and of rye.

Still, we might have maintained a plea for " both ", and have announced the mighty achievement, " This means that she has broken the record in both directions."

Many of our words have acquired idiomatic senses that diverge greatly from the primary sense. The preposition *with* is a good example. *With* meant " opposite to ". The original sense remains in many of our phrases. You contend *with* an enemy ; you compete *with* (or against) a rival ; you vie *with* your competitor ; you *withstand* an onslaught. But in the advice that was given to the unlucky Malvolio, " Be opposite with a kinsman, surly with servants ", the word implies no relation of physical position : it is transferred to a mental attitude.

Notice, too, these developments. In phrases like " She had a tongue with a tang " or in Milton's line " Now glowed the firmament with living sapphires " the word denotes accompaniment. In the patriotic sentiment " England, with all thy faults, I love thee still " the words mean " in spite of ".

Then we have phrases like—" I sympathise with you " (we have even, without any logic for it, " I disagree with you ") ; " The lady with the camellias " (where " with " signifies " characterised by always carrying ") ; " He writes with a fountain-pen " (by means of) ; " I'll do it with pleasure " (i.e. accompaniment) ; " I can do nothing with him " (i.e. I am unable to influence him).

Then you have the expressions, curious enough when you examine them—" I have parted with my best friend " ; " I can dispense with the money " (where " with " implies not company but separation) ; " With the best intentions he failed " (i.e. in spite of possessing).

IDYLL (sometimes spelled "*Idyl*" and always to be pronounced *ĭdĭl*, long *ĭ* and then short *ĭ*)

It is pleasant to fancy how Walton and Bunyan might have met and talked, under a plane-tree by the Ouse, while the May showers were falling. Surely Bunyan would not have likened the good old man to Formalist; and certainly Walton would have enjoyed travelling with Christian, though the book was by none of his dear bishops, but by a Nonconformist. They were made to like but not to convert each other; in matters ecclesiastical they saw the opposite sides of the shield. Each wrote a masterpiece. It is too late to praise *The Compleat Angler* or *The Pilgrim's Progress*. You may put ingenuity on the rack, but she can say nothing new that is true about the best romance that ever was wedded to allegory, nor about the best idyll of English life.

(ANDREW LANG, *Essays in Little.*)

An IDYLL is a picture, usually in verse, of what appeals strongly to sentiment, of scenes perhaps where the actors were shepherds and shepherdesses and their occupations the less sordid ones incident to country life. The *Idyll* is usually short, like Marlowe's " Come live with me and be my love "; though Tennyson's *Idylls of the King* is long enough to satisfy anybody.

IMPERSONAL VERBS

(*a*) It never rains but it pours.

(*b*) When it snoweth, it is good sitting by a good fire.

(*c*) Methought I heard a voice cry, " Sleep no more; Macbeth has murdered sleep, the innocent sleep."

In these sentences " rains ", " snoweth ", " methought " are IMPERSONAL VERBS. When used in their strict sense they are used only in the third person singular. There is an easy transference to a figurative sense, as when Marlowe writes " Fearful echoes thunder in mine ears ", or Donne " Till age snow white hairs on thee ".

The Old English form of the impersonal *methinks, methought* was distinct from the Old English form of the personal *I think, I thought*; *methinks* is " It seems to me ". Thus in Milton's sentence :

Methinks I see in my mind a noble and persistent nation

141

rousing himself like a strong man after sleep, and shaking his invincible locks. Methinks I see him as an eagle muing his mighty youth and kindling his undazzled eyes at the full midday beam.

Rossetti in *The Blessed Damozel* indulges in the old-fashioned use of the impersonal *her seemed*, " It seemed to her " :

> Her seemed she scarce had been a day
> One of God's choristers.

Probably the wise course, unless we wish to give some flavour of the distant past, is to say " It seems to me " rather than " Methinks ", and " It seemed to me " rather than " Methought ".

INDIRECT OBJECT. (See " Dative ", " Transitive Verb ")

INFINITIVE. (See " ' Split ' Infinitive ")

INFLEXIONS (also spelled " INFLECTIONS ")

(*a*) In many instances the old inflexions were dropped because they had become superfluous, owing to the growth of other and more efficient means of indicating the functions of words in the sentence.

(*b*) One reason for the scarcity of inflexions in modern English is that the accent is usually at the beginning of the words—*béau-ti-ful, im-mé-di-ate*—and, as a result, the end syllable loses distinction.

INFLEXIONS are those changes in words by which we indicate changes in meaning or application : the *s* in *ships*, the *er* in *smaller*, the *ed* in *walked* are inflexions. Compared with the Old English and with some modern languages, English has very few inflexions : our one adjective, for instance, *beautiful* does duty for the French *beau, bel, belle, beaux* and *belles*. Fixed words—prepositions mostly—play in modern English the part of the inflexions in other languages. Here is the Latin line :

> Tendebantque manus ripae ulterioris amore

a beautiful line you agree—and this whether or not you know Latin. And it owes much of its beauty to the full sounds of the word endings. We replace it by the English " And they were reaching forth their hands in longing for the farther shore ". So replacing the Latin line we have analysed the inflexions into separate words ; and in the process the beauty of the sound has in some measure vanished. Perhaps, indeed, we should place against the great benefit of simplicity in modern English the not great drawback that a poet nowdays has a harder task than his forerunner in creating music. For many musical vowels have gone and the noisy consonants for the most part have remained. Chaucer's line

> And smale foules maken melodie

(of eleven syllables, since *mel-od-i-e* has four) becomes " And small fowls make melody ". Our modern English is more useful, though less beautiful, than Chaucer's English.

INTERJECTIONS (EXCLAMATIONS). (See "Words ")

(*a*) " Did you ever remark that door ? " he asked ; and when his companions had replied in the affirmative, " It is connected in my mind," added he, " with a very old story."
    " Indeed ! " said Mr. Utterson, with a slight change of voice, " and what was that ? "

(*b*) " I gave in the cheque myself, and said I had every reason to believe it was a forgery. Not a bit of it. The cheque was genuine."
    " Tut-tut ! " said Mr. Utterson.

(*c*)   Fie, wrangling queen ;
Whom everything becomes, to chide, to laugh,
To weep ; whose every passion fully strives
To make itself, in thee, fair, and admired !

(*d*) O Charmian, I will never go from hence.

In (*a*) *indeed*, in (*b*) *tut-tut*, in (*c*) *fie*, in (*d*) *O*, are INTERJECTIONS. The first two quotations are from Stevenson's *Dr. Jekyll and Mr. Hyde*, the last two from Shakespeare's *Antony and Cleopatra*. It sometimes asks care to determine whether the exclamation mark or another stop is the appropriate one. Notice, for instance, how the irate Cleopatra alternates between question and exclamation :

Cleopatra :   Is he married ?
    I cannot hate thee worser than I do
    If thou again say *Yes*.

Messenger : He is married madam.
Cleopatra : The gods confound thee ! dost thou hold there still !

Though the last five words are in the form of a question they constitute in fact an exclamation ; and the exclamation mark, not the question mark, rightly follows.

INVERSION

    (*a*) And all the air a solemn stillness holds.

    (*b*) After Arica came Lima, the chief depot of all, where the grandest haul was looked for.

    (*c*) Surely never lighted on this orb, which she hardly seemed to touch, a more delightful vision.

    (*d*) Thee gentle Spencer fondly led ;
        But me he mostly sent to bed.

(LANDOR.)

To write good English you need to choose your words wisely —not always an easy task. You need also to arrange the words in an effective order and at times this task, too, presents difficulties. The usual order in an English sentence is Subject with its attendants, then Predicate with its attendants : " Brutus killed Cæsar " is the type. There is danger in departing from that type ; for it is the natural way, and your readers, expecting it, are apt to misinterpret the departure. Many of us, for example, do not see at first that " inevitable hour " is the Subject and that " the boast of heraldry " and so on is the Object, in Gray's lines :

    The boast of heraldry, the pomp of power,
      And all that beauty, all that wealth e'er gave,
    Awaits alike th' inevitable hour :
    The paths of glory lead but to the grave.

By his unusual order—his INVERSION, we say—Gray puzzled you a little. This usual order is, you note, changed almost of course when a statement becomes a question. Thus we have the interrogative, " What did he pay ? " as the counterpart of " He paid this amount."

Besides, in English, the place in the sentence serves very often to indicate the relations among the words composing the sentence. The three Latin words, *Brutus Cæsarem occidit*, mean much the same however they are arranged. But " Cæsar killed Brutus " and " Brutus killed Cæsar " have quite different meanings ; and " Brutus Cæsar killed " is hopelessly ambiguous. Still, inversion does not always deceive, and it may be quite pleasing. The extract from Pope under " Rising Rhythm " has several examples of effective inversion.

When a good writer does alter the usual order he has a reason for the inversion. He may want to make prominent, through its being in an unexpected place, a word or a phrase that otherwise you would have passed over lightly. Look at these instances of inversion ; read them aloud, re-arrange the words, and ask yourself why the inversion is better : " So ended this great siege, the most memorable in the annals of the British Isles " (doesn't the placing of " So ended " at the close of the sentence weaken the statement ?) " Whatsoever thy hand findeth to do, do it with thy might " (you agree that this admonition would be less stirring if it began with the imperative " do "). " Of Law there can no less be acknowledged than that her seat is the bosom of God, her voice the harmony of the world : all things in heaven and earth do her homage, the very least as feeling her care and the greatest as not exempted from her power."

> I strove with none, for none was worth my strife,
> Nature I loved and, next to Nature, Art :
> I warmed both hands before the fire of life ;
> It sinks, and I am ready to depart.
>
> (W. S. LANDOR.)

(" I loved Nature " is the prose order of the inversion.) In verse an unusual order of words may result from a difficulty in finding rhyme or rhythm. Thus :

> Who lets slip Fortune, her shall never find,
> Occasion, once passed by, is bald behind.

INVERTED COMMAS. (See **" Quotation Marks "**)

IRONY

(*a*) A drayman, in a passion, calls out, " You are a pretty fellow," without suspecting that he is uttering irony.

(MACAULAY.)

(*b*) Clap an extinguisher upon your irony, if you are unhappily blest with a vein of it. Remember you are upon your oath.

(CHARLES LAMB.)

The Greeks used their word " irony " for ignorance put on for a purpose. We have developed the idea : irony with us denotes the device whereby we impress a thought by using words in contradiction to their real meaning. We praise highly for instance : and our praise is felt to be sarcasm or ridicule. We thereby emphasise the contrast between what is actual and what is desirable. Mr. Justice Maule's attack on the old divorce law might have seemed at first view a laudatory explanation of the law : it was in fact a vigorous attack upon that law. He was passing judgment after the jury had brought in a verdict of " Guilty " :

Prisoner, you have been convicted upon clear evidence ; you have intermarried with another woman, your lawful wife being still alive. You have committed the crime of bigamy. You tell me, and indeed the evidence has shown that your first wife left her home and her young children to live in adultery with another man. You say this prosecution is an instrument of extortion on the part of the adulterer.

Be it so. I am bound to tell you that these are circumstances which the law does not in your case take notice of. You had no right to take the law into your own hands. Every Englishman is bound to know that when a wrong is done, the law, or perhaps I should say the Constitution, affords a remedy. Now listen to me and I will tell you what you ought to have done. Immediately you heard of your wife's adultery you should have gone to the attorney and directed him to bring an action against the seducer of your wife. You should have prepared your evidence, instructed counsel, and proved the case in court ; and recollect that it was imperative that you should recover—I do not mean actually obtain—substantial damages.

Having proceeded thus far, you should have employed a proctor and instituted a suit in the Ecclesiastical Courts for a divorce *a mensa et thoro.* Your case is a very clear one, and I doubt not you would have obtained your divorce. After this step your course was quite plain ; you had only to obtain a private Act of Parliament to dissolve your marriage. This you would get as a matter of course upon payment of the proper fees and proof of the facts ; you might then have lawfully married again. I perceive, prisoner, that you appear scarcely to understand what I am saying to you. But let me assure you these steps are constantly being taken by persons who are desirous to dissolve an unhappy marriage ; it is true, for the wise man has said it, that " a hated woman, when she is married, is a thing that the earth cannot bear," and that " a bad wife is to her husband as rottenness to his bones ". You, however, must bear the great evil, or must adopt the remedy prescribed by the constitution of your country.

I see you would tell me that these proceedings would cost you £1,000, and that your small stock-in-trade is not worth £100. Perhaps it may be so. The law has nothing to say to that ; if you had taken these proceedings you would have been free from your present wife, and the woman you have secondly married would have been a respectable matron. As you have not done so, you stand there a convicted culprit, and it is my duty to pass sentence upon you—you will be imprisoned for one day.

(MR. JUSTICE MAULE.)

As Charles Lamb suggests, irony is a dangerous weapon to use, and perhaps we should curb our propensity to it. For irony may be a boomerang :

Teacher (to scholar who has received his deserts for drawing caricatures) : " Well, Jones, what did the Head say about your funny picture ? "

Boy (with dignity) : " He said, sir, that only the lowest of the low would call it funny."

ITALICS

" Italic a Littera "—Italian Letter or Type—was the name given to that kind of printing type devised by Aldus Manutius of Venice. In this type, now called " italics ", the letters slope to the right.

The type is employed in order to give emphasis or distinction. If you should wish the printer to put a word or words in italics, instead of into the ordinary type, you underline the word, or words.

Italics are appropriate for the following purposes :

1. To make distinct words or phrases not yet fully a part of the English language. Here are instances :

(*a*) The writer may hope that his words will be studied, that the reader, coming upon an idea new to him, will stop, will consider, will decline to go on till he has this idea firmly in his mind. The speaker cannot hope for such deliberation. *Vox perit, litera scripta manet*, is his warning ; " the sound of my voice dies away, whereas the written word remains for a record ".

(*b*) 'Tis all mine, yet none mine (*Omne meum, Nihil meum*). As a good housewife out of divers fleeces weaves one piece of cloth, as a bee gathers wax and honey out of many flowers, I have laboriously collected out of divers writers.

2. For titles of books and so on, and names of fictitious characters. Here are instances :

(*a*) When he killed a calf he would do it in a high style and make a speech (*William Shakespeare*, in *Brief Lives* by John Aubrey).

(*b*) *Cob* was the strongest, *Mob* was the wrongest, *Chittabob's* tail was the finest and longest !

(*c*) *Oats*. A grain which in England is generally given to horses, but in Scotland supports the people. (*From Dictionary of the English Language* by *Samuel Johnson*.)

3. When you refer to a letter or a word as such, that is, where the letter is not doing its usual work as a symbol, nor the word its usual work as a constituent of a sentence. Thus :

> The long vowel *a* is indicated in one way in *pale*, in another way in *pail*.

4. Italics may be used to give emphasis. Thus : remember the *look* of a word ; it is this *look* that matters in spelling.

You should, perhaps be sparing in your italicising in order to give emphasis. This is so, even though some writers whom you admire make much use of the device. Charles Lamb is one. Here, for instance, is a paragraph from his Essay on *All Fools' Day* :

Many happy returns of this day to you—and you—and you, Sir—nay, never frown, man, nor put a long face upon the matter. Do not we know one another ? what need of ceremony among friends? we have all a touch of *that same*—you understand me—a speck of the motley. Beshrew the man who on such a day as this, the *general festival*, should affect to stand aloof. I am none of those squeakers. I am free of the corporation, and care not who knows it. He that meets me in the forest to-day, shall meet with no wise-acre, I can tell him. *Stultus sum.* Translate me that, and take the meaning of it to yourself for your pains. What ! man, we have four quarters of the globe on our side, at the least computation.

J

JARGON. (See "**Slang**")

(*a*) The hard-pressed reporter, anxious to fill up space and to give colour to his narrative, may speak of " extinguishing a conflagration " when all he means is " putting out a fire ", may expand " receive " into " be made the recipient of ", " eat " into " partake of some refreshment ", " portrait " into " a counterfeit presentment ", " house " into " domiciliary edifice ", " if " into " in the event of ". This is the journalistic jargon that journalists themselves laugh at.

(*b*) " Years have elapsed since I had an opportunity of ocularly perusing your lineaments," writes Mr. Micawber.

JARGON is the term applied loosely—and usually by unfavourable critics—to any speech or writing other than such as is expressed in plain straightforward terms. We must, it seems, call a spade a spade, not an agricultural implement ; we must prefer " it has been forgotten " to " it has gone into innocuous desuetude ". The writer fond of phrases like " the festive board ", " the cup that cheers but not inebriates ", " to trip the light fantastic toe ", and the others that come to your memory, may retort that simplicity may be carried too far. We don't ask for a great deal of such simplicity as :

> Well, after many a sad reproach,
> They got into a hackney coach
>   And trotted down the street.
> I saw them go ; one horse was blind,
> The tails of both hung down behind
>   Their shoes were on their feet.

Still, better simplicity than elaborate and affected jargon.

L

LACONICS. (See **" Conciseness "**)

(a) No man can be supremely eloquent in laconics. You
cannot express the rising and the expanding, the sweep
and the circling of eloquent feeling, in a style resembling
that which seamen call "a choppy sea". For such
thinking you must have at command a style of which
an oceanic ground-swell, or the Gothic interweaving of
forest-trees, is the more becoming symbol.

(Dr. Arnold.)

(b) Dr. Gaisford had the signal merit of speech, Spartan
brevity. When Lord Liverpool offered him the Greek
professorship, with profuse compliments on his erudition,
the learned man replied, " My Lord, I have received your
letter, and accede to the contents.—Yours, T. G." And
to the complaining parent of an undergraduate he wrote,
" Dear Sir,—Such letters as yours are a great annoyance
to your obedient servant T. Gaisford." This laconic gift
the dean evidently had not time to transmit to all of his
flock.

(John Morley, in his *Life of Gladstone*.)

(c) Let thy speech be short, comprehending much in few
words.

(*Ecclesiasticus*.)

The Lacedæmonians were notable for the fewness of their
words : laconic speech is an imitation of the Lacedæmonians in
their brevity of speech.

LANGUAGE AS A VEHICLE OF THOUGHT

" I knew it ; but I couldn't express it," laments the examination candidate. Can that really happen ; can there be a divorce
between thought and the means of expressing thought ? Perhaps
there can. Often enough you have thoughts and can find no
apt words for expression,—or perhaps have found them when too
late, when the chance to use them effectively has for ever vanished.
Esprit d'escalier the French call it, the witty answer, the crushing
retort that comes to us when the door is already closed and our
feet are on the staircase leading from the interview chamber.

Perhaps that writer, glorying in his own power of expression, was unduly disdainful of halting efforts who wrote, " A thought does not arrive at being a thought until we rightly express it : if people really have important thoughts in their minds they will coin them into beautiful ringing words and give them expression." Is not Browning's the truer statement, that apt words may not be forthcoming to embody the thought ?

> For me, I touched a thought, I know
>   Has tantalized me many times
> (Like turns of thread the spiders throw
>   Mocking across our path) for rhymes
> To catch at, and let go.

And you know Tennyson's couplet,

> And Thought leapt out to wed with Thought,
> Ere Thought, could wed itself with speech.

The hearer often needs to be very generous in interpreting what the speaker says. The broadcasting announcer tells us, for instance, " Elisabeth Schumann was singing those songs on both sides of H.M.V. Record No. . . ." If she had been, she would have been performing a curious feat. And, " These two songs are on either side of Columbia Record No. . . ." Well, they are not. One song is on one side, the other song on the other side. But the exact way of expression is a clumsy and lengthy way ; and we may well have sympathy for the harassed broadcaster. For it will be strange indeed if we ourselves are without spot or blemish in our speech.

You need not be greatly despondent though you say many things that could have been expressed otherwise, expressed more in keeping with recognised custom. These departures from what is customary—these " faults " if any one cares to attach that name to them—are incident to all speech. The Pharisee in speech, the person searching for faults in what others say, will not fail to find them. " I'm afraid she's not at home," said Mrs. X to an inquirer for Miss X. Did fear really enter into the matter ; was the hour deplorably late, and was the mother anxiously awaiting the laggard ? Probably not. The statement is convention only, a fashion to which most of us conform.

All this is only another way of saying that language is, at its best, not a perfect vehicle for the transmission of thought. The speaker puts his thought into words. Here at the outset there may be loss. For the speaker may be inept in his choice of words or in his arrangement of them ; and after all, series of sounds is a very different thing from a train of thought. This is the first difficulty, of putting thought into words.

There is little Titubus, the stammering law-stationer in Lincoln's Inn [Charles Lamb relates]. We have seldom known this shrewd little fellow engaged in an argument where we were not convinced he had the best of it, if his tongue would but fairly have seconded him. When he has been spluttering excellent broken sense for an hour together, writhing and labouring to be delivered of the point of dispute— the very gist of the controversy knocking at his teeth, which like some obstinate iron-grating still obstructed its deliverance—his puny frame convulsed, and face reddening all over at an unfairness in the logic which he wanted articulation to expose, it has moved our gall to see a smooth portly fellow of an adversary that cared not a button for the merits of the question, by merely laying his hand upon the head of the stationer, and desiring him to be *calm* (your tall disputants have always the advantage), with a provoking sneer carry the argument clean from him in the opinion of all the bystanders.

The other difficulty in the way of transmission is in the hearer or reader. You remember what Ruskin said about reading a good book :

There seems, to you and me, no reason why the electric forces of the earth should not carry whatever there is of gold within it at once to the mountain tops so that kings and people might know that all the gold they could get was there, and without any trouble of digging, or anxiety, or chance, or waste of time, cut it away, and coin as much as they needed. But Nature does not manage it so. She puts it in little fissures in the earth, nobody knows where ; you may dig long and find none ; you must dig painfully to find any. And it is just the same with men's wisdom. When you come to a good book, you must ask yourself " Am I inclined to work as an Australian miner would ? Are my pick-axes and shovels in good order, and am I in good trim myself, my sleeves well up to the elbow, and my breath good, and my temper ? " And, keeping the figure a little longer, even at cost of tiresomeness, for it is a thoroughly useful one, the metal you are in search of being the author's mind or meaning, his words are as the rock which you have to crush and smelt in order to get at it. And your pick-axes are your own care, wit, and learning; your smelting furnace is your thoughtful soul.

(Sesame and Lilies.)

That is a vivid and forceful way of saying this : in our use of language to express our thoughts, we need the co-operation of hearer or reader. And the co-operation may be absent. The hearer may be unable to co-operate. He may be ignorant of the words we use; he may not have heard them clearly—for, indeed, much of the speaking that goes on around us is not easily audible; or he may attach to them a meaning different from the one we intended. Or the hearer may be unwilling to co-operate. He may not accede to our implied demand upon his attention, may not trouble to listen; or listening, he may out of sheer perversity interpret our words in a sense that is possible, but that is unintended. On occasion, no doubt, the speaker purposely says what admits of two meanings : " I shall lose no time in reading your book," said a harassed Prime Minister to an importunate novelist. But these occasions should not occur frequently.

That miscarriage and misunderstandings arise through the use of speech is a fact. The fact imposes upon us the duty of care. Even in our speech we should give few occasions for offence; and in our writing, where deliberate consideration is possible, the occasions should be rare indeed.

LENGTH OF WORDS. (See also **"Syllable"**)

(*a*) Up in Will's valley only the wind and seasons made an epoch; the fish hung in the swift stream, the birds circled overhead, the pinetops rustled underneath the stars, the tall hills stood over all; and Will went to and fro, minding his wayside inn, until the snow began to thicken on his head. His heart was young and vigorous; and if his pulses kept a sober time they still beat strong and steady in his wrists. He carried a ruddy stain on either cheek, like a ripe apple; he stooped a little, but his step was still firm, and his sinewy hands were reached out to all men with a friendly pressure.

(ROBERT LOUIS STEVENSON, *Will o' the Mill.*)

153

(b) 1 Give me my robe, put on my crown; I have
     Immortal longings in me; now no more
     The juice of Egypt's grape shall moist this lip.
     Yare, yare, good Iras; quick. Methinks I hear
   5 Antony call; I see him rouse himself
     To praise my noble act; I hear him mock
     The luck of Cæsar, which the gods give men
     To excuse their after wrath: Husband, I come:
     Now to that name my courage prove my title!
  10 I am fire and air; my other elements
     I give to baser life. So, have you done?
     Come then, and take the last warmth of my lips.
     Farewell, kind Charmian; Iras, long farewell.
     Have I the aspic in my lips? Dost fall?
  15 If thou and nature can so gently part,
     The stroke of death is as a lover's pinch,
     Which hurts, and is desired. Dost thou lie still?
     If thus thou vanishest, thou tell'st the world
  19 It is not worth leave-taking.

                              (*Antony and Cleopatra.*)

The advice is sound: when a choice presents itself, use the
SHORT WORD RATHER THAN THE LONG. So doing you will be
following the example of the best writers, both in prose and in
verse. Not that great writers are afraid of long words: at times,
indeed, these writers may introduce a long word and produce
a great effect by doing so. Look at Macbeth's outburst:

> Will all great Neptune's ocean wash this blood
> Clean from my hand? No; this my hand will rather
> The multitudinous seas incarnadine,
> Making the green one red.

Are not the polysyllables, *multitudinous* and *incarnadine*, awe-
inspiring terms? And what a wonderful effect the words *absent*
and *felicity* have among the surrounding monosyllables of
Hamlet's cry:

> If thou didst ever hold me to thy heart
> Absent thee from felicity awhile
> And in this harsh world draw thy breath in pain
> To tell my story.

In scientific writing, too, long words may be plentiful. It is,

154

for instance, to be expected that a writer on the history of language should write : " It is a matter of general experience that a person who tries to learn a foreign language entirely by conversation finds the vocabulary easier to acquire than the grammar."

Short words, though, should be the rule ; long words the exception. Give a little time to the analysis of the Stevenson and Shakespeare extracts. In (a), which has in it 113 words, there are only four words—*overhead*, *underneath*, *vigorous*, *sinewy* —of more than two syllables ; and the first two of these are compounds of other words, the last two owe their third syllables to the adjective terminations *ous* and *y*, which turn the two-syllable nouns *vigour* and *sinew* into adjectives. There are 22 disyllables (including the compound *pine-tops*). The remainder, 87 in all, are monosyllables.

In the extract from *Antony and Cleopatra*, you will note that these lines are made up of ten monosyllables each—1, 12 ; in all the others there are only 2, 4, 5, 8, 10, 13 with two words not monosyllables. And you readily agree that a line does not of necessity lose in force because it is made up of single-syllable words. Look, for instance, at this most touching epitaph of Housman's :

> Here dead lie we because we did not choose
> To live and shame the land from which we sprung.
> Life, to be sure, is nothing much to lose ;
> But young men think it is, and we were young.

Because and *nothing* are the only words not monosyllables ; all the words are " ordinary " ; but how effective the lines are ! You note, too, that in the Shakespeare passage the proper names *Egypt, Iras, Antony, Cæsar, Charmian*—account for a good many of the two- or three-syllable words.

You will doubtless find writers—good writers, too—with a fondness for the longer words. This is how Macaulay writes of Judge Jeffreys :

> Tenderness for others and respect for himself were feelings alike unknown to him. He acquired a boundless command of the rhetoric in which the vulgar express hatred and contempt. The profusion of maledictions and vituperative epithets which composed his vocabulary could hardly have been rivalled in the fishmarket or the beargarden.

Lewis Carroll gets fun out of newspaper long words:

"You're a *very* poor *speaker*," said the King.

Here one of the guinea-pigs cheered, and was immediately suppressed by the officers of the court. (As that is rather a hard word, I will just explain to you how it was done. They had a large canvas bag, which tied up at the mouth with strings : into this they slipped the guinea-pig, head first, and then sat upon it.) "I'm glad I've seen that done," thought Alice, "I've often read in the newspapers at the end of the trials, 'There was some attempt at applause, which was immediately suppressed by the officers of the Court,' and I never understood what it meant till now."

Finally, ask yourself which of the two alternatives presented in Boswell's account would be likely to have the greater effect :

Johnson seemed to take pleasure in speaking in his own style ; for, when he had carelessly missed it, he would repeat the thought translated into it. Talking of the comedy of The Rehearsal, he said, It has not wit enough to keep it sweet. This was easy :—he therefore caught himself, and pronounced a more round sentence ; It has not vitality enough to preserve it from putrefaction.

LETTER-WRITING

(*a*) The style of letters ought to be free, easy, and natural ; as near approaching to familiar conversation as possible. Now, the two best qualities in conversation are good humour and good breeding ; those letters are therefore certainly the best that show the most of these two qualities.

(*b*) Lives of great men oft remind us
　　We may suffer in our turn,
And departing leave behind us,
　　Letters that we ought to burn.

(DEAN INGE's version of Longfellow's lines.)

(*c*) Oh, Little Woman ! you will come to our aid, if possible ; what on earth are we to do for eggs ? At this present Mr. C. is breakfasting on shop-eggs, and doesn't know it ; and I am every morning expecting to hear in my bed an explosion over some one too far gone for his making himself an illusion about it. All the people who kept fowls round about have, the maids say, during my absence ceased to keep them, and the two eggs from Addiscombe

156

three times a week are not enough for us both ; I, " as one solitary individual ", needing three in the day—one for breakfast, one in hot milk for luncheon, and one in my small pudding at dinner. When I left Holm Hill, Mrs. Russell was in despair over her hens ; thirty of them yielded but three eggs a day. Yours, too, may have struck work ; and in that case never mind. Only if you could send us some, it would be a mercy.

(A paragraph from a letter written by the
much-tried wife of Thomas Carlyle.)

Indeed, we should, as we write our letter, have our correspondent in mind. The letter is for *him*, or *her* ; and the kind of letter most effective depends much upon the recipient. That is, we must note, applicable to what is *really* a letter—a personal communication between familiars : Patmore's lines have many parallels :

> I hope you're well. I write to say
> Frederick has got, besides his pay,
> A good appointment in the Docks ;
> Also to thank you for the frocks
> And shoes for Baby.

> 5, CHEYNE ROW,
> *Tuesday,* 18*th October* 1860.

" LIKE " or " AS " in comparison

(1) Like mine, thy gentle numbers feebly creep ;
Thy tragic muse gives smiles, thy comic sleep.
Worthy burgers were long ago in bed, benight-capped like their domiciles.
He ran like a hare.
You are talking like a fool.
This is a hard world in winter for wolves and poor rogues like me.
All the light-footed tourists, all the pedlars laden with strange wares, were tending downwards like the river that accompanied that path.
All we like sheep have gone astray.
The barge she sat in, like a burnished throne,
Burned in the water.

(2) So do as thou hast said.
As is the matter, so is the man.

Montigny leaped up, swift as an adder, and stabbed him to the heart.

The baby was as good as gold.

She is as well as can be expected.

Ye shall be as Gods, knowing good and evil (i.e. as Gods are).

LIKE—an adjective though it does take an objective case after it, compares things :

So Lord Howard passed away with five ships of war that day
Till he melted like a cloud in the silent summer heaven.

AS—a conjunction, compares actions. For example :

For a dozen times they came with their pikes and musqueteers,
And a dozen times we shook 'em off as a dog that shakes his ears
When he leaps from the water to the land.

You will notice that, though *like* is in the examples an adjective, it can—like the transitive verb—take an Object : that is why in Shelley's lines we have *thee*, not *thou* :

What thou art we know not:
  What is most like thee ?
From rainbow clouds there flow not
  Drops so bright to see
As from thy presence showers a rain of melody.

Other adjectives denoting measurement also take an Object : in " ten years old " *years* is in the objective case, " governed " by *old* : in Tennyson's

Jewels five words long,
  That on the stretched forefinger of all time
  Sparkle for ever.

words is similarly in the objective case " governed " by the adjective *long*.

LITOTES

(*a*) I am a citizen of no mean city,

(*b*) Yet not the more
  Cease I to wander where the Muses haunt.

(Paradise Lost.)

It is often a quite effective way of expressing an affirmative by expressing the negative of its contrary. The Greeks called this rhetorical device a LITOTES.

LUCIDITY

(*a*) No doubt what I am writing will require much correction : but in the main, I think it will do. How little the all-important art of making meaning pellucid is studied now ! Hardly any popular writer, except myself, thinks of it. Many seem to aim at being obscure. Indeed, they may be right enough in one sense ; for many readers give credit for profundity to whatever is obscure, and call all that is perspicuous, shallow. But corragio ! and think of A.D. 2850. Where will your Emerson be then ? But Herodotus will still be read with delight. We must do our best to be read too.

(In MACAULAY's Diary for 12th January, 1850.)

(*b*) I may truly say that I have never been in the practice, since I was a boy, of attempting to write well, or to form an elegant style. I think I have never written for writing's sake, but my one and single desire and aim has been to do what is so difficult, namely, to explain clearly and exactly my meaning ; this has been the whole principle of all my corrections and re-writings.

(CARDINAL NEWMAN.)

There is LUCIDITY—clearness—in your composition when an intelligent reader gets your meaning without needing to spend much time or thought. Your clear expressions and your orderly arrangement of them have served to economise your reader's attention. You are not vague (indefinite in thought or expression) or obscure (hard to understand). In short you are easily intelligible and in one interpretation only.

Lucidity is one of the great merits of composition. *Clarté est politesse*—the courteous person tries to make you understand easily—say our neighbours. Macaulay himself, whose commendation of lucidity is above, makes his practice accord well with his theory. Does anyone, for instance, have much trouble in getting the meaning of this little extract ? It is from an Essay dealing with the German Emperor :

But the mind of Frederick William was so ill-regulated,

that all his inclinations became passions, and all his passions partook of the character of moral and intellectual disease. His parsimony degenerated into sordid avarice. His taste for military pomp and order became a mania, like that of a Dutch burgomaster for tulips, or that of a member of the Roxburghe Club for Caxtons. While the envoys of the court of Berlin were in such a state of squalid poverty as moved the laughter of foreign capitals, while the food placed before the princes and princesses of the blood-royal of Prussia was too scanty to appease hunger, and so bad that even hunger loathed it, no price was thought too extravagant for tall recruits. The ambition of the king was to form a brigade of giants, and every country was ransacked by his agents for men above the ordinary stature. These researches were not confined to Europe. No head that towered above the crowd in the bazaars of Aleppo, of Cairo, or of Surat, could escape the crimps of Frederick William. One Irishman, more than seven feet high, who was picked up in London by the Prussian Ambassador, received a bounty of near thirteen hundred pounds sterling, very much more than the ambassador's salary. This extravagance was the more absurd, because a stout youth of five feet eight, who might have been procured for a few dollars, would in all probability, have been a much more valuable soldier. But to Frederick William, this huge Irishman was what a brass Otho, or a Vinegar Bible, is to a collector of a different kind.

The judgments delivered in the High Courts of Justice are usually fine instances of lucidity. Here is an example that bears upon our topic of English composition. The point at issue— in *Cummins* v. *Bond* (1926)—was, " Who is the first author of this ? To whom, accordingly, does the copyright adhere ? "

The plaintiff had written, so she declared, the *Chronicle of Cleopas* ; she had written it while under the influence of a psychic visitant introduced by the defendant. The defendant, moreover, had transcribed and annotated the writing ; and he claimed to be joint author with the plaintiff. The plaintiff, however, got the declaration she sought, Mr. Justice Eve saying

So far as this world is concerned there can be no doubt who is the author here ; for the plaintiff has written every word of this script. But the plaintiff and the defendant are of opinion that the true originator is some being, no longer inhabiting this world, and who has been out of it long enough to hope that he has no reason for wishing to return to it. It would seem as though the individual who has been dead and buried for some 1900 years and the plaintiff ought to be regarded as the joint authors and owners of the copyright. But, inasmuch as I do not feel myself competent to make any declaration in his favour, and recognising as I do that I have no jurisdiction extending to the sphere in which he moves, I think I ought to confine myself, when inquiring who is the author, to individuals who were alive when the book first came into existence, and to conditions which the legislature of 1911 may reasonably be presumed to have contemplated. The defendant invites me to declare that the authorship and copyright rest with someone already domiciled on the other side of the inevitable river. But I can only look upon the matter as a terrestrial one, of the earth earthy, and I deal with it on that footing. The plaintiff has made out her case, and the copyright rests with her.

LYRIC

Lyric poetry is the expression by the poet of his own feelings.

(RUSKIN.)

The lyre was the stringed instrument used by the Greeks to accompany their songs; the LYRIC was once made to be sung. We now apply the term, as in Ruskin's definition, to a poem directly expressing the poet's own thoughts and sentiments. We class Wordsworth's great poem *Intimations of Immortality* along with delightful little songs like :

> Oh! Mistress mine, where are you roaming?
> O stay and hear! your true-love's coming
>   That can sing both high and low;
> Trip no further, pretty sweeting,
> Journeys end in lovers meeting—
>   Every wise man's son doth know.

Lyric, however, may be used with a less elastic scope. The term is applied to the lighter forms, lovers' protestations in particular, of verse—very charming forms, though Milton does disparage them. " Why," he asks, " take incessant care "

> To tend the homely, slighted shepherd's trade
> And strictly meditate the thankless Muse?

Why make preparations for an elaborate epic when these trifles are so easy to produce :

> Were it not better done, as others use,
> To sport with Amaryllis in the shade
> Or with the tangles of Neæra's hair ?

But of course, these delightful little poems of Herrick and Lovelace, of whom perhaps Milton thought, are very rare things,— not at all easy to produce. Milton himself wrote many lovely lyrics—" Sweet Echo " in *Comus* is one of our greatest treasures —and it may be that you would be willing to give up a long poem like *Paradise Regained* for half-a-dozen more of such songs.

M

MALAPROPISM

(*a*) Mr. Lewes is sending what a Malapropian friend called a " missile " to Sara.

(George Eliot.)

(*b*) I would by no means wish a daughter of mine to be a progeny of learning. But I would send her, at nine years old, to a boarding-school in order to learn a little ingenuity and artifice. Then, sir, she would have a supercilious knowledge in accounts—and, as she grew up, I would have her instructed in geometry that she might know something of the contagious countries,—but above all, Sir Antony, she should be mistress of orthodoxy, that she might not mis-spell and mis-pronounce words so shamefully as girls usually do ; and likewise that she might reprehend the true meaning of what she is saying. This, Sir Antony, is what I would have a woman know ; and I don't think there is a superstitious article in it.

(Sheridan, *The Rivals*.)

A word, or an action, is *á propos* when it is to the purpose, when it is appropriate ; a word, or an action, is *mal á propos* when it is ill-fitted, awkward, ill-timed. The misuse is—on occasion— amusing to others than the user ; and Mrs. Malaprop (in Sheridan's play *The Rivals*) gives her name to the ludicrous misuse of words. But such misuse has existed since the beginning of language and will continue so long as language exists. For no language is a perfect vehicle of thought and no one a perfect user of it.

Perhaps you will, for instance, rejoice in reading a little of what Miss Winifred Jenkins (in *Humphrey Clinker*) wrote to her friend in Wales. Winifred, during her visit to London, had " seen the park, and the paleass of Saint Gimse's, and the king's and queen's magisterial pursing, and the sweet young princes, and the hilly-fents, pyebald ass, and all the rest of the royal family "; and she ends her letter with some sound advice.

DEAR MARY JONES,

An' please God, when I return I'll bring you a new cap, with a turkey-shell coom, and a pyehouse sermon, that was preached in the Tabernacle; and I pray of all love, you will mind your writing and your spilling for, craving your pardon Molly, it made me suet to disseyffer your last scrabble, which was delivered by the hind at Bath.

O, voman! voman! if thou hadst but the least consumption of what pleasure we scullers have, when we can cunster the crabbidst buck off hand, and spell the echnitch words without looking at the primmer. As for Mr. Klinker, he is qualified to be clerk to a parish. But I'll say no more. Remember me to Saul—poor sole! it goes to my heart to think she don't know her letters. But all in God's good time. It shall go hard, but I will bring her the ABC in gingerbread, and that you nose, will be learning to her taste.

Mistress says we are going a long gurney to the North; but go where we will, I shall ever be

Dear Mary Jones,
Yours with true infection,
WIN JENKINS.

LONDON,
3rd June.

METAPHOR

(a) I fall upon the thorns of life! I bleed!
    A heavy weight of hours has chained and bowed
    One too like thee—tameless, and swift, and proud.
        (SHELLEY, *Ode to the West Wind*.)

(b) Fish not with this melancholy bait
    For this fool's gudgeon, this opinion.
        (*Merchant of Venice*.)

163

(c) " To what base uses we may return, Horatio."
" 'Twere to consider too curiously, to consider so."

(*Hamlet.*)

(d) 'Tis true, there is an edge in all firm belief, and with an easy metaphor we may say, the *Sword* of Faith ; but in these obscurities I rather use it in the adjunct the Apostle gives it, a *Buckler*, under which I conceive a wary combatant may be invulnerable.

(SIR THOMAS BROWNE, *Religio Medici.*)

(e) *Orinthia :* Heaven is offering you a rose ; and you cling to a cabbage.
Magnus : That is a very apt metaphor, beloved. But what wise man, if you force him to choose between doing without roses and doing without cabbages, would not secure the cabbages ? Besides, all these old married cabbages were once roses ; and though young things like you don't remember that, their husbands do. They don't notice the change. (G. B. SHAW, *The Apple Cart.*)

In these quotations you have instances of what is so common in our English language, the transfer of a name or descriptive term to something to which it is not in strictness applicable. " METAPHOR " is the name given to this transfer. Some of the transfers you can hardly overlook. You know well enough that the trials and troubles in Shelley's life were not really " thorns ". They gave pain indeed, but it was mental, not physical, pain. Shelley would not have defined his thorns as " stiff, sharppointed woody processes on the stem of a plant ". Nor can you suppose that the Merchant of Venice was being counselled against angling in a stream. Such implied comparisons, where we are quite conscious that the words do not bear their literal meaning, are sometimes called " live metaphors ".

But " consider " in (c) is a metaphor too. It does not, however, at once bring into mind a vision of something other than the intended meaning ; hearing the word you do not conjure up a view of the astrologer, surveying the stars and seeking from them reliable conclusions. Yet the word is connected with " sidereal " (belonging to the stars). The metaphor is similar to that of " examine " : we do not think—when we hear such a sentence as " I was examined in Latin "—of the weighing accurately in a balance. Yet *examen* is the Latin word for the tongue of a balance; and " to examine " is literally " to weigh in the balance ". The implied comparison has been made so often, it is so familiar to us, that we are unaware of our departure from the strictly literal sense. More of our language consists of such " dead " metaphors than we perhaps suppose.

We have, indeed, an irresistible tendency to slip, often without noticing the fact of our doing so, from one meaning of a word to another meaning. That is why it is rarely possible to define a word—" book ", for instance—in isolation. You need to have the context before you are able to interpret the present meaning. Being asked the meaning of a word you would most likely do well to imitate the prudent Scot and ask for further information : " Give me the context, and I may be able to tell." The original meaning of " book " was a writing-tablet, the wood of the beech-tree. But now look at the varied ideas that come to us when we hear the name. You say " This book weighs six ounces " ; and you have in mind the material contents. To define " book " then you say : " A book is a collection of sheets, of paper or other substance, fastened together to make a whole and protected by covers." You say " This book has been translated into many languages " ; and you have in mind the product of the labour of a great mind. This is Milton's sense when he speaks of a good book as the product of " a master spirit, preserved and treasured up on purpose to a life beyond life ".

Then you have the several, metaphorical uses where neither the tangible book nor its intangible message are intended. " To be in someone's good books " is to be in his favour : your name is in the record, the imaginary record, of those whom he delights to honour. " To bring a person to book " is to put him to the test : he is constrained to bring forward the authority upon which he based his statement. " To speak like a book " is to speak with complete accuracy of information : it is as though you had the written record before you. And " to take a leaf out of a person's book " is to follow his example : you follow the instructions that, it would appear, he has engraved upon his mind.

When the comparison implied in a metaphor is apt, that is, people not only get delight from it, but they use it so that it becomes part of the language. The metaphor may retain its vividness for long. " They smote him with their tongues " could hardly appear to be other than a metaphor. It has kept its liveliness when such an expression as " A blow with a word strikes deeper than a blow with a sword " has perhaps lost some.

Many of Shakespeare's metaphors have, indeed, become so much a part of the language that not only do we forget their origin but we sometimes use them with little consciousness of the implied comparison. Many a time maybe, you have used the phrase " the sere and yellow leaf " without thinking of Macbeth's, " My way of life is fallen into the sere, the yellow leaf " ; many a time Hamlet's phrase " caviare to the general " without thinking of his shrewd note that the thing approved by competent critics does not always please the populace ; or his oft-repeated phrases, sometimes with no very apt application, " slings and arrows of outrageous fortune ", " take arms against a sea of troubles ", " a consummation devoutly to be wished ", " whips and scorns of time ", and a hundred others ; many a time spoken of a merciless creditor wanting " his pound of flesh " without bringing into mind Shylock and his insistence on his forfeit.

Your metaphors will be to the advantage of your style when they arise naturally from your subject matter. For you readily realise that a style may be too flowery. Here is what William Cowper says about Pope's translation of Homer :

> The garden in all the gaiety of June is less flowery than his translation. Metaphors of which Homer never dreamt, which he did not seek, and which probably he would have disdained if he had found, follow each other in quick succession like the sliding pictures in a show box.

The metaphors, too, may call into mind images that clash with one another, " Mixed metaphor " is the name sometimes given to this kind of ineptitude. The traditional example is " Mr. Speaker, I smell a rat ; I see him forming in the air and darkening the sky ; but I'll nip him in the bud."

METATHESIS

Her hair was crull as it were laid in press. (CHAUCER.)

Wrought iron is *worked iron*, Old English *axian* is *ask*, *kers* is *cress*, *thridda* is *third*, *nosthryl* is *nostril*, *brid* is *bird*, *wyrhta* is *wright*, *crull* in the Chaucer line is now *curl[ed]*.

The sounds of a word, and more particularly the sounds of *r* and *l*, may move from one position to another. At times the changed position, as in *ask*, becomes the recognised position so that *ax* is looked on as an error to be avoided. The change in position is METATHESIS.

METONYMY

> The glories of our blood and state
>   Are shadows, not substantial things ;
> There is no armour against fate ;
>   Death lays his icy hand on kings :
>   Sceptre and Crown
>   Must tumble down
> And in the dust be equal made
> With the poor crooked Scythe and Spade.
>
> (J. SHIRLEY.)

METONYMY is " change of name " : *meta* is the Greek prefix for *instead of* ; *onymy* for *name* is seen in *anonymous* (without a name), and *pseudonym* (a fictitious name). In metonymy the name of an accompaniment suggests the name really intended. The " Sceptre " suggests authority and power (here the King or the Queen), and the " Scythe " suggests the peasant worker. In a sense, to be sure, we are inaccurate when we say " the bench " when we mean " the judges in their official capacity " or " Lombard Street " when we mean " the money market, the whole body of financiers " ; we have, in fact, sacrificed accuracy in our attempt to be impressive. But, provided that our audience can reasonably be assumed to get the literal from the figurative, well-judged metonymy is quite effective. Thus " The pen is mightier than the sword " (where you have the instrument as a name for the books written or the battles fought) ; " Ye bring down my grey hairs with sorrow to the grave " (where an accompaniment of old age serves as the name for old age itself) are good instances of metonymy.

METRE

(*a*) The curfew tolls || the knell of parting day

(*b*) Haste thee, Nymph, || and bring with thee
    Jest and youthful jollity.

(*c*) And the stately ships || go on
    To their haven || under the hill ;

But Ó for the tóuch || of a vánished hánd,
And the sóund of a vóice || that ĭs stíll.

(d) Ĭ spráng to the stírrŭp || ănd Jóris ănd hé;
Ĭ gálloped, Dírck gálloped, || we gálloped áll thrée;
"Góod spéed!" cried the wátch, || as the gáte-bolts undréw;
"Spéed!" echoed the wáll || to us gállopĭng thróugh.

In English verse there is regularity in the coming of the strongly accented syllable : it may come regularly after each weakly accented syllable, ("A little learning is a dangerous thing"), or regularly before each weakly accented syllable ("Mirth, admit me of thy crew"), or after two unaccented syllables, ("To the West, to the West, to the Land of the Free, Where the mighty Missouri rolls down to the sea"), and so on. Each line of verse will have one or more of the regular groups, or FEET. METRE in poetry corresponds to TIME in music : the regular recurrence of the strong accent in the verse corresponds to the regular beat of the music. This note gives a little light on English metre ; a full account would take up many pages.

METRE (or measure) is the name given to the particular form of verse, having regard to the kind and number of the groups.

By far the most used metre in English is the line of five groups, each having a weak accent followed by a strong—a RISING RHYTHM, it is sometimes called. This is the metre of Shakespeare's blank verse, "In maiden meditation, fancy-free", and of Milton's epics, "Sonorous metal blowing martial sounds". The group, or foot, is called an IAMBIC or an IAMBUS.

It is accident that gives this name to the particular group : the Greek satirists used such groups ; and the Greek word for "assail, attack", is connected with *iambic*.

Since the verse lines of the blank verse plays have five groups, the blank verse is called an Iambic Pentameter. Those savage satires of Dryden are, for example, in Iambic Pentameter :

> The rest to some faint meaning make pretence,
> But Shadwell never deviates into sense.

The Iambic Pentameter is also called "Heroic Verse" used as

it (or its equivalent) was in the long poems (" epics ") relating to the deeds of heroes.

The group like *happy*, *angry*, with their *falling rhythm*—consisting of a strongly accented followed by a weakly accented syllable is a TROCHEE. The word is connected with " tripping ", " running ", and the trochee is, in fact, well suited to indicate light movement. Contrast, for example, the slow movement of :

> Oh ! what can ail thee, knight-at-arms,
> Alone and palely loitering ?
> The sedge has withered from the lake,
> And no birds sing.

with the lively movement of :

> Come and trip it as you go
> On the light fantastic toe.

Much less frequent than the two-syllable groups are the three-syllable groups. The group where the strongly accented syllable precedes the two weakly accented syllables—*dolefully, sacrament, scrutiny*—is called a DACTYL. Like the other words descriptive of the various groups, *dactyl* comes from the Greek, where it means a finger, one long joint being followed by two smaller joints. The prevailing group in this poem of Browning's, you will note, is the dactyl :

> This is a spray the Bird clung to,
> Making it blossom with pleasure,
> Ere the high tree-top she sprung to,
> Fit for her nest and her treasure.
> Oh ! what a hope beyond measure
> Was the poor spray's, which the flying feet hung to,
> So to be singled out, built in, and sung to !

The three-syllable group, or foot, in which the strongly accented syllable follows the two weakly accented syllables—a group like *to the West*—is called an ANAPÆST. The prevailing foot in this poem of Byron's is the *anapæst* :

> The Assyrian came down like the wolf on the fold,
> And his cohorts were gleaming in purple and gold ;
> And the sheen of their spears was like stars on the sea,
> When the blue wave rolls nightly on deep Galilee.

Like the leaves of the forest when Summer is green,
That host with their banners at sunset were seen:
Like the leaves of the forest when Autumn hath blown,
That host on the morrow lay wither'd and strown.

For the Angel of Death spread his wings on the blast,
And breathed in the face of the foe as he pass'd;
And the eyes of the sleepers wax'd deadly and chill,
And their hearts but once heaved, and for ever grew still!

And there lay the steed with his nostril all wide,
But through it there roll'd not the breath of his pride;
And the foam of his gasping lay white on the turf,
And cold as the spray of the rock-beating surf.

And there lay the rider distorted and pale,
And the dew on his brow, and the rust on his mail:
And the tents were all silent, the banners alone,
The lances unlifted, the trumpet unblown.

And the widows of Ashur are loud in their wail,
And the idols are broke in the temple of Baal:
And the might of the Gentile, unsmote by the sword,
Hath melted like snow in the glance of the Lord!

The number of feet in each line of verse varies from one to six or even seven. The four-foot line is the one favoured by beginners; the five-foot line, that of Chaucer's *Canterbury Tales* and of the blank-verse plays, is the most numerous. A poet may produce some delightful effects by varying the length of lines in his stanza, or grouping of lines. Look for instance at Herrick's lines *To Daffodils*:

> Fair daffodils, we weep to see
>   You haste away so soon:
> As yet the early rising sun
>   Has not attained his noon.
>   Stay, stay
>   Until the hasting day
>   Has run
>   But to the even-song
> And having prayed together we
>   Will go with you along.

We have short time to stay, as you,
 We have as short a Spring:
As quick a growth to meet decay
 As you or any thing.
  We die
 As your hours do, and dry
  Away
 Like to the Summer's rain;
Or as the pearls of morning dew
 Ne'er to be found again.

MIXED METAPHOR. (See " Metaphor ")

MOCK-HEROIC. (See " Parody ")

N

NAME-MAKING : SOUND ECHOING SENSE : ONO-MATOPŒIA

(*a*) swish : cackle : flip : flash : bang : mumble : pop : whirr : zip

(*b*) (1) The lisp of leaves and the ripple of rain.
 (2) Season of mists and mellow fruitfulness.

(*c*) The fair breeze blew, the white foam flew,
 The furrow followed free,
We were the first that ever burst
 Into that silent sea.

Down dropt the breeze, the sails dropt down,
 'Twas sad as sad could be :
And we did speak only to break
 The silence of the sea.
     (COLERIDGE, *The Ancient Mariner*.)

ONOMATOPŒIA is the Greek word for " name-making ". It signifies the natural instinct to form a name or other word by an imitation of the sound associated with the thing or action designated. A noise, or what makes it, may create its own name.

" Echo words " these may be called—like *bang, cackle, fizz, gibber, giggle, hiss, mumble, cuckoo.*

The term is extended to the use of such words as by their sounds suggest the sense : as, for instance, in Browning's lines suggestive of the galloping of horses :

I sprang to the stirrup, and Joris, and he ;
I galloped, Dirck galloped, we galloped all three ;
" Good speed ! " cried the watch, as the gate-bolts undrew ;
" Speed ! " echoed the wall to us galloping through.

In the example (*c*) you have the first stanza filled with rush and movement, the *r*'s and *l*'s giving the ripple of the water, the *f*'s the onrush of the ship ; in the second stanza you have the contrasted heavy syllables suggestive of stagnation.   Look, too, for something of the same effect at the whole poem of Browning's *Up at a Villa, Down in the City*.   Here are a few lines :

Is it ever hot in the square ?   There's a fountain to spout
    and splash !
In the shade it sings and springs ; in the shine such foam-
    bows flash
On the horses with curling fish-tails that prance and paddle
    and pash
Round the lady atop in the conch—fifty gazers do not
    abash,
Though all that she wears is some weeds round her waist
    in a sort of sash !

Language is, no doubt, primarily a tool, a well-nigh indispensable machinery in the mouths of men for transmitting thought. By way of its symbols, those black marks on white paper, language also transmits thought through boundless time and space.   Perhaps we are right in regarding this utility side of language, this service as a vehicle of thought, as the more important aspect of language.

We know very well, though, that language is a plaything also ; it is a toy, in which we all take delight, as well as a tool.   For words have a musical appeal to the ear as well as an intellectual appeal to the mind.   At times, indeed, this play aspect of language seems to be the thing of importance.   The thought to be expressed goes into the background ; the mode of expression appears to have been the writer's problem. You have, maybe, read an extraordinary poem of Browning's in which his main effort was seemingly to string together all sorts of strange rhymes. Here is a little of it :

> While treading down rose and ranunculus,
> You Tommy-make-room-for-your-Uncle us !
> Troop, all of you—man or homunculus,
> Quick march ! for Xanthippe, my housemaid,
> If once on your pates she a souse made
> With what, pan or pot, bowl or skoramis,
> First comes to her hand—things were more amiss !

You read the lines—read them aloud : and you are interested in the sounds rather than in the sense. A thought does underline the strange combination : the crowding intruders are warned off under penalty of an onslaught by the maid. But you hardly attend to the thought because you are noting things like the amazing rhymes—*ranunculus* with *Uncle us*, *skoramis* with *more amiss*, and the more amazing verb in the second line.

The pranks played with words are seldom so startling as those. They delight, not amaze. Rossetti, for instance—Dante Gabriel Rossetti, that is—has a poem *The Stream's Secret*. He thinks of the phrase " wandering water " and he plays a melody upon it. See how the sounds of the phrase are echoed in varied ways through the lines :

> What thing unto mine ear
> Would'st thou convey—what secret thing,
> O wandering water ever whispering ?
> Surely thy speech shall be of her,
> Thou water, O thou whispering wanderer,
> What message dost thou bring ?

We need not complain of this playing with words even when the playing is prompted because of the writer's poverty of thought, or because he is obliged to relate an incident that has been related a thousand times before. The promising journalist sets out to write an exercise in the style of the newspaper leading articles ; he explains : " the kind of thing in which one makes a column out of what would fill six lines of respectable prose. You call a cigar a ' convoluted weed ', and so on, you know ".

NOMINATIVE ABSOLUTE. (See " The Detached Phrase ")

> My story being done,
> She gave me for my pains a world of sighs.
>
> *(Othello.)*

" Story ", we say, is in the NOMINATIVE ABSOLUTE case, the participle " being done " supplying by implication the intended statement, " When my story was done ". That is to say, the Nominative Absolute is equivalent to an adverbial clause : in these two lines of Dryden, for instance :

> All human things are subject to decay,
> And, when Fate summons, monarchs must obey.

the clause " when Fate summons " is " fate summoning ". So too, in Froude's sentence : " All that August night the fight continued, the stars rolling over in their sad majesty, but unseen through the sulphur clouds which hung over the scene ", we could replace the Nominative Absolute and its participles by the adverbial clause " while the stars rolled over in their sad majesty but were unseen . . ."

Notice that the Absolute Phrase is usually separated from the rest of the sentence by a comma. Thus : " Judgment being given, the Court rose."

NOMINATIVE CASE

(*a*) If it be a sin to cover honour, I am the most offending soul alive.

(*b*) Sigh no more, ladies, sigh no more ;
> Men were deceivers ever ;
> One foot in sea and one on shore,
> To one thing constant never.
>
> *(Much Ado About Nothing.)*

In English a noun or a pronoun is in the NOMINATIVE CASE when it is :

  (1) the subject of a finite verb (as *I* in the first quotation) ;

  (2) the subject of a participle, express or understood, in the absolute construction (as *foot* in the second quotation) ;

  (3) the complement of the verb (as *soul* in the first quotation) ;

(4) the name of the person addressed, the VOCATIVE CASE in Latin (as *ladies* in the second quotation).

As regards (3), see "*Copulative Verb*".

"NONE" (PRONOUN) : NUMBER OF

(*a*) No one ever took him for a fool; but none, except his intimate friends, know he has a great deal of wit.

(*The Spectator*.)

(*b*) None but the brave deserves the fair.

(DRYDEN.)

(*c*) None does offend, none I say, none; I'll able 'em.

(SHAKESPEARE, *King Lear*, IV, VI.)

"None" in (*a*) is equivalent to "no people", and takes a plural verb "know". In (*b*) "none" is equivalent to "no one", and takes a singular verb "deserves".

There is no need to lash oneself into a fury because of another's trivial fault. All of us, many and many a time, must make the petition :

Be to my virtues ever kind,
And to my faults a little blind.

In matters of language this is particularly so. Is there one of us quite impervious to censure ? He that gloats over the defective sentence from a national newspaper may himself be at some time or other a suppliant for his reader's complacency.

The sentence was : "With regard to German journalists recently asked to leave the country, it is pointed out by the authorities that none of them has been ordered out because of their journalistic work." Some palliation of the error in the sentence, if error there is, may be found in the fact that careful and leisurely revision is rarely possible for the journalist.

The point debatable is the number of the pronoun "none". Is this singular or plural ? Well, there can be no doubt about its being either at the choice of the user. In Goldsmith's sentence, "None of these, however, are known to us", the verb "are" shows that the phrase "none of these" is looked upon as plural. In Tennyson's "There is none like her, none", the verb "is" gives the notion of singular. Logic can be brought into defence of either construction. "None" may be expanded into "no persons", and this apparently is the more common expansion. For you find " none " more often in modern English with the plural than with the singular. Perhaps that is why Dryden's " None but the brave deserves the fair " is more often than not misquoted, " deserve " taking the place of " deserves ".

But, though singular or plural may be justified, it is rather awkward to have the two in the same sentence ; and this is what one may, reasonably enough, animadvert against in the newspaper sentence. " None of them *has* " interprets " none " as singular ; " *their* journalistic work " interprets " none " as plural. We had better alter " has " into " have " or, less eligible, change " their " into " his or her ".

NOUNS, VERBS, ADJECTIVES

(a) Thou hast most traitorously corrupted the youth of this land in erecting a grammar school. It will be proved to thy face that thou hast men about thee that usually talk of a noun and a verb, and such abominable words as no Christian ear can endure to hear.

(Jack Cade in SHAKESPEARE'S *Henry VI*.)

(b) Alas, poor Yorick ! I knew him, Horatio : a fellow of infinite jest, of most excellent fancy : he hath borne me on his back a thousand times.

(*Hamlet*.)

The child learning its language gets first to know the names of things (nouns), of actions (verbs), and of qualities (adjectives). Its mother will very likely be able to interpret these when uttered : they are the essentials of thought. Others, however, want to have these words connected—by prepositions or conjunctions or adverbs or relative pronouns—in order to reach to the thought. Can you interpret this assembly ? " Alice came three-legged table, solid glass, tiny gold key, idea, doors hall, locks too large, key too small, not open." Well, you guess a great deal and yet are not at all sure. But you are sure when the substantive words are fitly joined together :

Suddenly Alice came upon a little three-legged table all made of solid glass ; there was nothing on it but a tiny gold key, and Alice's first idea was that this might belong to one of the doors of the hall ; but alas ! either the locks were too large, or the key was too small, but at any rate it would not open any of them.

" Noun " is the part of speech that names a person or thing :
in the Hamlet quotation *Yorick, Horatio, fellow, jest, fancy, back,
times,* are nouns ; and *I, him, he, me, his,* are substitutes for nouns.
These are " pronouns ".

" Verb " is the part of speech that expresses action or being :
in the Hamlet quotation *knew, hath borne,* are verbs.

" Adjective " is the part of speech dependent on the noun
as its attribute : in the Hamlet quotation, *poor, infinite, most
excellent, thousand,* are adjectives.

NUMBER OF NOUNS (PECULIARITIES IN)

(*a*) The eight has been out this morning.

(*b*) Snuff or the fan supply each pause of chat.

(POPE, *Rape of the Lock.*)

Strict grammar at times conflicts with logic ; and, as in the
two instances, English idiom calls upon grammar to give way.
Eight, though a plural, takes *has, snuff or the fan,* though in
grammar singular, take *supply.*

A plural may be thought of as a unity : " he hit a six and
a four " ; " O that we now had here But one ten thousand of
those men in England." In many instances we are so used to
look upon the unity that the essential plurality hardly comes to
mind : we say " a fortnight ", and rarely think of " fourteen
nights " ; we say " The United States is the chief factor to be
considered."

Here lies the explanation of the idiom seen in such expressions
as " Twice two makes four " (not *make*) ; " Three times six
makes eighteen." Those who use the singular verb look upon
two or *six* as a single group : " This group thrice repeated makes
eighteen." Those who prefer *make*—and apparently there is no
great difference between the numbers of those using *makes* and
those using *make*—regard *two* or *six* as a plural. We should
notice also that the singular frequently comes where strict
grammar calls for the plural. In the verse " And now abideth
faith, hope, charity, these three ; but the greatest of these is
charity ", some would have " abide ". In Portia's submission
" My self and what is mine, to you and yours is now converted "
—the strict grammarian would have " are " for " is ". Note,
too, Milton's :

The mind and spirit remains
Invincible, and vigour soon returns.

Moreover, just as two subjects joined by *and* may be in logic one idea and then, quite naturally, be used with a singular, two subjects with *or* are in logic plural and take a plural verb. It is absurd to call such an idiom an error.

O

OBJECT : OBJECTIVE CASE. (See also **" Transitive Verb "**)

(*a*) The village street its ancient *mansion* lacks.

(*b*)　　　　　Some loss of habit's power
　　Befalls *me* wandering through this upland dim.

(*c*) I see *her veil drawn soft across the day*.

(*d*) I ask *if thou hast passed their quiet place*.

(*e*) The red rose cries, " *She is near, she is near* " ;
　　And the white rose weeps, " *She is late* " ;
　　The larkspur listens, " *I hear, I hear* " ;
　　And the lily whispers, " *I wait*."

(*f*) Come into the *garden*, Maud.

(*g*) I said to the *lily*, " *There is but one
　　With whom she has heart to be gay*."

We speak of a transitive verb—like *lacks* in (*a*) and *befalls* in (*b*)—as " governing " a noun or pronoun, or a phrase, or a clause, in the " objective case ". In (*c*) we have as " object " the phrase " her veil draw soft across the day ". In (*d*) we have a " noun clause " as " object " of the transitive verb " ask ", " If thou hast passed their quiet place ". And in (*e*) we have other instances of a noun clause as object.

We also speak of the objective case as being " governed " by a preposition : in (*f*) *garden* is a noun governed in the objective case by the preposition *into*. In (*g*) " whom " is a relative pronoun governed in the objective case by the preposition " with ".

In English our nouns have long ceased to have a special form for the objective case : we have " O, to be in England Now that April's there "—(where " April " is in the nominative case), and also " And after April, when May follows " (where " April " is in the objective case).

We retain, however, different forms for most of our pronouns : in " here and here did England help me : how can I help England ? " *I* is in the nominative case, subject of the verb " can help "—*me* is in the objective case governed by the transitive verb " did help ".

OCTET—at times spelled " OCTETTE ". (See " Sonnet ")

The Latin word " eight " is " octo " ; and " octet " (applied to a group of eight lines of verse, and also to a group of eight singers) is akin to " octave " and " octavo ".

ORATORY. (See " Rhetoric ")

ORATORY is the art of public speaking, particularly when such speaking is eloquent and is likely to move deeply the feelings of the hearers. In Cicero's Dialogue, *De Oratore*, stress was laid upon the following qualities of an orator : *natural gifts* (among which memory stood high, the comforting safeguard of type-written notes being only available in our days), *experience* (i.e. practice in speaking and wide knowledge of affairs), *understanding of human nature* (this being essential if the orator is to sway the minds of his hearers), *self-confidence* (we sometimes call this " bounce " or " cheek "), and *style* (this comprising whatever goes to make a fine speech—its choice of phrase, its being understood without trouble, its skill in bringing out the points desired by the speaker). Perhaps Milton had such an orator—unluckily on the wrong side—in mind when describing Belial :

> he seemed
> For dignity composed, and high exploit,
> But all was false and hollow ; though his tongue
> Dropt manna, and could make the worse appear
> The better reason, to perplex and dash
> Maturest counsels : for his thoughts were low—
> To vice industrious, but to nobler deeds
> Timorous and slothful. Yet he pleased the ear,
> And with persuasive accent thus began.

ORNATE SPEECH. (See under " Verb ")

For as the silk-worm eateth itself out of a seed to become a little worm ; and there feeding on the leaves of mulberries it grows till its coat be off and then works itself into a house of silk ; then casting its pearly seeds for the young to breed it leaveth its silk for man, and dieth all white and winged in the shape of a flying creature. So is the progress of Souls. When they are regenerate by baptism, and have cast off their first stains and the skin of worldly vanities, by feeding on the leaves of Scriptures, and the fruits of the Vine, and the joys of the Sacrament, they encircle themselves in the rich garments of holy and virtuous habits ; then by leaving their blood, which is the Church's seed, to raise up a new generation to God, they leave a blessed memory and fair example, and are themselves turned into Angels, whose felicity is to do the will of God, as their employment was in this world to suffer it.

(From a sermon by JEREMY TAYLOR.)

This kind of talk, crammed with illustrations, was objected to by some of the great preacher's critics. Most readers, however, find it very delightful ; and, no doubt, the preacher's congregation thought it to be fine indeed. Still, you will agree, there may well be a superfluity of ornament. Where important things are to be considered it is not desirable to have one's attention diverted from the real points at issue.

ORTHOGRAPHY. (See "Spelling")

Ortho is the Greek word for *straight, right* ; *graphé* is the Greek word for *writing*.

The current meaning of "orthography" is the spelling of words in accordance with usage, whether or not that usage is in keeping with the pronunciation.

OVER-STOPPING

You punctuate your writing so as to afford some guidance to your reader. From your various stops he will know how you intend your words to be grouped, and also, it may be, how you intend them to be expressed. Still, there is no need to be lavish of your commas and semi-colons. Your reader has intelligence, and you are entitled to expect him to exert it ; you pay your reader a pleasant compliment when you require much from him in order to reach your intended meaning. Not too much, you understand : there may be UNDER-STOPPING as well as OVER-STOPPING. But this latter, too annoys. Indeed, at times it may distort the meaning. Moderation is the word for our rule in punctuation as in most other things. It would be absurd to mark off every, even the slightest, pause in our sentence.

For instance, *Alice's Adventures in Wonderland* is admirable in its punctuation ; your pleasure in reading the book is greatly enhanced by the judicious stopping, not excessive but just enough. Here is a taste :

> Alice did not wish to offend the Dormouse again, so she began very cautiously : " But I don't understand. Where did they draw the treacle from ? "
>
> " You can draw water out of a water-well," said the Hatter ; " so I should think you could draw treacle out of a treacle well—eh, stupid ? "
>
> " But they were *in* the well," Alice said to the Dormouse, not choosing to notice this last remark.
>
> " Of course they were," said the Dormouse ; " —well in."

Here is a curious instance of over-stopping. The fine old hymn that you sing to the tune of the Old Hundredth has the line,

> " The Lord ye know is God indeed."

That is the correct way to write it. For the paraphrase of the line is

> " The Lord whom ye know is really God."

The line puts in an emphatic way the contrast between the gods of the heathen, " the work of men's hands ", and the true God. A sad ruin of the line is made in some editions by punctuating it in this way.

> " The Lord, ye know, is God indeed."

To make " ye know " into a parenthesis is to represent the hymn writer as a gossip not quite sure of what he is saying.

P

PARADOX

(*a*) These are old fond paradoxes to make fools laugh i' the alehouse.

(*Othello.*)

(*b*) The child is father to the man.

(WORDSWORTH.)

(c) A paradox, you know, is simply that which contradicts the popular opinion—which in too many cases is the false opinion.

(DE QUINCEY.)

Dox is a shortening of the Greek word meaning " opinion " or " belief " : to be " orthodox " is to have (so those think that agree with us) the right belief ; to be " heterodox " is to have the wrong belief. *Para*, here, implies " contrary to ". A PARADOX, therefore, is an expression startling one into attention by asserting what at first sight is false : on further examination, though, truth may be discerned in it.

PARAGRAPH

. . . at the sight of nature my fancy, poor as it is, droops and closes up its leaves, like flowers at sunset. I can make nothing out on the spot :—I must have time to collect myself.

In general, a good thing spoils out-of-door prospects : it should be reserved for table-talk. Lamb is for this reason, I take it, the worst company in the world out of doors ; because he is the best within. I grant, there is one subject on which it is pleasant to talk on a journey ; and that is, what one shall have for supper when we get to our inn at night. The open air improves this sort of conversation or friendly altercation, by setting a keener edge on appetite. Every mile of the road heightens the flavour of the viands we expect at the end of it.

How fine it is to enter some old town . . .

(WILLIAM HAZLITT, " On Going a Journey ".)

A PARAGRAPH is a section connected with, but more or less distinct from, the paragraph before and after. In the Hazlitt example we have the closing words of the preceding paragraph (where he explains that in general he dislikes talk while walking), the paragraph in which he expands upon this topic, and the opening words of the following paragraph (where he dilates upon the thought already suggested). A paragraph usually consists of a group of sentences explaining and supporting one another.

This analysis of Ruskin's paragraph speaking of " The Roman Campagna at Eventide " will perhaps better explain :

First is the topic sentence, the statement that the other sentences support.
The second sentence ushers in the supporting facts.

The third sentence gives the first supporting fact.

The remaining sentences add further facts reaching a climax in the closing sentence with its impressive comparison.

Perhaps there is no more impressive scene on earth than the solitary extent of the Campagna of Rome under evening light. Let the reader imagine himself for a moment withdrawn from the sounds and motion of the living world and sent forth alone into the wild and wasted plain. The earth yields and crumbles beneath his foot, tread he never so lightly; for its substance is white and hollow like the dusty wreck of the bones of men. The long knotted grass waves and tosses feebly in the evening wind, and the shadows of its motion shake feverishly along the banks of the ruins that lift themselves to the sunlight. A dull purple, poisonous haze stretches level along the desert, veiling its spectral wrecks of massy ruins, remnants of mighty edifices. Watchtowers of dark clouds stand along the peaks of the Apennines. From the plain to the mountains, shattered aqueducts, pier beyond pier, melt into the darkness like shadowy troops of funeral mourners passing from a nation's grave.

You will probably keep your reader's attention the better by making your paragraphs fairly short—not more than half a dozen sentences. The long paragraph is apt to find its reader mind-wandering before the end, just as the express train journey lulls one to sleep. The short paragraphs give repeated calls to attention, just as the stoppages of a slow train jerk one away from the oncoming nap.

Here, as an example of a well-built paragraph, is one of Macaulay's : it is from his account of the trial of the Bishops in the reign of James the Second :

The jury was sworn ; it consisted of persons of highly

respectable station. The foreman was Sir Roger Langley, a baronet of old and honourable family. With him were joined a knight and ten esquires, several of whom are known to have been men of large possessions. There were some Nonconformists in the number; for the Bishops had wisely resolved not to show any distrust of the Protestant Dissenters. One name excited considerable alarm, that of Michael Arnold. He was brewer to the palace, and it was apprehended that the government counted on his voice. The story goes that he complained bitterly of the position in which he found himself. "Whatever I do," he said, "I am sure to be half ruined. If I say NOT GUILTY, I shall brew no more for the King; and if I say GUILTY, I shall brew no more for anybody else."

The drawing of a short horizontal line below the line beginning a new section was the early way of marking off a paragraph. The modern way is by indenting the line.

PARALLELISM. (See "Repetition")

(a) They that sow in tears shall reap in joy : and he that goeth forth and weepeth shall doubtless come home with rejoicing, bringing his sheaves with him.

(*Psalms.*)

(b) Every man is not a proper champion of truth, nor fit to take up arms in the cause of verity.

(SIR THOMAS BROWNE.)

(c) Punish not thyself with pleasure ; glut not thy sense with palative delights ; nor revenge the contempt of temperance by the penalty of satiety.

(SIR THOMAS BROWNE.)

(d) Many waters cannot quench love, neither can the floods drown it.

(*Song of Solomon.*)

In Hebrew poetry the PARALLELISM consists in this : the second phrase repeats the first in other words. Thus : " O death, where is thy sting ? O grave, where is thy victory ? " is such a Parallelism.

PARAPHRASE

(a) And now for the person of her self : she was laid under a pavilion of cloth of gold of tissue, apparelled and attired like the goddess Venus, commonly drawn in picture : and hard by her, on the either hand of her, pretty fair boys apparelled as painters do set forth God Cupid, with little fans in their hands, with the which they fanned wind upon her. Her ladies and gentlewomen also, the fairest of them, were apparelled like the nymphs nereids (which are the mermaids of the waters) and like the Graces, some steering the helm, others tending the tackle and ropes of the barge, out of the which there came a wonderful passing sweet savour of perfumes, that perfumed the wharf's side, pestered with innumerable multitudes of people. Some of them followed the barge all along the riverside : others also ran out of the city to see her coming in. So that in the end there ran such multitudes of people one after another to see her, that Antonius was left post alone in the market-place, in his imperial seat to give audience : and there went a rumour in the people's mouths, that the goddess Venus was come to play with the god Bacchus, for the general good of all Asia.

(From NORTH's translation of *Plutarch*.)

(*b*) *Enobarbus* :   For her own person,
It beggar'd all description ; she did lie
In her pavilion, cloth-of-gold of tissue,
O'er-picturing that Venus where we see
The fancy outwork nature : on each side her
Stood pretty dimpled boys, like smiling Cupids,
With divers-coloured fans, whose wind did seem
To glow the delicate cheeks which they did cool,
And what they undid did.
Agrippa : O, rare for Antony.
Enobarbus : Her gentlewomen, like the Nereides,
So many mermaids, tended her i' the eyes,
And made their bends adornings : at the helm
A seeming mermaid steers : the silken tackle
Swell with the touches of those flower-soft hands,
That yarely frame the office. From the barge
A strange invisible perfume hits the sense
Of the adjacent wharves. The city cast
Her people out upon her ; and Antony,
Enthroned in the market-place, did sit alone,
Whistling to the air ; which, but for vacancy,
Had gone to gaze on Cleopatra too,
And made a gap in nature.

(From SHAKESPEARE's *Antony and Cleopatra*.)

A line alongside another line is parallel to it. An expression in other words of the sense of a passage is a PARAPHRASE. The paraphrase is a translation in which the author gives himself freedom to amplify; the original is kept in view, but the words are not so strictly followed as the sense. You paraphrase when you simplify an obscure document, when you re-arrange a sentence so that no possibility of misunderstanding haunts it, when you smooth an unduly rough reply, when you make polite a brusque, churlish one. Consideration of your readers is with you, as it always is with good writers. It is this consideration that impels you to make changes whereby your writing becomes more intelligible, more forcible, more pleasing.

Doctor Johnson paraphrased the proverb : " Take care of the pence and the pounds will take care of themselves " into the ponderous :

> The proverbial oracles of our parsimonious ancestors have informed us that the fatal waste of fortune is by small expenses, by the profusion of sums too little singly to alarm our caution, and which we never suffer ourselves to consider together.

Perhaps we should notice this caution given by the Board of Education :

> Written paraphrase is both a good test of the pupils' under-standing and an exercise in the power of expressing their own meaning, which in this case is the amount of meaning that the passage actually conveys to them. It has, however, dangers of its own. It may easily lead to the pernicious belief that one word is as good as another so long as it conveys something like the same meaning, and to the equally pernicious result of mangling the beauty of a fine phrase or passage.

Here, as a capital instance of excellent prose put into excellent poetry, is Shelley's account of Pompeii. Here is the prose account :

> Above and between the multitudinous shafts of sunshining columns was seen the sea, reflecting the purple heaven of noon above it, and supporting as it were, on its line the dark lofty mountains of Sorrento, of a blue inexpressibly deep and tinged towards their summits with streaks of new-fallen snow. Between was one small green island. Behind was the single summit of Vesuvius, rolling forth volumes of thick white

smoke, whose foamlike column was sometimes darted into the clear dark sky, and fell in little streaks along the wind. Between Vesuvius and the nearer mountains, as through a chasm, was seen the main line of the loftiest Apennines, to the east. The day was radiant and warm. Every now and then we heard the subterranean thunder of Vesuvius ; its distant deep peals seemed to shake the very air and light of day, which interpenetrated our frames, with the sullen and tremendous sound.

The Tombs were the most impressive things of all. The wild woods surround them on either side ; and along the broad stones of the paved road which divides them you hear the late leaves of autumn shiver and rustle in the stream of inconstant wind, as it were, like the steps of ghosts.

And this is his poetical version :

> I stood within the city disinterred,
> And heard the autumnal leaves like light foot-falls,
> Of spirits passing through the streets, and heard
> The mountain's slumbrous voice at intervals
> Thrill through those roofless halls.
>
> The oracular thunder penetrating shook
> The listening soul in my suspended blood.
> I felt that Earth out of her deep heart spoke,
> I felt, but heard not. Through white columns glowed
> The isle-sustaining ocean-flood.

PARENTHESIS

(a) There are no voices, O Rhodope, that are not soon mute, however tuneful ; there is no name, with whatever emphasis of passionate love repeated, of which the echo is not faint at last.

(W. S. LANDOR.)

(b) A difference of colour in the stars—oftener read of than seen in England—was really perceptible here.

(THOMAS HARDY.)

(c) In despair she put her hand in her pocket, and pulled out a box of comfits (luckily the salt water had not got into it), and handed them round as prizes.

(*Alice in Wonderland.*)

(d) " ' Afore I see you, I thought all women was alike.' "

" So they are," observed the elder Mr. Weller, parenthetically.

" ' But now,' " continued Sam, " ' now I find what a reg'lar soft-headed, inkred love turnip I must ha' been ; for there ain't nobody like you, though I like you better than nothin' at all.' I thought it best to make that rayther strong," said Sam, looking up.

(Sam Weller submits his composition to his father's criticism.)

A PARENTHESIS is a word, a clause, or a sentence, inserted into a sentence for purposes of explanation or modification : it is marked off by brackets, or dashes, or commas. The plural form is PARENTHESES. The danger attending the use of the parenthesis comes from the fact that it interrupts the even flow of the narrative. The reader is diverted from the main sentence and, before he reaches the end of the parenthesis, he may have lost the thread of that main sentence. It may be, for instance, that the insertion into Lord Morley's sentence is too long-drawn-out—

I am well aware that to try to write Mr. Gladstone's life at all—the life of a man who held an imposing place in many high national transactions, whose character and career may be regarded in such various lights, whose interests were so manifold, and whose years bridged so long a span of time— is a stroke of temerity.

Would it not have been better to make of this two separate sentences ? " I am well aware that to try to write Mr. Gladstone's life at all is a stroke of temerity. For it is the life of a man . . . time."

(See also " *Digressions* ".)

PARODY : MOCK-HEROIC

<blockquote>
I marvelled why a simple child
   That lightly draws its breath,
Should utter groans so very wild,
   And look as pale as Death.

Adopting a paternal tone,
   I asked her why she cried ;
The damsel answered with a groan,
   " I've got a pain inside."
</blockquote>

> " I thought it would have sent me mad
>   Last night about eleven " ;
> Said I, " What is it makes you bad ?
> How many apples have you had ? "
>   She answered, " Only seven ! "
>
> " And are you sure you took no more,
>   My little maid ? " quoth I,
> " Oh ! please, sir, Mother gave me four,
>   But *they* were in a pie ! "
>
> " If that's the case," I stammered out,
>   " Of course you've had eleven " ;
> The maiden answered with a pout,
>   " I ain't had more nor seven."

A PARODY imitates, recalls to our minds, and very often makes us laugh a little at its original—its PROTOTYPE. Wordsworth's " We are Seven " is, you recognise, the prototype of the parody above. The parody is by H. S. Leigh, who makes the whimsical apology in the " Postscript " :

> To borrow Wordsworth's name was wrong,
>   Or slightly misapplied ;
> And so I'd better call my song,
>   " Lines after *Ache-Inside* ".

Pope in *The Rape of the Lock* parodies the great poems of antiquity by speaking of little things in the style fitting big things : " mock-heroic " is the term sometimes applied to his poem. The modern girl might ask, " Was it for that impertinent cutting of her curls that she had gone to such trouble to get a good perm ? " Pope asks :

> Was it for this you took such constant care
> The bodkin, comb, and essence to prepare ?
> For this your locks in paper durance bound ?
> For this with torturing irons wreathed around ?
> For this with fillets strained your tender head,
> And bravely bore the double loads of lead ?

John Milton sings of country joys :

> As one who, long in populous city pent,
> Where houses thick and sewers annoy the air,

> Forth issuing on a summer's morn to breathe
> Among the pleasant villages and farms
> Adjoined, from each thing met conceives delight:
> The smell of grain, or tedded grass, or kine,
> Or dairy, each rural sight, each rural sound.

Sydney Smith, parodying the lines, sings of town joys:

> As one who, long in rural hamlets pent,
> (Where squires and parsons deep potations make,
> With lengthened tale of fox, or timid hare,
> Or antlered stag, sore vext by hound and horn),
> Forth issuing on a winter's morn, to reach
> In chaise or coach the London Babylon
> Remote, from each thing met conceives delight:
> Or cab, or car, or evening muffin-bell,
> Or lamps—each city sight, each city sound.

PARSE
> The curfew tolls the knell of parting day.

Curfew is a Common Noun ; Third Person ; Singular Number ; Neuter Gender ; Nominative Case to the Verb " tolls ".

Tolls is a Verb : Transitive : Regular Conjugation ; Active Voice ; Indicative Mood ; Third Person, Singular Number, agreeing with its Nominative " curfew ".

To PARSE a word is to set out at length, as in the example above, its ACCIDENCE—that is to say, its part of speech, its inflexions, and its relation to the rest of the sentence.

PARTICIPLE. (See " Nominative Absolute ")

PARTS OF SPEECH. (See also " Nouns, Verbs, Adjectives ")

(*a*) The words we use are divided into classes in accordance with the work they do. The various classes are " parts of speech ".

(*b*) Few features of the English language are more striking than the ease with which a word may be transferred from one part of speech to another.

We classify our words into various PARTS OF SPEECH in accordance with the work the words do in the sentence. Thus *rose* is an adjective in " Gather ye rose buds while ye may " ; it is a noun in " A rose by any other name would smell as sweet " ;

it is a verb in " Then rose a little feud betwixt the two ". *But* is an adverb in " I can but try " ; it is a preposition in " I have no friend but you " ; it is a conjunction in " The rest to some faint meaning make pretence, but Shadwell never deviates into sense."

It is, in other words, the work and not the look of a word that determines its proper classification. *Chariot*, for instance, is usually a noun, a name. But in Shelley's lines, " Thou that chariotest to their dark wintry bed, The winged seeds ", *chariotest* is a verb. Ask yourself what work the word *after* does in these five sentences :

1. After him then, and bring him back.
2. After he came all went wrong.
3. You go first ; I will come after.
4.   I hear him mock
 The luck of Cæsar, which the gods give men
 To excuse their after wrath.
5. After me cometh a man that is preferred before me.

In (1) *after* is clearly a verb, a doing word ; it is an emphatic form of the imperative *go after*. A verb it is, but it serves also as a preposition. In (2) *after* introduces the clause " he came " and indicates the relation of that dependent clause to the principal clause " all went wrong " : *after* is, therefore, a conjunction, a linking word. In (3) *after* " modifies "—adds a particular to— the meaning of the verb *will come*. *After* is therefore an adverb (of place, we may say). In (4) *after* describes *wrath* : it is an adjective. In (5) *after* expresses the relation between *a man* and *me* : it is, therefore, a preposition.

PASSIVE VOICE : ACTIVE VOICE

(a) For centuries they have been outraged and oppressed, banished from this place, imprisoned in that, deprived of their money, deprived of their teeth, convicted of the most improbable crimes on the feeblest evidence, dragged at horses' tails, hanged, tortured, burned alive. When manners became milder, they have still been subject to debasing restrictions and exposed to vulgar insults, locked up in particular streets in some countries, pelted and ducked by the rabble in others, excluded everywhere from magistracies and honours.

       (MACAULAY, writing of the Jews.)

(b) Sir king, I closed mine eyelids, lest the gems
   Should blind my purpose, for I never saw,
   Nor shall see, here or elsewhere, till I die,
   Not though I live three lives of mortal men,
   So great a miracle as yonder hilt.
   Then with both hands I flung him, wheeling him ;
   But when I looked again, behold ! an arm,
   Clothed in white samite, mystic, wonderful,
   That caught him by the hilt, and brandished him
   Three times, and drew him under in the mere.

(TENNYSON, " Morte d'Arthur.")

In " each horseman drew his battle blade " the subject of the sentence (horseman) is the active agent ; the verb (drew) is in the ACTIVE VOICE ; and *battle blade* is the Object. In " Men were driven by want to desperate courses " we have made the Object of the action (*men*) into the Subject of the sentence. We have made the effect of the activity, not the activity itself, into the matter of importance : the verb (*were driven*) is in the PASSIVE VOICE. Note the difference in effect given when we turn the statement into the Active Voice : " Want drove men to desperate courses ".

The Passive Voice is fitting when (as in the Macaulay passage) the sense of compulsion and suffering is prominent. The Active Voice is fitting when (as in the Tennyson passage) the sense of vigorous action is prominent.

PECULIAR PLURALS. (See " Number of Nouns ")

PERIPHRASIS. (See " Circumlocution ")

(a) *Yorick* had no impression but one, and that was what arose from the nature of the deed spoken of ; which impression he would usually translate into plain *English* without any periphrasis ;—and too oft without much distinction of either person, time, or place ; so that when mention was made of a pitiful or an ungenerous proceeding—he never gave himself a moment's time to reflect who was the hero of the piece,—what his station,—or how far he had power to hurt himself hereafter :—but if it was a dirty action, without much ado,—the man was a dirty fellow,—and so on.

(STERNE, *Tristram Shandy*.)

(*b*) Dr. Grainger, it should seem, had become sensible that introducing *rats*, in a grave poem, might be liable to banter. He, however, could not bring himself to relinquish the idea ; for they are thus periphrastically exhibited in his poem : " Nor with less waste that whiskered vermin race, A countless clan despoil the lowland cane."

(Boswell, *Johnson*.)

(*c*) " In short "—the preacher before Charles the Second at Whitehall ended his sermon—" if you don't live up to the precepts of the Gospel, but abandon yourselves to your irregular appetites, you must expect to receive your reward in a certain place, which 'tis not good manners to mention here."

When you go a roundabout way to express an idea, using many words where one or a few suffice, you use a PERIPHRASIS. In these lines of Pope's :

Close by those meads, for ever crowned with flowers,
Where Thames with pride surveys his rising towers,
There stands a structure of majestic frame,
Which from the neighbouring Hampton takes its name.

instead of *Hampton Court* you have the periphrasis " a structure of majestic frame Which from the neighbouring Hampton takes its name ". Siegfried Sassoon (" The Blues at Lords ") goes one better than the sports reporter by calling the cricket-ball not " the leather " or " the pill " but " the five-ounce fetish ".

The stalwart teams, capped with contrasted blue,
Exert their skill ; adorning the arena
With modest, manly, muscular demeanour,
And (while the five-ounce fetish they pursue)
Admired by gloved and virginal gentility.

You may at times use a periphrasis in order to emphasise a particular element of your sentence. When you say " I met him on Monday ", you give no prominence to " on Monday ". When, however, you say " It was on Monday that I met him ", you do give prominence to " on Monday ".

PERSONAL PRONOUNS

(*a*) The Miss Nightingale of fact was not as facile fancy painted her. She worked in another fashion, and towards another end ; she moved under the stress of an impetus which finds no place in the popular imagination. A Demon possessed her. Now demons, whatever else they may be, are full of interest. And so it happens that in the real Miss Nightingale there was more that was interesting than in the legendary one ; there was also less that was agreeable.

(LYTTON STRACHEY, Eminent Victorians.)

(b) O thou, that, with surpassing glory crowned,
Look'st from thy sole dominion like the god
Of this new world ; at whose sight all the stars
Hide their diminished heads ; to thee I call,
But with no friendly voice, and add thy name,
O Sun ! to tell thee how I hate thy beams,
That bring to my remembrance from what state
I fell, how glorious once above thy sphere ;
Till pride and worse ambition threw me down.

(MILTON, Paradise Lost, Book IV.)

The PRONOUN is a substitute for a noun, for a name. It is a PERSONAL PRONOUN when it is a substitute for the name of a definite person or thing : *she* and *her* in (*a*) are PERSONAL PRONOUNS, substitutes as they are for *Miss Nightingale* ; *I, me, my, thou, thee, thy, their* in (*b*) are PERSONAL PRONOUNS. *It*, however, in " it happens " is an Impersonal Pronoun.

The pronoun gives us scope for indulging in our liking for variety in our talk : by the use of the pronoun we can avoid repetition of a name, *Miss Nightingale* for instance. We must note, however, that care in using the pronoun is called for. *He* may be *king* or *beggar* ; *it* may be *dog*, or *horse* or *book* ; and our sentences should be so framed that no doubt arises about the reference of the pronoun. We note, too, that a substitute is not always desirable : " in the real Miss Nightingale " is better than " in the real her ".

PERSONIFICATION : PROSOPOPŒIA (*Prosopopia*)

(*a*) She sat like Patience on a monument
Smiling at grief.

(SHAKESPEARE, Twelfth Night.)

(*b*) By fairy hands their knell is rung,
By forms unseen their dirge is sung.

There Honour comes a pilgrim grey
To bless the turf that wraps their clay,
And Freedom shall awhile repair
To dwell, a weeping hermit, there.

(COLLINS.)

You PERSONIFY when you write of an imaginary person as representing an abstract idea or an intangible thing : " Patience ", " Honour ", " Freedom " in the quotations are instances ; and you note that the practice is to write the personification with a capital.   Here are other striking instances in Shelley's lines about Melancholy :

She dwells with Beauty—Beauty that must die ;
    And Joy, whose hand is ever at his lips
Bidding adieu ; and aching Pleasure nigh,
    Turning to Poison while the bee-mouth sips ;
Ay, in the very temple of Delight
    Veiled Melancholy has her sovran shrine,
    Though seen of none save him whose strenuous tongue
    Can burst Joy's grape against his palate fine ;
His soul shall taste the sadness of her might,
    And be among her cloudy trophies hung.

When these lifeless things are endowed with life and feeling are we to regard them as men or women ?   Shall we make the corresponding pronouns masculine or feminine ?   It is in great measure a matter of taste.   Wordsworth, thinking of the beauty and of the cheering, comforting nature of *Hope*, makes it feminine :

Hope rules a land for ever green ;
The powers that serve the bright-haired Queen
    Are confident and gay ;
    Clouds at her bidding disappear ;
Points she to aught, the bliss draws near
    And Fancy smooths the way.

Turbulence and uncouthness being its marks, Collins makes *Anger* masculine—

Next, Anger rushed, his eyes on fire,
    In lightnings owned his secret stings ;
In one rude crash he struck the lyre
    And swept with hurried hand the strings.

Knowledge and *Wisdom* being considered, unjustly indeed, the

195

attribute of men rather than of women, Cowper makes these masculine—

> Knowledge is proud that he has learned so much,
> Wisdom is humble that he knows no more.

PHONETICS

Speech is a series of sounds. The study of these sounds, including the mode of representing them, is called PHONETICS. The word—akin to *phonograph* and *telephone*—from the Greek, suggests that the study is worthy of being dignified as a science. As regards English the study is more difficult than in most tongues since our letter symbols have in many instances lost touch with the sounds, and there is a good deal of confusion in the ordinary representation. Another complication comes from the fact that, among educated people themselves, a good deal of diversity exists : the word *vase*, for instance, is given in the *Oxford Dictionary* the pronunciations : *vāz* (the *a* being the same vowel sound as in *alms*), *vſz* (the *ſ* being the same vowel sound as in *fought*), and " earlier and still United States ", *vās*, *vāz* (the *a* being the same vowel sound as in *rain*). That is, the vowel has three pronunciations, the *s* has two.

PHRASE. (See " Rhythm ")

Reader, | have you | ever seen a fight ? | If not, | you have a pleasure to come, | at least | if it is a fight | like that | between the Gas-man and Bill Neate. | The crowd was very great | when we arrived | on the spot ; | open carriages were coming up, | with streamers flying | and music playing, | and the country people were pouring in | over hedge and ditch | in all directions, | to see their hero beat | or be beaten. |

(HAZLITT, The Fight.)

A sentence is made up of single words (like " Reader " above) or of more or less compact groups of words (like the groups marked off above). These groups are PHRASES often, though by no means always, marked off by one or other of the punctuation marks.

PLACE OF PREPOSITION

(*a*) I grew weary *of* the *sea*, and intended to stay *at home with my wife* and family.

(*b*) *At length* the little squadron came *to the place of peril*.

Usually a preposition precedes its noun or pronoun. But is it a serious fault, or fault at all, to have the noun or pronoun before the preposition ?

A notion prevails that the answer should be " yes ". Dryden in one of his Prefaces alludes to " the preposition in the end of the sentence ; a common fault with him " ; and we are told that, influenced by this superstition, he carefully eliminated from later editions the end prepositions of his first editions. But the instinct of the language finds such placings quite comfortable ; and the superstition has no warrant from the usage of speakers and writers entitled to be looked upon as authorities. " To poor people, looking up under moist eyebrows, it seemed a wonder where it all came from." That is a sentence from the paragraph ushering in Robert Louis Stevenson's short story : " A Lodging for the Night ". Would anyone in his senses dream of revising and putting " from where it all came " ?

We do not, it will be understood, refer to sentences like Byron's, " From peak to peak the rattling crags along Leaps the Live thunder " (where *along* is, for the sake of effect, detached from its customary place), or like Hazlitt's, " The Bath mail I had set my mind upon " (where " The Bath mail " is emphasised by precedence over its preposition " upon "). We refer to ordinary practice.

Certainly, the word " preposition " itself suggests that its usual and natural place is before the noun or pronoun in the objective case : " They that sow in tears shall reap in joy." Obviously the one place for *in* is before *tears* and before *joy*. Yet it is sound English idiom on occasion to have the preposition after the noun or pronoun, and even at the end of a sentence. We do, in fact, quite naturally speak of " the people I was travelling with ", " The book I found it in ". It would sound stilted and absurd to say, " These are people to whom it is worth while talking " ; and no schoolboy would say, " For what are you hitting me ? " The curiosity is that, when we take pen in hand, we think proper to diverge from the custom of speech.

At times we cannot avoid the end preposition. We cannot when the defining relative *that* is used : " Better bear those ills we have than fly to others that we know not of." And when the interrogative pronoun occurs, it is more comfortable to have the preposition later in the sentence. " What do you take me for ? " comes trippingly to the tongue ; you could hardly express the same intended indignation by " For what do you take me ? " And look at this instance from Lamb's Essay on " New Year's Eve " : " It was better that our family should have missed that legacy, which old Dorrell cheated us of, than that I should be without the idea of that specious old rogue " (not " of which old Dorrell cheated us ").

PLAGIARISM (pronounced *plajiarism*)

(*a*) *Beefeater :* Perdition catch my soul, but I do love thee.
   Sneer : Haven't I heard that line before ?
   Puff : No, I fancy not,—Where pray ?
   Dangle : Yes, I think there is something like it in " Othello ".
   Puff : Gad ! now you put me in mind on't, I believe there is—but that's of no consequence ; all that can be said is, that two people happened to hit on the same thought—and Shakespeare made use of it first, that's all.
   (A comment on Puff's play in *The Critic*.)

(*b*) As a good housewife out of divers pieces weaves one piece of cloth, as a bee gathers wax and honey out of many flowers, I have laboriously collected this out of divers writers. The matter is theirs most part, and yet mine : we can say nothing but what hath been said ; the composition and method is ours. Yet I say, " A dwarf standing on the shoulders of a giant may see farther than a giant himself : I may likely add, alter, and see farther than my predecessors."

   (The apology of ROBERT BURTON for his borrowing
      —his " liftings " from a multiplicity of authors,
                              ancient and modern.)

(*c*) Next, o'er his Books his eyes began to roll,
   In pleasing memory of all he stole.

                              (POPE, *Dunciad*.)

(*d*) Il m'est permis de reprendre mon bien ou je le trouve.
                              (MOLIÈRE.)
   (On the assumption that I can make good use of it,
It is quite right for me to take my material wherever I find it.)

A good illustration of (*d*) above is Dryden's comment on Ben Jonson :

> He was deeply conversant in the Ancients, both Greek and Latin, and he borrowed boldly from them : there is scarce a poet or historian among the Roman authors of those times whom he has not translated in *Sejanus* and *Cataline*. But he has done his robberies so openly that one may see he fears not to be taxed by any law. He invades authors like a monarch ; and what would be theft in other poets is only victory in him.
>
> (An Essay of Dramatic Poesy.)

To PLAGIARISE is to borrow without acknowledgement another's literary product and to present it as one's own. Such purloining is in some measure restricted by the operation of the copyright law. Where this law is invoked in defence of literary property, the controversy usually bears upon the question whether or not there has been a " new " work or merely a copying of an old work. For to work upon another's material is no infringement of copyright. Nor does the use of another's ideas of itself constitute plagiarism.

You would not call Wordsworth a plagiarist because " The Daffodils " runs into verse the ideas in his sister's prose :

> We saw a few daffodils close to the waterside. But as we went along there were more and yet more ; and at last, under the boughs of the trees, we saw that there was a long belt of them along the shore. They grew among the mossy stones, above and about them. Some rested their heads upon these stones, as on a pillow, for weariness ; and the rest tossed and reeled and danced, and seemed as if they verily laughed with the wind that blew upon them over the lake, they looked so gay, ever glancing, ever changing.

This becomes " Beside the lake beneath the trees, Fluttering and dancing in the breeze ", and so on.

The trouble about borrowings from others is that the borrowed plumes may offer too severe and too startling a contrast to our own products. The reader might be tempted to say :

> Thou wear a lion's hide ! doff it for shame,
> And hang a calf-skin on those recreant limbs.

See how Sterne—who borrowed as copiously as Falstaff did—speaks of the matter :

I'm to preach at court next Sunday, said *Homenas*—run over my notes—so I hummed over the doctor *Homenas's* notes —the modulation's very well—'twill do, *Homenas*, if it holds on at this rate—so on I humm'd—and a tolerable tune I thought it was ; and to this hour, may it please your reverences, had never found out how low, how flat, how spiritless and jejune it was, but that all of a sudden, up started an air in the middle of it, so fine, so rich, so heavenly,—it carried my soul up with it into the other world ; now had I (as *Montaigne* complained in a parallel accident)—had I found the delivery easy, or the ascent accessible—certes I had been outwitted. Your notes, *Homenas*, I should have said, are good notes ;—but it was so perpendicular a precipice—so wholly cut off from the rest of the work, and by the first note I hummed I found myself flying into the other world, and from thence discovered the vale from when I came, so deep, so low, and dismal, that I shall never have the heart to descend into it again.

A dwarf who brings a standard along with him to measure his own size—take my word, is a dwarf in more articles than one.

And a little of Macaulay on the matter will be welcome :

A few more lines, as bad as those which we have quoted, bring us to one of the most amusing instances of literary pilfering which we remember. It might be of use to plagiarists to know, as a general rule, that what they steal is, to employ a phrase common in advertisements, of no use to any but the right owner. We never fell in, however, with any plunderer who so little understood how to turn his booty to good account as Mr. Montgomery. Lord Byron, in a passage which everybody knows by heart, has said, addressing the sea :

Time writes no wrinkle on thine azure brow.

Mr. Robert Montgomery very coolly appropriates the image, and reproduces the stolen goods in the following form :

And thou, vast Ocean, on whose awful face
Time's iron feet can print no ruin—trace.

So may such ill-got gains ever prosper !

We must note, however, that there must be many an unintended and unconscious copying or imitation. Thus, in Essay 8 of *The Friend*, Coleridge has " The dwarf sees farther than the giant when he has the giant's shoulder to mount on." This is something like Burton in example (*b*) ; but it is not of necessity plagiarism. And very likely the two later writers of the sentences below were not aware that they were imitating the earliest writer .

He had a head to contrive, a tongue to persuade, and a hand to execute any mischief.

(LORD CLARENDON, of Hampden in *History of the Great Rebellion*.)

Whether it be the heart to conceive, the understanding to direct, or the hand to execute.

(JUNIUS, in *Letter* 37.)

In every deed of mischief he had a heart to resolve, a head to contrive, and a hand to execute.

(GIBBON, of Commenus in *Decline and Fall of the Roman Empire*.)

PLURAL NOUNS (SPELLING OF). (See also under "Idiom ")

Towns : Soldiers : Years : Tresses : Churches.

The usual spelling of plural nouns is as above : *s* or *es* is added to singular noun. The spellings below, however, need notice.

In such a word as *calf* we automatically transfer to the *f* some of the hissing sound of the plural sign *s*, and so turn the *f* into *v*. So we have the plurals : *calves, knives, loaves, sheaves*. In other words, we retain *f*—*chiefs, briefs, roofs, fifes*—the instruments of music that is (*fives* is the name of a game), *hoofs*.

The single vowel *y* unites with *e* to make it *ie* ; so *ladies* (*lady*), *rubies* (*ruby*), *soliloquies* (*soliloquy*), where the *u* belongs to *q*, making the sound *kw*, and *y* is a single vowel.

In words like *key, bay, day*, the *y* is not a single vowel, but forms part of the double vowel (or diphthong), *ey, oy, ay* ; we have, therefore, as plurals—*keys, donkeys* (contrast this word with *ponies*), *boys, days*.

There are remnants of old forms, as well as new arrivals, in modern English. *Men, feet, mice, children, oxen*, all bear traces of their Old English origin. *Radii* (*radius* is the singular); *maxima* (*maximum*) (*maximums* will displace the foreigner after a while); *strata* (*stratum*); *species* (singular also *species*); *theses* (singular, *thesis*); *bases* (singular, *basis*); *opera* (singular, *opus*); are Latin plurals. *Ellipses* (*ellipsis*); *analyses* (*analysis*); *parentheses* (*parenthesis*); *phenomena* (*phenomenon*); are Greek plurals. We occasionally see even the French plurals *beaux*, *messieurs* (*monsieur*), of which the abbreviation " *Messrs.*" serves as our plural of " *Mr.*"; the Italian *banditti*, *libretti* (for books of words); and the Hebrew *cherubim* and *seraphim* (but mostly *cherubs* and *seraphs*); and *stigma* has its foreign form *stigmata*, but also *stigmas*.

Some curious plurals are :

Irides, the plural of *iris*, meaning " an appearance like the rainbow "; and, like the plural, we have a describing word, *iridescent*, meaning " gaily coloured ".

Miasmata, the plural of *miasma*, meaning " infectious and polluting matter in the air ".

Dilettanti, the plural of *dilettante*, an Italian word that signifies one who dabbles in art, who loves painting or music but gives no serious study to them.

Genera, the plural of *genus*, the Latin word that means " a group of similar things that may again be divided into smaller groups called *species* ".

Corps, used for both singular and plural. In writing we make no distinction. In speaking we do : we sound the *s* in the plural (*kors*), we do not in the singular (*kor*).

Hiatus (pronounced (*hī-āt-ŭs*) is properly the succession of two vowel sounds without an intervening consonant—as in " no others "—and by transference a gap in a series : the Latin plural is *hiatūs* (the *u* being long); but *hiatuses* is found.

Octopus, a Greek word signifying of eight arms (or legs); its plural is properly *octopodes* (though *octopuses* will doubtless prevail).

PLURAL OF COMPOUND WORDS. (See **"Hyphen"**)

(*a*) Dark bluebells drenched with dews of summer eves.

(*b*) Home through flooded fields foot-travellers go.

In general, when a noun is composed of two or more elements, the plural sign appears on the last element only : we have *girl clerks, boy messengers, bookcases, coach-houses, apple-trees.* Yet we find instances where both elements take the sign. This appears to be invariably so when *man* or *woman* is the first element : contrast *men-servants* and *women-servants* with *maid servants.*

When the compound noun consists of two titles there seems to be a tendency to add the plural sign to both elements : *lords-lieutenants, lords justices, knights templars,* and so on. We cannot say, however, that the rule is observed universally, *Lord Chancellors* is found with *Lords Chancellor* and *Lords Chancellors.* Nor is there uniformity where a noun consists of a title and name. Thus, the plural of *Miss Brown* is usually written " *The Miss Browns* " ; but where it is desirable to retain the old formality, as in lists of guests, and so on, *The Misses Brown* is still found. Note, for instance, the distinction implied between " the Miss Inderwicks, as the girls called them, or the Misses Inderwick, as they call themselves ". Perhaps the modern preference of *The Miss Browns* for *The Misses Brown* is that *Misses* may easily be confused with *Mrs.*

When the compound word—as in *letter-patent, court-martial, knight-errant, attorney-general, account-current*—consists of a noun and its attendant adjective, the general rule is to place the plural sign with the noun. The two words, though, may be so welded together that we cannot but look upon them as a unit. Then the plural sign is added to the whole word. *Court-martials* is, for instance, the ordinary plural, though in more formal writing *courts-martial* is still found. *Governor-Generals* is perhaps more frequent than *Governors-General.*

PLURALS OF COURTESY TITLES

Plurals of proper names are common enough, and you experience no difficulty about them : " We must keep up with the Joneses " ; " Shall we ask the Robinsons to the wedding ? " A difficulty does present itself, though, in regard to courtesy titles. How do you indicate that you are referring to more than one Mr. Brown, more than one Mrs. Brown, more than one Miss Brown ? Modern English usage has certainly evolved some curious customs in the matter.

"Misters" as a courtesy title seems to be confined to talk, talk intended to be jocular, and to the writing representing such talk. You do not find it in literary English. In talk also, "the two Mr. Browns" is customary. In formal and commercial language, however, we go to France for a plural; we write "Messrs." the abbreviated form of "Messieurs" (the plural of "Monsieur"). We write "the two Messrs. Brown".

"Mrs." with its *s* ending raises a problem. We can hardly say "missesses"; our instinct to prefer easy instead of difficult sounds impels us to transfer the plural sign to the second element and say, as well as to write, "the two Mrs. Browns" or even to allow the plural to be understood from "two" and write "the two Mrs. Brown".

POETRY

(*a*) "Sir, what is poetry?"
   "Why, Sir, it is much easier to say what it is not. We all *know* what light is, but it is not easy to tell what it is."
                              (BOSWELL, *Life of Johnson*.)

(*b*) A poet soaring in the high region of his fancies with his garland and singing robes about him.
                                                            (MILTON.)

(*c*)   Lady of the Mere,
   Sole-sitting by the shores of old romance.
                                                      (WORDSWORTH.)

You write POETRY when you express beautiful or lofty thoughts, lively imagination, or strong feeling in fit language, your language having as a rule a regular rhythm and a recurrent metre. "Composition" in verse or metrical language does not always come within this description; but, then, a good deal of metrical composition is no more than the form of poetry. When a poet offers a definition of the poetry he makes you are, perhaps, not much enlightened. But you are greatly interested. In his Preface to the *Lyrical Ballads*, Wordsworth writes: "Poetry is the spontaneous overflow of powerful feelings: it takes its origin from emotion recollected in tranquillity." Milton has "Thoughts that voluntary move harmonious numbers"; and Keats seems to be of the same opinion; "If," he writes, "poetry comes not as naturally as leaves to a tree it had better not come at all."

And this is how Macaulay explains what poetry is :

> By poetry we mean not all writing in verse, nor even all good writing in verse. Our definition excludes many metrical compositions which, on other grounds, deserve the highest praise. By poetry we mean the art of employing words in such a manner as to produce an illusion on the imagination, the art of doing by means of words what the painter does by means of colours. Thus, the greatest of poets has described it, in lines universally admired for the vigour and felicity of their diction, and still more valuable on account of the just notion which they convey of the art in which he excels :

> As imagination bodies forth
> The forms of things unknown, the poet's pen
> Turns them to shapes, and gives to airy nothings
> A local habitation and a name.

POSSESSIVE CASE. (See " Apostrophe ")

PREDICATE. (See " Subject and Predicate ")

PREFIX

(a) Unhappy, never, oncoming.

(b) Avert, ambidexterous, omniscience.

(c) Amphitheatre, hemisphere, monograph.

In the words above a particle has been added, the English *un, n, on*, the Latin *a, anti, omni* ; the Greek *amphi, hemi, mono*. The particle placed at the beginning of the word is a PREFIX, making a DERIVATIVE. Thus *never* is *not-ever, ambidexterous* is *dexterous* with both hands ; *hemisphere* is *half a sphere*.

Latin and Greek prefixes are these :

LATIN	MEANING	EXAMPLE
a-, ab-, abs-	from : away	avert, abduct, abstract
ad- (taking by assimilation the forms *ac-, af-, ag-, al-, an-, ap-, ar-, as-, at-*)	to : at	adhere, accede, affirm, aggregate, allude, annex, applaud, arrogant, assume, attribute
amb-, ambi-	on both sides	ambitious, ambidextrous
ante-	before	antedate, antecedent

LATIN	MEANING	EXAMPLE
bi-, bis-	twice : two ways : double	biennial, biscuit
circum-	around : all round	circumspect
cis-	on this side of	cisalpine
com-, col-, con-, cor-, co-	with : together : altogether (intensively)	combine, collect, connect, correspond, co-exist
contra-, contro-, Gallicised into counter-	against	contradict, controvert, counterfeit
de-	down : from : off	deduce
demi-	half	demi-semiquaver, demi-god
dis-, di-, dif-	apart : asunder : not	disarm, divulge, differ
ex-, e- before d, l, m, n, ef- before f	out of : out : from	exacerbate, educe, elucidate, emanate, enervate, effect
equi-	equally	equidistant
extra-	beyond : without	extraordinary, extra-judicial
in-, modified into il- before l, im- before m, p, Gallicised into em-, en-	in : into : on : against (used with verb)	include, illuminate, immure
in- before h and vowels, modified into il- before l, im- before m, ir- before r	not (used with adj.)	inhuman, illegal, immeasurable, irrational
inter-, Gallicised into enter-	between : among	intercede, entertain
intro-	within	introduce
juxta-	near : nigh	juxtaposition
mal-, male-	ill : badly	maladministration, malefactor
manu-	hand	manuscript
non-	not	nonentity
ob-, modified into oc-, before c, of- before f, op- before p	against : in front of	obstacle, occurrence, offend, opposition
omni-	all	omniscient
per-	through : thoroughly	perforate
post-	after	post-mortem
pre-	before	precede
preter-	beyond : past	preternatural
pro-, Gallicised into pur-	before : forth : forward	proceed, purpose
re-, red-	back : again	rehearse, redeem
retro-	backwards	retrospective
se-	apart	seclusion
semi-	half	semicircle

LATIN	MEANING	EXAMPLE
sub-, modified into *suc-* before *c*, *suf-* before *f*, *sug-* before *g*, *sup-* before *p*, *sur-* before *r*, *su(s)-* before *s*	under	substitute, succour, suffice, suggest, support, surrender, su(s)-spect
super-, Gallicised into *sur-*	above	superabundant, surfeit
trans-, *tra-*, Gallicised into *tres-*	across	transport, tramontane, trespass
tri-	thrice	tricolour
ultra-	beyond : advance	ultramarine
uni-	one	university, uniform

GREEK	MEANING	EXAMPLE
a-, modified into *an-* before vowels	no : without	amorphous, apathy, anarchy, anonymous
amphi-	about : around : on both sides	amphitheatre, amphibious
ana-	up : through : according to	analogy, analysis
anti-, *ant-*	against : opposite to	antagonist, antiseptic, antipodes
apo-, *aph-*	away : apart : off	apostrophe, apostle, aphelion
arch-, *archi-*	chief : head : ruling	archbishop, architect
auto-, *auth-*, *aut-* before a vowel	self : oneself	autograph, autobiography, autopsy, authentic
cata-, *cath-*, *cat-*	down : through : according to	catastrophe, cathedral, cataract, categorical
deca-	ten	decagon, decametre
di-	two : double	dilemma, dimorphous, di(s)syllable
dia-	through : between	dialogue, diameter, diadem
dys-	bad : ill	dysentery, dyspeptic
ec-, modified into *ex-* before a vowel	out : forth	eclipse, ecstasy, eccentric, exodus
en-, modified into *em-* before *b*, *l*, *el-* before *p*	in : on	encomium, enthusiasm, emblem, emphasis, elliptical
endo-	within	endogenous, endogamous

GREEK	MEANING	EXAMPLE
epi-, modified into *ep-* before a vowel or *h*	upon : over	epistle, epitaph, epigram, epoch, ephemeral
eu-	well	eulogy, euphony
exo-	outside	exogenous, exotic
hemi-	half	hemisphere
hexa-	six	hexameter, hexagon
hetero-	other : different	heterodox, heterogeneous
hepta-	seven	heptagon
hier-	sacred	hierarchy
holo-	whole : entire	holocaust
homo-	same : similar : together	homonym, homogeneous
hyper-	over : beyond : too	hyperborean, hypercritical
hypo-, modified into *hyp-* before *h*	under : beneath	hypocrite, hypotenuse, hypothesis, hyphen
meta-, *met-* before vowel or *h*	beyond : after (denoting change)	metathesis, metaphor, method, metonymy
mono-, modified into *mon-* before a vowel	alone	monograph, monogram, monarch, monk
ortho-	right	orthoepy, orthography
oxy-, modified into *ox-* before a vowel	sharp : acid	oxytone, oxygen, oxopia
pan-	all	pan-Anglican, panoply, pantomime, panorama
para-, modified into *par-* before a vowel	eside	parasite, paraphrase, parable, paragraph, parallel
penta-	five	pentameter
peri-	round : around	perimeter, periphrasis, period
philo-, modified into *phil-* before a vowel	love : loving	philology, philosopher, philanthropy
poly-	many	polyarchy, polygamy, polysyllable, polygon
pro-	before	prophecy, programme
pros-	towards	proselyte
pseudo-, modified into *pseud-* before a vowel	false	pseudo-metallic, pseudonym
syn-, modified into *syl-* before *l*, *sym-* before *b*, *m*, *p*, *sy-* before *s*	with	synthesis, synchronise, syllable, symbol, symmetry, sympathy, system, syzygy
tele-	afar	telegram, telephone, telepathy, telescope
tri-	thrice : three	tripod, trigonometry, trihedral, trisyllable

A particle added to a word and making a derivative is a SUFFIX. Thus, *ness* added to the adjective *sweet* makes the abstract noun, *sweetness*; *en* added to the adjective makes the verb, *sweeten*; *ly* added to the adjective makes the adverb, *sweetly*; a *baker* is one who *bakes*, a *guardian* one who *guards*; a *student* one who *studies*. (See "*Diminutives*", "*Frequentative Verbs*", "*Causative Verbs*".)

PREPOSITION. (See also "**Appropriate Preposition**" and "**Place of Preposition**")

(*a*) They that sow *in* tears shall reap *in* joy.

(*b*)   Thy plaintive anthem fades
    Past the near meadow, *over* the still stream,
    Up the hill-side; and now 'tis buried deep
        In the next valley glades.

(*c*) From peak to peak the rattling crags *along*
    Leaps the live thunder.

A PREPOSITION is a word used to indicate the relation between two notional words, like *anthem* and *meadow* above. *Past* gives us the idea of the relation between *anthem* and *meadow*. The word following the preposition is usually a noun or pronoun, and is said to be "governed" in the objective case by the preposition.

Occasionally as in (*c*) inversion ("along the rattling crags" is the direct order) occurs for the sake of effect.

To a very great extent the preposition in modern English does the work once done by inflexions. Note how the meaning changes when we vary the preposition showing relation. When Mr. Churchill said, "Never in the history of the world has so much been owed by so many to so few" he meant a very different thing from what the spendthrift, confronted with a host of bills, meant, "Never in the history of the world has so much been owed to so many by so few."

PROLOGUE

(*a*) It is a foolish thing to make a long prologue, and to be short in the story itself.

(*Maccabees.*)

(b)   Two truths are told
          As happy prologues to the swelling act,
          Of the Imperial theme.

                                            (*Macbeth.*)

(c) It is not the fashion to see the lady the epilogue : but
    it is no more unhandsome than to see the lord the prologue.
                        (Rosalind in *As You Like It.*)

The PROLOGUE is the introduction, the preface, as the Epilogue
is the speech, or writing, that takes leave of the audience or
readers.   It is often used by the dramatist to put his audience
into possession of the knowledge that will enable them the
better to understand his play.   Look, for instance at the opening
lines spoken by " Chorus " in *Henry V* ; where, after apologies
for the inadequate means of showing so great a theme, the
author asks for the co-operation of the audience :

          Piece out our imperfections with your thoughts ;
          Into a thousand parts divide one man,
          And make imaginary puissance ;
          Think, when we talk of horses, that you see them
          Printing their proud hoofs i' the receiving earth ;
          For 'tis your thoughts that now must deck our kings,
          Carry them here and there ; jumping o'er times,
          Turning the accomplishment of many years
          Into an hour-glass ; for the which supply,
          Admit me Chorus to this history ;
          Who, prologue-like, your humble patience pray,
          Gently to hear, kindly to judge, our play.

(See " *Epilogue* ".)

PRONOUN.   (See also "Relative Pronoun ")

(a) Tell *it* not in Gath, publish *it* not in the streets of Askelon.
(b) When *I* said *I* would die a bachelor, *I* did not think *I*
    should live till *I* were married.
(c) *They* seemed to *those who* saw *them* meet
    The worldly friends of every day,
    Her smile was undisturbed and sweet,
    His courtesy was free and gay.

A PRONOUN is a word used instead of a noun.   It signifies
an object without naming it.   That which is designated by the

pronoun is known from the context, or it has already been indicated, or, being unknown, it is the subject of inquiry.

There is sometimes an instinctive reluctance to repeat, and the pronoun obviates the need to do so. We read, in a Lesson for the Day, " the sound of the cornet, flute, harp, sackbut, psaltery, and all kinds of music "; we probably think that comprehensive " they " or " them " might well stand for the collection afterwards, but the whole range recurs, and becomes indeed impressive and welcome. Perhaps the repetition in our Parliamentary statutes is less welcome :

> If any person receives any sketch, plan, model, article, note, document, or information knowing, or having reasonable ground to believe, at the time when he receives it, that the sketch, plan, model, article, note, document, or information is communicated to him in contravention of this Act, he shall be guilty of a misdemeanour, unless he proves that the communication to him of the sketch, plan, model, article, note, document, or information was contrary to his desire.

PRONUNCIATION

(a) By Pronunciation the ancients understood both Elocution and Action.

(b) Speak the speech, I pray you, as I pronounced it to you, trippingly on the tongue.

(Hamlet.)

(c) The standard of English Pronunciation, as far as a standard may be said to exist, is the usage that now prevails among the educated and cultured people to whom the language is vernacular ; but, since somewhat different pronunciations are used by the cultivated in different regions too large to be ignored, we must frankly admit the fact that, at present, uniformity of pronunciation is not to be found throughout the English-speaking world.

(Webster's New International Dictionary.)

Our PRONUNCIATION of a word is the manner in which we turn the written symbols into audible sounds. Differences in this manner exist and will continue to exist. Nor is this surprising. The dictionary-makers themselves differ, for they do not try to show how a word *should* be pronounced but how people *do* pronounce ; and people—even educated and cultured people—have no uniform way of speaking.

Dr. Johnson, for instance, has a word or two to say upon the matter:

Boswell: It may be of use, Sir, to have a Dictionary to ascertain the pronunciation.

Johnson: Why, Sir, my Dictionary shows you the accent of words, if you can remember them.

Boswell: But, Sir, we want marks to ascertain the pronunciation of the vowels. Sheridan, I believe, has finished such a work.

Johnson: Why, Sir, consider how much easier it is to learn a language by the ear, than by any marks. Sheridan's Dictionary may do very well, but you cannot always carry it about with you, and when you want a word, you have not the Dictionary. It is like a man who has a sword that will not draw. It is an admirable sword, to be sure, but while your enemy is cutting your throat, you are unable to use it. Besides, Sir, what entitled Sheridan to fix the pronunciation of English? He has, in the first place, the disadvantage of being an Irishman: and if he says he will fix it after the example of the best company, why they differ among themselves. I remember an instance: when I published the Plan for my Dictionary, Lord Chesterfield told me that the word *great* should be pronounced so as to rhyme to *state* and Sir William Yonge sent me word that it should be pronounced so as to rhyme with *seat*, and that none but an Irishman would pronounce it *grait*. Now here were two men of the highest rank, the one, the best speaker in the House of Lords, the other, the best speaker in the House of Commons, differing entirely.

PROPER NOUNS BECOMING COMMON NOUNS. (See also "Prototype")

(*a*) Some village-Hampden that with dauntless breast
The little tyrant of his fields withstood,
Some mute, inglorious Milton here may rest.

(GRAY, *Elegy*.)

(*b*) A Daniel come to judgment! yea, a Daniel!

(*The Merchant of Venice*.)

(*c*)   Sage he stood,
With Atlantean shoulders, fit to bear
The weight of mightiest monarchies.

(*Paradise Lost*.)

(d) The English winter—ending in July,
   To recommence in August.

(Byron, Don Juan.)

A particular person or place becomes well-known for one reason or another. It may become a type and its name be applied to persons or things like it: " the Manchester of the United States " is the cotton market town ; the " Benedick " is the man married, the man who excuses himself by " When I swore I would die a bachelor, I did not think I should live till I were married." The " mute inglorious Milton " is one with the poet's nature and capacity. The " village-Hampden " is one that in less trying conditions of life might have been a statesman of renown :

> But Knowledge to their eyes her ample page,
> Rich with the spoils of time, did n'er unroll ;
> Chill Penury repressed their noble rage,
> And froze the genial current of the soul.

You encourage a diffident batsman by assuring him that he is becoming another " Grace ". The individual names have acquired a meaning ; they have become generic, names applicable to a class.

A further development is when—as in (c)—an adjective has been made from the noun : Atlas was the god supposed to hold up the pillars of the universe ; he bequeathed his name to the Libyan mountains ; he also gave us the adjective " Atlantean ".

Compare *July* and *August*, keeping in perpetual record the names of the great Romans, *Julius Cæsar* and *Augustus Cæsar* ; *bayonet*, reminding us of *Bayonne* ; *currants*, the dried grapes of *Corinth* ; *jovial*, as being born under *Jupiter* (*Jove*) the lucky planet ; *quixotic*, resembling *Don Quixote* ; *utopian*, desirable but found nowhere in *Utopia*, which is nowhere (or *Erewhon*).

PROPORTION IN COMPOSITION

It is no more than common sense—which applies to English composition as to other affairs of life—that due proportion should be observed. Important matters must be dealt with in an important way ; subordinate matters are to be dealt with in a subordinate way.

The lack of a sense of proportion, the inability to discriminate

213

between the thing that matters immensely and the thing that matters little, is a drawback in all concerns of life ; it is often disastrous in an examination. You are asked to answer four questions out of seven ; you have two hours for your task ; the same number of marks is allotted to each question. Surely reason dictates that you will give approximately the same amount of time and thought to each of your four answers ? Yet how often does an examiner encounter that most exasperating paper where the candidate has dilated at large upon one question, has found that the sands of time are quickly running out, and has unmercifully " skimped " the other questions ! After all, the examiner cannot give more than full marks to an answer. He cannot supplement the defective answers—he is often tempted to do so, and he sometimes yields to the temptation—by carrying over a few marks from the brilliant answer.

The same remarks apply—*mutatis mutandis*, as the lawyers say, the necessary modifications being made—to the answering of a single question. Just as it is inexpedient to spend an unduly long time over a single question when many are clamouring for answers, so it is inexpedient to spend an inordinate time over one point in a question when many points demand notice.

Suppose, for example, you are tackling such a question as examiners are fond of setting—fond of setting because it is easy to set and because it allows of much latitude in marking. This is the giving of a quotation and the requiring of a comment. Thus—

> " The larger the firm, the greater is the need to recruit separately its administrative staff, the less its power to do other than promote from existing subordinates."
> Discuss.

You will not grumble that this statement of an inherent difficulty in all large concerns, the clash between what scientific reasoning dictates and what practical expediency dictates, gives too little scope for your powers. Rather, it calls for severe self-abnegation. You could write at great length about the need for a highly trained specialist to control one particular aspect of the large concern, its technical aspect, or its personal aspect, or its financial aspect, a specialist too, trained to envisage the whole in relation to its parts. You could also write at great length upon the troubles that are likely to ensue upon the introduction of an administrative head from outside, troubles that may well counterbalance the introduction of even a highly competent administrator. You would not, in your wisdom, indulge your power in either direction; you would exercise a wise discretion and divide your answer fairly evenly. Part would be devoted to the advantages of outside recruiting—the advantages that many heads of businesses know would accrue from introduction, the advantages that they must forgo because they know how incentives among the staff would vanish. Part would be devoted to the almost inevitability, in an enormous concern, of staff promotion. And one part would not be developed to such an extent as makes the other part neglected.

PROPRIETY (FITNESS OF EXPRESSION)

(*a*) Whatever his theme the orator will speak as becomes it; neither meagrely where it is copious, nor meanly where it is ample, nor in *this* way when it demands *that*. He will keep his speech level with the actual subject and adequate to it.

(*b*) 1. The house was soon on fire; much sympathy is expressed with the sufferers. (*The fact.*)
2. In a moment the edifice was enveloped in shooting tongues of flames; the appalling catastrophe has plunged the whole street into the gloom of night. (*The newspaper reporter.*)

(*c*) 1. The strike is bound to have ill effects. (*The fact.*)
2. The strike is bound to have disastrous repercussions. (*The " Times " reporter.*)

(*d*) 1. Since the leaders know that so much will be lost and so little gained, we think that there will be no strike. (*The fact.*)
2. It is difficult to believe that the responsible leaders of Labour and Capital will now jeopardize a recovery which has brought them both so much benefit by plunging into a conflict from which neither is likely to derive any advantage comparable with the inevitable sacrifices. (*The " Times " reporter.*)

The quality of fitness—of propriety—is highly desirable; proper words in proper places is the very definition of a style. Whether you are speaking or writing, you do well to choose words suited to your topic, suited also to your audience. Your own taste will most likely be your best guide. You will, having consideration for your audience, prefer the simple expressions to the difficult. You will say " He was fond of fishing " rather than " He was an ardent devotee of the piscatorial art "; you will speak of " lectures suitable to boys and girls " rather than " lectures adapted to a juvenile auditory "; and you will think *Proverbs* more effective than Dr. Johnson. The version of the *Proverbs* is :

> Go to the Ant, thou Sluggard, consider her ways, and be wise : which having no guide, overseer, or ruler, provideth her meat in summer, and gathereth her food in the harvest. How long wilt thou sleep, O sluggard ? When wilt thou arise out of thy sleep ? Yet a little sleep, a little slumber, a little folding of the hands to sleep. So shall thy poverty come as one that travelleth, and thy want as an armed man.

Dr. Johnson's version is

> Turn on the prudent Ant thy heedless eyes,
> Observe her labours, Sluggard, and be wise ;
> No stern command, no monitory voice,
> Prescribes her duties, or directs her choice ;
> Yet timely provident, she hastes away
> To snatch the blessings of a plenteous day ;
> When fruitful Summer loads the teeming plain,
> She crops the harvest, and she stores the grain.
> How long shall sloth usurp thy useless hours,
> Unnerve thy vigour, and enchain thy powers ?
> While artful shades thy downy couch enclose,
> And soft solicitation courts repose,
> Amidst the drowsy charms of dull delight,
> Year chases year with unremitted flight,
> Till Want now following, fraudulent and slow,
> Shall spring to seize thee, like an ambushed foe.

During the dismal spring of 1947 the Government issued a White Paper designed to make every man and woman fully understand how badly off the country was and how much it needed everyone's efforts to make things better. The Prime

Minister's statement was that the White Paper " is written in simple language and I am sure the bulk of the people can read it and understand it ". But words like " formulate ", " objectives ", " ultimately " appeared ; and here are two sentences that cannot be called crystal clear at the first reading, " The gap between resources and requirements will in the end be closed by some of the requirements being left unsupplied." " The objectives of this paper embody the Government's determination to put first things first." One may well think the Prime Minister's notion of " simple language " a strange one.

PROSE

(a) Al shal passyn that men prose or ryme.

(CHAUCER.)

(b) In prose and verse was held without dispute,
Lord of the realms of nonsense absolute.

(DRYDEN, on his rival Shadwell.)

(c) The words in prose ought to express the intended meaning, and no more ; if they attract attention to themselves, it is in general a fault. In the very best styles you read page after page, understanding the author perfectly, without once taking notice of the medium of communication ; it is as if he had been speaking to you all the while. But in verse you must do more : there the words, the media, must be beautiful, and they ought to attract your notice —yet not so much and so perpetually as to destroy the unity which ought to result from the whole poem.

(COLERIDGE.)

(d) M. *Jourdain :* Quoi ? quand je dis : " Nicole, apportez-moi mes pantoufles, et me donnez mon bonnet de nuit ", c'est de la prose ?
Maitre : Oui, monsieur.
M. *Jourdain :* Par ma foi ! il y a plus de quarante ans que je dis de la prose sans que j'en susse rien.

(MOLIÈRE, *Le Bourgeois Gentilhomme.*)

(M. *Jourdain :* What ? When I say : " Nicole, fetch me my slippers, and give me my night-cap ", that's prose, is it ?
Master : Yes, sir.
M. *Jourdain :* Well, well ! for more than forty years I've been talking prose without knowing it.)

PROSE is straightforward speech. The Latin is *prosa oratio*, straightforward discourse, as distinct from verse where there is ever a turning back as a line is finished. Prose is the usual form of written or spoken language. In English prose there is no regular succession of strongly-accented and weakly-accented syllables ; in English verse there is such regular succession. Here are a few sentences of excellent prose. You note that the accented syllables follow no regular beat :

> It is almost a definition of a gentleman, to say he is one who never inflicts pain. This description is both refined and, as far as it goes, accurate. He is mainly occupied in merely removing obstacles which hinder the free and unembarrassed action of those about him ; and he concurs with their movements rather than take the initiative himself. His benefits may be considered as parallel to what are called comforts or conveniences in arrangements of a personal nature ; like an easy chair or a good fire, which do their part in dispelling cold and fatigue, though nature provides both means of rest and animal heat without them.
>
> (CARDINAL NEWMAN.)

Contrast with this straightforward speech, in which the accents have no regular sequence, the speech, turned into lines, and with its weak and strong accents arranged so as to correspond with the beats of music. Read aloud these lines—at times misquoted—of Pope :

> A little learning is a dangerous thing :
> Drink deep, or taste not the Pierian spring :
> There shallow draughts intoxicate the brain,
> And drinking largely sobers us again.

Though we use the adjective " prosy " in the sense of " dull and wearisome ", prose is not of necessity boring and heavy. It may, as Dryden implies, have a harmony of its own. In the *Preface* to his *Fables* he writes :

> Thoughts come crowding in so fast upon me, that my only difficulty is to choose or reject,—to run them into verse or to give them the other harmony of prose.

There are, as our various examples show, glorious passages of prose as of verse. Hamlet's prose gives us much the same thrill as his verse soliloquy does :

> I have of late—but wherefore I know not—lost all my mirth, foregone all custom of exercise ; and indeed it goes so heavily with my disposition that this goodly frame, the Earth, seems to me a sterile Promontory ; this most excellent Canopy, the Air, look you, this brave o'erhanging Firmament, this Majestical Roof fretted with golden fire, why, it appears no other thing to me than a foul and pestilent congregation of vapours. What a piece of work is a man ! How noble in Reason ! How infinite in faculty ! In form and moving, how express and admirable ! In Action how like an Angel ! In apprehension how like a God ! The beauty of the world ! The Paragon of Animals ! And yet, to me, what is this Quintessence of Dust ? Man delights not me ; no, nor Woman neither, though, by your smiling, you seem to say so.

PROTOTYPE : ANTITYPE : PARALLEL. (See also "Proper Nouns becoming Common Nouns ")

When a particular person or place possesses a quality in great measure, the person or place may be taken as a TYPE. The name, the PROTOTYPE, is no longer a mere label of a particular person or place. It has a meaning. It conveys a definite idea to the mind, because we have come to associate with the name the special qualities pre-eminently possessed by the owner of the name. It has, in effect, ceased to be a proper noun (a name appropriated to one particular person or place) and has become a common noun (a name significant of a class of things).

So " a mute, inglorious Milton " is a compact phrase to describe one who has the poet's nature, but who from the lack of education has never made verse nor gained fame. " A Daniel come to judgment " is an expressive way of saying " a wise and upright judge ". A Jonah is one that brings ill-luck to the company ; a Machiavelli is one that gets his way by subtlety. The use of the word may become so common that its original application to a particular person or place is in the background. We write the word then with the small letter.

The adjectival use of the name is a further development. Thus " fabian " implies delaying action like that of Fabius Maximus, who foiled Hannibal by his dilatory tactics.

The names of characters in literature at times comes to have a place in the language : a Scrooge is a miser ; a Shylock is one insistent on his utmost rights ; " lilliputian " recalls the tiny folk in *Gulliver's Travels* ; the " socratic method " recalls Socrates who was for ever wanting to know.

PROVERB

(a) A proverb is much matter decocted into few words.
(THOMAS FULLER, *Worthies of England*.)

(b) " While the grass grows ",—the proverb is something musty.

(*Hamlet*.)

(c) Pride goeth before destruction, and an haughty spirit before a fall.

(*Proverbs*.)

(d) Better is a dinner of herbs where love is, than a stalled ox and hatred therewith. (*Proverbs*.)

A PROVERB is a concise expression of a truth that is understood to be based upon experience and long-continued observation. " Yet ", says Sir Thomas Browne, " all is not true that is proverbial." And, indeed, some of our common proverbs go about in pairs that appear to contradict one another : " Many hands make light work " seems to run counter to " Too many cooks spoil the broth ". The proverb being an expression of conclusion drawn from long experience, the utterance of proverbs is supposed—probably erroneously—to be a peculiar characteristic of mature age : The Justice, in the Seven Ages of man is, for example, " Full of wise saws and modern instances ".

PUNCTUATION, PURPOSE OF

Punctuation is the practice of inserting " points " or " stops " in order to give help towards the correct interpretation of writing or of printing. The stops indicate the groups of words into which the writer intends his sentences to be divided. The comma after " merry " in the carol prevents you from the absurd misreading of which the carol-singers seem to be obsessed. It is " God rest you merry, Gentlemen "—not, " God rest you, merry gentlemen ". The stops also help, though in a less measure, to indicate the tone in which he would like his words to be read. Sensible punctuation saves the reader's time and guards him against possible misinterpretation. Reading would be difficult if, as in the old manuscripts, the writing were continuous. We are accustomed to helps, nowadays, and even a little sentence like :

Takecareofthesenseandthesoundswilltakecareofthemselves

would impede us. The sentence following, for instance, easily grasped when heard, clamours when written for indications of how its words are to be grouped :

Unquestionably as a general proposition when an offer is made it is necessary in order to make a binding contract not only that it should be accepted but that the acceptance should be notified.

True, a little patience will determine the matter ; but the stops are welcome :

Unquestionably, as a general proposition, when an offer is made, it is necessary, in order to make a binding contract, not only that it should be accepted, but that the acceptance should be notified.

So, too, even if you wrote without troubling about stops, your reader would in the end be able to place into proper groups these words—

I'll tell you how I came to think of it said the Knight you see I said to myself the only difficulty is with the feet the head is high enough already now first I put my head on the top of the gate then the heads high enough then I stand on my head then the feet are high enough you see then Im over you see

Yes I suppose youd be over when that was done Alice said thoughtfully but dont you think it would be rather hard

I havent tried it yet the Knight said gravely so I cant tell for certain but Im afraid it would be a little hard

The devices of the printer in order to economise the reader's attention enable the reader to group the words, and so to grasp the intended meaning much more speedily :

" I'll tell you how I came to think of it," said the Knight.

"You see, I said to myself, 'The only difficulty is with the feet : the head is high enough already.' Now, first I put my head on the top of the gate—then the head's high enough—then I stand on my head—then the feet are high enough,—you see—than I'm over, you see."

"Yes, I suppose, you'd be over when it was done," Alice said thoughtfully ; "but don't you think it would be rather hard ? "

"I haven't tried it yet," the Knight said gravely : "so I can't tell for certain—but I'm afraid it *would* be a little hard."

PUNS. (See " Homonyms ")

(*a*) He that would pun would pick a pocket.

(*b*) "Prithee, friend," said the Oxford scholar to the porter, "is that thine own hare—or a wig ? "

(*c*) Said she : My taste will never learn
　　　To like so huge a man,
　　So I must beg you will come here
　　　As little as you can.

(HOOD.)

You make a pun when you use one word so as to suggest two meanings at the same time. The learned word for a pun is *paronomasia* (a play on words, *onoma* being the Greek for name) :

You see this pebble-stone ? It's a thing I bought
Of a bit of a chit of a boy i' the mid o' the day—
I like to dock the smaller parts-o'-speech,
As we curtail the already curtail'd cur,
(You catch the paronomania, play on words ?).

(C. S. CALVERLEY.)

Lamb's comment on the example in (*b*) is :

There is no excusing this, and no resisting it. A man might blur ten sides of paper in attempting a defence of it against a critic who should be laughter-proof. The quibble in itself is not considerable. It is only a new turn given, by a little false pronunciation, to a very common, though not very courteous inquiry. Put by one gentleman to another at a dinner-party, it would have been vapid ; to the mistress of the house, it would have shown much less wit than rudeness. We must take in the totality of time, place, and person ; the pert look of the inquiring scholar, the desponding looks of the puzzled porter; the one stopping at leisure, the other hurrying on with his burthen; the innocent though rather abrupt tendency of the first member of the question, with the utter and inextricable irrelevancy of the second; the place— a public street, not favourable to frivolous investigations; the affrontive quality of the primitive inquiry (the common question) invidiously transferred to the derivative (the new turn given to it) in the implied satire; namely, that few of that tribe are expected to eat of the good things which they carry, they being in most countries considered rather as the temporary trustees, than owners of such dainties,—which the fellow was beginning to understand; but then the *wig* again comes in, and he can make nothing of it; all put together constitute a picture: Hogarth could have made it intelligible on canvas.

Q

QUESTION MARK (NOTE OF INTERROGATION)

(*a*) Young Castlewood came clambering over the stalls before the clergy were fairly gone, and, running up to Esmond, eagerly embraced him. " My dear, dearest old Harry," he said, " are you come back? Have you been to the wars? You'll take me with you when you go again? Why didn't you write to us? Come to mother."

(THACKERAY, Henry Esmond.)

(*b*) No one knows how good the world is, till grief comes to try us.

(*c*) What hands are here? Ah, they pluck out my eyes! Will all great Neptune's ocean wash this blood Clean from my hand? No; this my hand will rather The multitudinous seas incarnadine, Making the green one red.

(Macbeth.)

The QUESTION MARK is the appropriate stop to end a sentence that consists of a *direct* question: see the instances in the Thackeray passage. It is not appropriate for an *indirect* question: note the instance in (*b*) above. The direct question is " How good is the world? "

QUOTATIONS

(a)   —The *fight*, the *fight's* the thing,
Wherein I'll catch the conscience of the king.

Where there's a will there's a way—I said to myself, as I
walked down Chancery Lane, about half-past six o'clock
on Monday the 10th of December, to inquire at Jack
Randall's where the fight the next day was to be ; I found
" the proverb nothing musty " in the present instance.
I was determined to see this fight, come what would, and
see it I did, in great style. It was my *first fight*, yet it more
than answered my expectations. Ladies ! it is to
you I dedicate this description ; nor let it seem out of
character for the fair to notice the exploits of the brave.
Courage and modesty are the old English virtues ; and
may they never look cold and askance on one another !
Think, ye fairest of the fair, loveliest of the lovely kind,
ye practisers of soft enchantment, how many more ye kill
with poisoned baits than ever fell in the ring ; and listen,
with subdued air and without shuddering, to a tale tragic
only in appearance and sacred to the FANCY !

(WILLIAM HAZLITT, The Fight.)

(b) " Do you know what day it is ? " she continued. " It is
the 29th December—it is your birthday ! But last year
we did not drink it—no, no. My lord was cold, and my
Harry was likely to die : and my brain was in a fever ;
and we had no wine. But now—now you are come again,
bringing your sheaves with you, my dear." She burst
into a wild flood of weeping as she spoke ; she laughed
and sobbed on the young man's heart, crying out wildly,
" bringing your sheaves with you—your sheaves with you."

(THACKERAY, Henry Esmond.)

(c) By necessity, by proclivity,—and by delight, we all quote.
(EMERSON.)

You have a thought that has been well expressed in writing
you admire. What more natural than to quote ! And, indeed,
when the quotation is apt, and especially when it brings into
the reader's mind pleasant memories, it is a great delight.
Besides, our quotation may be so much a real part of everyday
language that we do not recognise it as a quotation. The Bible
and Shakespeare have, as we should expect, provided these
ready-made phrases in plenty : the Bible quotation in the

Thackeray extract and the *Hamlet* quotations in the Hazlitt extract we all know as quotations. Others that come to mind spontaneously may not be recognised as quotations. Which of these, for example, from the Bible can you place correctly— " bring down my grey hairs with sorrow to the grave ", " the apple of his eye ", " the stars in their courses ", " entreat me not to leave thee ", " to cast pearls before swine ", " the eleventh hour ", " hoping against hope ", " a howling wilderness ", "a labour of love ", " a perfect babel ", " a painted Jezebel ", " the shibboleth of his party " ? And can you tell off-hand from which of Shakespeare's plays these " household words " come : " to eat the leek ", " here's metal more attractive ", " hoist with his own petard ", " caviare to the general ", " full of sound and fury signifying nothing ", " a Daniel come to judgment ", " a Triton among the minnows " ? Why, a single speech of Hamlet supplies a dozen or more phrases that have become real parts of the language ; they are constantly used by people quite unaware that they are quoting. Look at a few lines of the speech :

> To be, or not to be—that is the question—
> Whether it is nobler in the mind to suffer
> The slings and arrows of outrageous fortune,
> Or to take arms against a sea of troubles,
> And by opposing end them ?—To die,—to sleep,
> No more, and by a sleep to say we end
> The heart-ache and the thousand natural shocks
> That flesh is heir to,—'tis a consummation
> Devoutly to be wished. To die,—to sleep,—
> To sleep ! perchance to dream : ay, there's the rub.

You notice that Hazlitt has, as his custom is, adapted a little his opening quotation. Some object to this treatment of quotations ; but there seems to be no great harm in it. At any rate it is a widespread practice.

There is another danger about quotations. It is this. Those unfamiliar with the quotation may resent it. They may think it introduced to display the writer's knowledge rather than to inform the reader's ignorance. This is especially so when the quotation is in another language. Here, for instance, is this clever little snatch of R. H. Barham's :

> *Eheu fugaces.*
> What Horace says is—
> > *Eheu fugaces*
> > *Anni labuntur, Postume, Postume!*
> > Years glide away, and are lost to me, lost to me!

Delightful this is to the Latin scholar; but one with but a nodding acquaintance with Latin will brush it away with impatience and turn to something more intelligible.

QUOTATION MARKS (INVERTED COMMAS)

(*a*) " There are ", says the author of *Lacon*, " three difficulties in authorship, to write anything worth publishing, to find honest men to publish it, and to get sensible people to read it when published."

(*b*) " Do you mean that you think you can find out the answer to it ? " said the March Hare.

"Exactly so," said Alice.

"Then you should say what you mean," the March Hare went on.

" I do," Alice hastily replied, " at least—at least I mean what I say—that's the same thing, you know."

" Not the same thing a bit ! " said the Hatter. " Why, you might just as well say that ' I see what I eat ' is the same as ' I eat what I see ' ! "

> (*Alice in Wonderland.*)

QUOTATION MARKS are helps that a writer, or more often his printer, provides for the reader. Not always, though ; for here and there you find a writer requiring you to decide for yourself which are the quoted words. The use of the quotation mark is, indeed, quite modern. Nor do we have great trouble in supplying them when we read older writings. Thus, we do not miss them greatly in :

> And when he came to himself, he said, How many hired servants of my father have bread enough and to spare, and I perish with hunger.

or

> Mizpah ; for he said, The Lord watch between me and thee, when we are absent one from another.

Sterne is one of these rebels against convention.

Thou hast read the sermon extremely well, *Trim*, quoth my father. If he had spared his comments, replied *Dr. Slop*, —he would have read it much better. I should have read it ten times better, Sir, answered *Trim*, but that my heart was so full.

In the *Alice in Wonderland* passage you notice that the quotations inside the quotation—the phrases ' I see what I eat ' and ' I eat what I see '—are marked off by single commas or " quotes ". Such is the usual method ; but you may come across a writer that prefers the single commas for the main quotation. This is perhaps the more logical. But, after all, an internal quotation is rare ; and the double commas do make the quotation more conspicuous.

You notice that the comma sign is turned upside down (inverted) at the opening of the quotation and is also raised above the line. " The close of the quotation, however, is marked by commas in the ordinary form but raised above the line.

R

REALISM

(*a*) When daffodils begin to peer
　　With heigh ! the doxy over the dale,
Why, then comes in the sweet o' the year ;
　　For the red blood reigns in the winter's pale.

The white sheet bleaching on the hedge,
　　With heigh ! the sweet birds, O, how they sing !
Doth set my pugging tooth on edge ;
　　For a quart of ale is a dish for a king.
　　　　　(Autolycus, sings this in *The Winter's Tale*.)

(*b*) Just now the lilac is in bloom,
All before my little room ;
And in my flower-beds, I think,
Smile the carnation and the pink ;
And down the borders, well I know,
The poppy and the pansy blow. . . .
Oh ! there the chestnuts, summer through,

Beside the river make for you
A tunnel of green gloom, and sleep
Deeply above ; and green and deep
The stream mysterious glides beneath
Green as a dream and deep as death.
—Oh damn ! I know it ! and I know
How the May fields all golden show,
And when the day is young and sweet,
Gild gloriously the bare feet
That run to bathe . . .
                    Du lieber Gott !
Here am I, sweating, sick, and hot,
And there the shadowed waters fresh
Lean up to embrace the naked flesh.
        (So RUPERT BROOKE, writing from a Berlin café,
                        says in *Grantchester*.)

The modern tendency of writers is to speak of things as they
are—" to exclude nothing as common or unclean " so long as it
can in any way strengthen the impression of life and variety.
This may be called REALISM ; it is the method of the Dutch
painting, which makes even sordid details add to the truth of
the picture. The tramp and his sweetheart, the washing put
to dry, the thieving appetite looking for a quart of ale as a
reward—most poets would shun these. But here Shakespeare
makes them into real poetry and is as modern as anyone !

To be sure the modern writer making good literature out of
actuality, sometimes out of ugliness and squalor, has fore-
runners from as far away as Chaucer's days. Chaucer's Wife
of Bath—the large woman with the red face and loud laugh,
with her new shoes and her scarlet stockings—is very much
alive still. And here, from the eighteenth century, is how
Goldsmith makes things commonplace into literature. It is his
" Description of an Author's Bedchamber " :

Where the Red Lion flaring o'er the way,
Invites each passing stranger that can pay ;
There in a lonely room, from bailiffs snug,
The Muse found Scroggen stretched beneath a rug ;
A Window, patched with paper, lent a ray
That dimly showed the state in which he lay ;

The sanded floor that grits beneath the tread ;
The humid wall with paltry pictures spread ;
The royal game of goose was there in view,
And the twelve rules the royal martyr drew ;

And brave Prince William showed his lamp-black face ;
The morn was cold, he views with keen desire
The rusty gate unconscious of a fire ;
With beer and milk arrears the frieze was scored
And five cracked teacups dressed the chimney board ;
A nightcap decked his brows instead of bay,
A cap by night—a stocking all the day !

REDUNDANCY. (See " Relevance : Tautology ")

RELATIVE PRONOUN

(a) I met a traveller from an antique land,
Who said, " Two vast and trunkless legs of stone
Stand in the desert."

(SHELLEY.)

(b) He that shall live this day, and see old age,
Will yearly on the vigil feast his neighbours.

(SHAKESPEARE.)

(c) Surely never lighted on this orb, which she hardly seemed
to touch, a more delightful vision.

(BURKE.)

(d) I am bold to say that I ask no ill thing for you, when on
parting from this place I pray that whomever you choose
to succeed me, he may resemble me exactly in all things,
except in my abilities to serve and my fortune to please
you.

(BURKE.)

(e) The people of a free commonwealth cannot suffer their
executory system to be composed of persons on whom
they have no dependence and whom no proofs of the
public love and confidence have recommended to power.

(BURKE.)

The RELATIVE PRONOUN—like *who* in (a), *that* in (b), *which*
in (c), *whomever* in (d), and *whom* in (e)—is a noun-substitute
and, at the same time, a joining word. Thus, *who* in (a) is
equivalent to " and he ". The Relative may be added to define
a preceding noun : " They stared at the dead *that* had been so

valiant and true"; "This mob was one of many thousands *that* were going about the country at that time." The Relative may also add a new fact: "He had all the play-books to read, and a hundred childish pursuits and pastimes, *which* made this time very pleasant."

You notice that the Relative may have a different "case" from that of the noun to which it relates. Here, for instance, is Antony's exclamation:

> What, girl! though grey
> Do something mingle with our younger brown, yet have we
> A brain that nourishes our nerves and can
> Get goal for goal of youth.

The noun *brain* is in the objective case governed by the transitive verb *have*. The Relative *that*, however, takes its case from its work in its own clause; and, since it is the Subject of the clause "that nourishes our nerves", it is in the nominative case.

You notice, too, that the Relative is nearly always placed near the beginning of its clause. Perhaps that is why we are apt to put the nominative *who* when the objective *whom* is required. *Whomever* in (*d*) is the correct word: some of us might slip into *whoever*.

RELEVANCE

Relevance is the quality of being to the point, of being pertinent.

Your speech or your writing is RELEVANT when it bears directly upon the matter discussed; it is full of IRRELEVANCIES when a number of topics only indirectly connected with the main topic are introduced. If I say, "No accumulation of facts can establish an irrelevant conclusion" you understand me to imply that the facts brought forward give no support to the conclusion.

Jane Austen's *Miss Bates* in *Emma* supplies plentiful illustrations of irrelevancy:

"But where could you hear it? Where could you possibly hear it, Mr. Knightley? For it is not five minutes since I received Mrs. Cole's note—no, it cannot be more than five, or at least ten, for I had only gone down to speak to Patty again about the pork—Jane was standing in the passage, were not you, Jane?—for my Mother was so afraid that we had

not any salting-pan ' Shall I go down instead ? for I think
you have a little cold, and Patty has been washing the kitchen.'
' O my dear,' said I—well, and just then came the note. A
Miss Hawkins, that's all I know—a Miss Hawkins of Bath.
But Mr. Knightley, how could you possibly have heard it ?
for the moment Mr. Cole told Mrs. Cole of it she sat down
and wrote to me."

A speech like this fine one of Edmund Burke illustrates
relevance in composition. He is withdrawing his candidature
to represent Bristol :

> Gentlemen : I decline the election. It has ever been my
> rule through life to observe a proportion between my efforts
> and my objects. I have never been remarkable for a bold,
> active, and sanguine pursuit of advantages that are personal
> to myself.
> I have not canvassed the whole of this city in form. But
> I have taken such a view of it as satisfies my own mind that
> your choice will not ultimately fall on me. Your city, Gentle-
> men, is in a state of miserable distraction ; and I am resolved
> to withdraw whatever share my pretensions may have had in
> its unhappy divisions. I have not been in haste ; I have tried
> all prudent means ; I have waited for the effect of all con-
> tingencies. If I were fond of a contest, by the partiality of
> my numerous friends (whom you know to be among the most
> weighty and respectable people of the city), I have the means
> of a sharp one in my hands. But I thought it far better with
> my strength unspent, and my reputation unimpaired, to do,
> early and from foresight, that which I might be obliged to
> do from necessity at last.
> I am not in the least surprised, not in the least angry at
> this view of things. I have read the book of life for a long
> time, and I have read other books a little. Nothing has hap-
> pened to me but what has happened to men much better than
> me, and in times and in nations full as good as the age and
> country that we live in. To say that I am no way concerned,
> would be neither decent nor true. The representation of
> *Bristol* was an object on many accounts dear to me ; and I
> certainly should very far prefer it to any other in the kingdom.
> My habits are made to it ; and it is in general more unpleasant
> to be rejected after long trial, than not to be chosen at all.
> But Gentlemen, I will see nothing except your former kind-

ness, and I will give way to no other sentiment than those of gratitude. From the bottom of my heart I thank you for what you have done for me. You have given me a long term, which is now expired. I have performed the conditions, and enjoyed all the profits to the full; and I now surrender your estate into your hands, without being in a single tile or a single stone impaired or wasted by my use. I have served the public for fifteen years. I have served you in particular for six. What is passed is well stored. It is safe, and out of the power of fortune. What is to come is in wiser hands than ours; and He, in whose hands it is, best knows whether it is best for you and me that I should be in Parliament, or even in the world.

Gentlemen, the melancholy event of yesterday reads to us an awful lesson against being too much troubled about any of the objects of ordinary ambition. The worthy Gentleman, who has been snatched from us at the moment of election and in the middle of the contest, whilst his desires were as warm and his hopes as eager as ours, has feelingly told us what shadows we are, and what shadows we pursue.

It has been usual, for a candidate who declines, to take his leave by a letter to the sheriffs; but I received your trust in the face of day; and in the face of day I accept your dismission. I am not,—I am not at all ashamed to look upon you; nor can my presence discompose the order of the business here. I humbly and respectfully take my leave of the sheriffs, the candidates, and the electors, wishing heartily that the choice may be for the best at a time which calls, if ever time did call, for service that is not nominal. It is no plaything you are about. I tremble when I consider the trust I have presumed to ask. I confided perhaps too much in my intentions. They were really fair and upright; and I am bold to say that I ask no ill thing for you when on parting from this place I pray that whomever you choose to succeed me, he may resemble me exactly in all things, except in my abilities to serve and my fortune to please you.

You write an essay. Well, one test of a good essay is this: can you, from the essay itself, deduce the title of the essay? If you can, there is some likelihood that the essay is not to be condemned for irrelevance.

REPETITION

(*a*) They went down to the camp in black, but they came back to the town in white ; they went down to the camp in ropes, but they came back in chains of gold ; they went down to the camp with their feet in fetters, but came back with their steps enlarged under them ; they went also to the camp looking for death, but they came back from thence with assurance of life ; they went down to the camp with heavy hearts, but came back again with pipe and tabor playing before them. So, as soon as they were come to Eyegate, the poor and tottering town of Mansoul adventured to give them a shout, and they gave such a shout as made the captains in the Prince's army leap at the sound thereof.

(The Pilgrim's Progress.)

(*b*) With thee conversing, I forget all time :
All seasons and their change : all please alike :
Sweet is the breath of Morn, her rising sweet,
With charm of earliest birds, pleasant the sun
When first on this delightful land he spreads
His orient beams, on herb, tree, fruit and flower,
Glist'ring with dew ; fragrant the fertile earth
After soft showers ; and sweet the coming on
Of grateful evening mild ; then silent Night
With this her solemn bird and this fair moon,
And these the gems of heaven, her starry train :
But neither breath of morn when she ascends
With charm of earliest birds, nor rising sun
On this delightful land, nor herb, fruit, flower
Glist'ring with dew, nor fragrance after showers,
Nor grateful evening mild, nor silent Night
With this her solemn bird, nor walk by moon,
Or glittering starlight, without thee is sweet.

(Paradise Lost.)

(*c*) Break, break, break,
    On thy cold grey stones, O Sea !
And I would that my tongue could utter
    The thoughts that arise in me.

O well for the fisherman's boy,
    That he shouts with his sister at play !
O well for the sailor lad
    That he sings in his boat on the bay !

And the stately ships go on
  To their haven under the hill ;
But O for the touch of a vanished hand,
  And the sound of a voice that is still !

Break, break, break,
  At the foot of thy crags, O Sea !
But the tender grace of a day that is dead
  Will never come back to me.

(Tennyson.)

(d) " The British people and their Grecian Allies need assist-
ance, and that they will get. They need ships. From
America they will get ships. They need planes. From
America they will get planes. Yes, from America they
need food. From America they will get food. They need
tanks and guns and ammunition and supplies of all kinds.
From America they will get tanks and guns and ammunition
and supplies of all kinds." (President Roosevelt.)

(e) Multitudes, multitudes in the valley of decision ; for the
day of the Lord is near in the valley of decision.

(Joel iii. 14.)

(f)   Though fallen on evil days,
On evil days though fallen and evil tongues.

(Milton.)

REPETITION, well managed, need not be a distasteful same-
ness. It may, as in the examples, be very effective. A writer,
indeed, may be so fond of the device that we get a little
impatient with it. Perhaps, for example, Matthew Arnold,
counselling " the Philistines " to seek after " sweetness and
light " indulges to excess in repetition :

The pursuit of perfection is the pursuit of sweetness and
light. He who works for sweetness and light, works to make
reason and the will of God prevail. He who works for
machinery, he who works for hatred, works only for confusion. Culture hates hatred ; culture has one great passion,
the passion for sweetness and light. It has one passion yet
greater—the passion for making them prevail. It is not
satisfied until *all* come to a perfect man ; it knows that the
sweetness and light of the few must be imperfect until the
raw and unkindled masses of humanity are touched with
the same sweetness and light.

The poet Wordsworth, too, at times indulges in such childish repetition as makes you wonder whether his critical faculty had fallen into a deep sleep for a while. He begins one poem with the astonishing lines :

> Oh ! what's the matter ? what's the matter ?
> What is't that ails young Harry Gill ?
> That evermore his teeth they chatter,
> Chatter, chatter, chatter still !
> Of waistcoats Harry has no lack ;
> Good duffle grey, and flannel fine ;
> He has a blanket on his back,
> And coats enough to smother nine.

Akin to this actual repetition of word or phrase is the parallelism of the Hebrew poetry. Thus in the Psalms :

> Keep thy tongue from evil
>   And thy lips from speaking guile.
> Depart from evil
>   And do good
> Seek peace
>   And ensue it.

Each injunction is there expressed twice over. Now and again you meet with threefold reiteration : Thus

The Lord bless thee, and keep thee :
The Lord make his face shine upon thee, and be gracious unto thee :
The Lord lift up his countenance upon thee, and give thee peace.

How very effective is the repetition in those companion speeches of Brutus and Antony in *Julius Cæsar* ! Here is Brutus's with his reiterated question in varied form :

Who is here so base that would be a bondman ? If any, speak ; for him have I offended. Who is here so rude that would not be a Roman ? If any, speak ; for him have I offended. Who is here so vile that will not love his country ? If any, speak ; for him have I offended. I pause for a reply.

And here is Antony with his cunning play upon the phrase, " Brutus is an honourable man " :

> Here, under leave of Brutus and the rest,
> (For Brutus is an honourable man ;

So are they all, all honourable men ;)
Come I to speak in Cæsar's funeral.

Read the speech through and see how skilfully the orator used the repetition.

REPORT

(a) *Messenger :* The nature of bad news infects the teller.
Antony : When it concerns the fool or coward. On :
Things that are past are done, with me. 'Tis thus ;
Who tells me true, though in his tale lie death,
I hear him as he flattered.

(Antony and Cleopatra.)

(b) *Othello :* I pray you, in your letters,
When you shall these unlucky deeds relate,
Speak of me as I am ; nothing extenuate,
Nor set down aught in malice.

(Othello.)

(c) All our friends took their share and fought like men in the great field. All day long, whilst the women were praying ten miles away, the lines of the dauntless English infantry were receiving and repelling the furious charges of the French horsemen. Guns which were heard at Brussels were ploughing up their ranks, and comrades falling, and the resolute survivors closing in. Towards evening, the attack of the French, repeated and resisted so bravely, slackened in its fury. They had other foes beside the British to engage, or were preparing for a final onset. It came at last : the columns of the Imperial Guard marched up the hill of Saint Jean, at length and at once to sweep the English from the height which they had maintained all day, and spite of all : unscared by the thunder of the artillery, which hurled death from the English line—the dark rolling column pressed on and up the hill. It seemed almost to crest the eminence, when it began to wave and falter. Then it stopped, still facing the shot. Then at last the English troops rushed from the post from which no enemy had been able to dislodge them, and the Guard turned and fled.

No more firing was heard at Brussels—the pursuit rolled miles away. Darkness came down on the field and city : and Amelia was praying for George, who was lying on his face, dead, with a bullet through his heart.

(W. M. THACKERAY, *Vanity Fair*, Chap. XXXII.)

With a utilitarian report we are all familiar. Out goes the patrol and, maybe after " moving accidents by flood and field ", brings in a report. And what would its recipient like it to be ? It is, you say, an accurate account of the enemy's position, the likely strength of that enemy, the possibility of an attack by him, the possibility too of a gain of ground at his expense. These are the things a leader craves to know in order to determine upon his action ; these are what he asks from a report.

The well-written report should, in short, be a reliable guide to action.

You become a secretary. Well, among the most onerous of your duties will be the writing of a report of a meeting ; you will enter the minutes in the minute book. These minutes are a report in a concise—but yet clear and complete—form of what happened at the meeting, in particular what decisions were reached. An *aide-mémoire* people call the account when they speak of high policy ; the matters transacted, the conclusions reached, are placed upon record lest there should be a future conflict of testimony concerning them. For it would appear that in diplomacy, far more than in other transactions among men, the maxim applies, *Vox perit, litera scripta manet* : negotiators are apt to forget what they said, spoken words may be distorted, only half-remembered, even wholly forgotten ; but the written account endures, a lasting memorial.

Your report, you will agree, will emphasise the results of the meeting rather than the process by which those results were reached. The speeches, the interjections, the many irrelevancies that a weak chairman permits, will be subordinated to the decisions ultimately agreed upon. Doubtless, there will sometimes be a strong reason why a particular person's attitude to a proposal should be recorded. If there is, you will record it : but normally you will content yourself with " It was decided that . . ." rather than " Mr. Smith proposed and Mr. Jones seconded the proposition that . . ."

As secretary you will have prepared an agenda—a word that means, though chairmen sometimes seem unaware of the fact, " things to be *done* at the meeting ". You will have arranged the items so that one follows logically upon its predecessor—you have indicated an order from which the wise chairman will not lightly deviate. Such an agenda helps you in noting the decisions reached and in recording them. As secretary, too, you may take a part, even a prominent part, in the discussions leading to the decisions. As reporter, however—as minute-taker—your one aim is to state, without bias or prejudice, what happened. For when, at a following meeting, the minutes are confirmed by the appending of the chairman's signature, the preliminary question he asks is, " Do you agree that the minutes as presented are a correct record of what was done at the meeting ? "

The stock phrases of the harassed " official spokesman " suggest one ever-present difficulty for the reporter : how is he to avoid reproach for telling too little or censure for telling too much ? To be precise and definite would be giving information to the enemy. Better say that things have gone " according to plan ". This phrase, you agree, admits of elastic interpretation. It may mean in accordance with the enemy's plan : it may mean the smooth working out of a scheme of conquest or the more or less orderly retreat that could bear another name. It leaves the actual happenings to your imagination. The hearer hungry for news gets little from the report. Yet the reporter must be reserved while he appears frank ; and you, too, must at times be reticent while appearing voluble.

REPORTED SPEECH : ORATIO OBLIQUA

(a) The snow fell over Paris. . . . To poor people, looking up under moist eyebrows, it seemed a wonder where it all came from. Master François Villon had propounded an alternative that afternoon, at a tavern window : was it only Pagan Jupiter plucking geese upon Olympus ? Or were the holy angels moulting ? He was only a poor Master of Arts, he went on ; and, as the question somewhat touched upon divinity, he durst not venture to conclude.

(ROBERT LOUIS STEVENSON.)

(b) Mr. Pickwick observed (says the secretary) that fame was dear to the heart of every man. Poetic fame was dear to the heart of his friend Snodgrass ; the fame of conquest was equally dear to his friend Tupman ; and the desire of earning fame in the sports of the field, the air, and the water, was uppermost in the breast of his friend Winkle.

(CHARLES DICKENS.)

The DIRECT SPEECH (*oratio recta*), the actual words, of Master François Villon would have been the French equivalent of, " Is it only Pagan Jupiter plucking geese upon Olympus ? Or are the holy angels moulting ? I am only a poor Master of Arts ; and, as the question somewhat touches upon divinity, I dare not venture to conclude." The direct speech of Mr. Pickwick was, " Fame is dear to the heart of every man. Poetic fame is dear to the heart of my friend Snodgrass ; the fame of conquest is equally dear to my friend Tupman ; and the desire of earning fame in the sports of the field, the air, and the water, is uppermost in the breast of my friend Winkle."

REVISION (ITS DESIRABILITY)

(*a*)   Doeg, without knowing how or why
Made still a blundering kind of melody,
Spurred boldly on, and dashed through thick and thin,
Through sense and nonsense, never out nor in.
He was too warm on picking work to dwell,
But fagotted his notions as they fell,
And if they rhymed and rattled, all was well.

(DRYDEN.)

(*b*) The best writers, in their beginnings, imposed upon themselves care and industry : they did nothing rashly : they obtained first to write correctly, and then custom made it easy and a habit.

(BEN JONSON.)

(*c*) " He never blotted out a line," was the Players' praise of Shakespeare. " My answer hath been," said Ben Jonson, " would he had blotted out a thousand ! "

(*d*) Pope was not content to satisfy ; he desired to excel ; and therefore always endeavoured to do his best : he did not court the candour, but dared the judgment of his reader, and, expecting no indulgence from others, he showed none to himself. He examined lines and words with minute and punctilious observation, and retouched every part with indefatigable diligence, till he had left nothing to be forgiven.

(DR. SAMUEL JOHNSON.)

Of course you appreciate a well-turned phrase, in prose as well as in poetry. " Isn't this capital ? " you say, " the choice of words and the manner of their combination make the passage irresistible. It couldn't be bettered." Perhaps you stop at that ; you decline to trouble yourself with an examination into the reason why the phrase differs from the ordinary, humdrum phrase you hear in talk or read in the papers. Yet the examination is worth making.

The thought expressed makes notable some of the expressions over which you chuckle. When Mr. Pepys recorded : " 4th—Home and being washing-day, dined upon cold meat ", he had no wish to delight readers with his manner of expression. Indeed he wanted no readers ; he simply recorded in his diary the sense of irritation that he dare not utter to his wife, " poor wretch ! " So, too, when Doctor Johnson rejects his friend's invitation to travel in Ireland, what delights you is the way in which the Doctor twists his friend's words : " Is not the Giant's Causeway worth seeing ? " asks Boswell. " Worth seeing ? " answers Johnson. " Yes, but not worth going to see."

It is the manner of expression that is notable in other phrases. The thought, no doubt, has weight, but the thought goes into the background as we rejoice in its expression. Why do we linger over " In maiden meditation, fancy free " ? Hasn't the mode of expression taken precedence in our minds of the bare thought, ' She lived unmarried " ? Here, too, are lines you very likely know well ; they are from Wordsworth's " Solitary Reaper "—

> No Nightingale did ever chant
>   More welcome notes to weary bands
> Of travellers in some shady haunt
>   Among Arabian sands.

Now try, as a substitute for the second line, this : " So sweetly to reposing bands " ; and try the preposition " Amid " for " Among " in the fourth line. Do you agree that the first version is the better ? In Coleridge's *Ancient Mariner*, the first edition has :

> The breezes blew, the white foam flew,
>   The furrow followed free,
> We were the first that ever burst
>   Into that silent sea.

Don't you agree that the alteration of the first line into :

> The fair breeze blew, the white foam flew,

effects an improvement ?

Look again at these famous lines about the nightingale's song—

> The same that oftimes hath
> Charmed magic casements, opening on the foam
> Of perilous seas in fairy lands forlorn.

Perhaps you know that Keats at first wrote " keelless seas ". Now, why did he prefer the adjective " perilous " ? Why did he choose to have the echo " opening " with " perilous ", instead of the echo " casements " with " keelless " ? Is your ear better pleased with the first than with the second ?

Consider another example. Milton in his *Comus* wrote first

> And airy tongues that lure night wanderers.

Evidently the last three words did not please him greatly, and he revised :

> And airy tongues that syllable men's names
> On sands and shores and desert wildernesses.

You agree that he wrought a tremendous improvement. It was a much better revision than the one suggested by Wordsworth : " Tell me ", he wrote to a correspondent, " if you approve of the following alteration " :

> The City now doth on her forehead wear
> The glorious crown of morning ; silent, bare,
> Ships, towers, etc. . . .

You cannot think this better than :

> This City now doth like a garment wear
> The beauty of the morning ; silent, bare,
> Ships, towers, etc. . . .

You may, indeed, revise too much ; and the labour of the file —*labor limae*, Horace calls it—may result in worse instead of better. Not often, though, we may be pretty sure. The " first sprightly runnings " are preferable on only rare occasions. Most of us need to make the old apology for our work :

> I might indeed (had I wisely done) have observed that

precept of the poet,—*nonumque prematur in annum*, kept it a-maturing to the ninth year—and have taken more care : or as Alexander the physician would have done by lapis lazuli, fifty times washed before it be used. I should have revised, corrected, and amended this tract ; but I had not that happy leisure, no amanuenses or assistants.

RHETORIC

(*a*) Bridget is so sparing of her speech on most occasions that, when she gets into a rhetorical vein, I am careful how I interrupt it.

(CHARLES LAMB.)

(*b*) It is now sixteen or seventeen years since I saw the Queen of France, then the Dauphiness, at Versailles ; and surely never lighted on this orb, which she hardly seemed to touch, a more delightful vision. I saw her just above the horizon, decorating and cheering the elevated sphere she just began to move in—glittering like the morning-star, full of life and splendour and joy. Oh ! what a revolution ! And what a heart must I have, to contemplate without emotion that elevation and that fall ! Little did I dream when she added titles of veneration to those of enthusiastic, distant, respectful love, that she should ever be obliged to carry the sharp antidote against disgrace concealed in that bosom ; little did I dream that I should have lived to see such disasters fallen upon her in a nation of gallant men, in a nation of men of honour, and of cavaliers. I thought ten thousand swords must have leaped from their scabbards to avenge even a look that threatened her with insult. But the age of chivalry is gone.

(EDMUND BURKE.)

RHETORIC is the art of using speech so as to persuade or influence others. It was an important part of their deliberate study to men of old ; and it is quite certain that, while there is much less ostentation about the matter, many do in our own days give a deal of time and thought to the art of persuading by means of speech. We have, indeed, seen abroad amazing results achieved by the power of the spoken word. In our grandfathers' days people thought it to be astonishing that Benjamin Disraeli, beginning his political career under heavy handicaps, should have become Prime Minister and the acknowledged leader of the Conservative party. It was astonishing. But Disraeli's achievement is dwarfed by the recent instances of accession to power by way of talk. The pen is mightier than the sword; words accomplish more than deeds. That is why the publicity expert is convinced that, whereas excellence of quality and moderation of price sell their thousands, effective advertisement sells its hundreds of thousands.

Among us rhetoric is a little suspect. We are inclined to couple it with the talk that is meant to mislead, talk that turns us away from the exercise of calm reason. We are moved at the moment; yet we may come to think " his tongue dropped manna, and could make the worse appear the better reason, to perplex and dash maturest counsels ". So it is that the really effective orator poses as none other than a quite ordinary speaker. He disclaims all artifice: no persuasive rhetoric sleeks his tongue. He is another Antony, cunningly disguising his art. " I am no orator ", he says, " as Brutus is ": " I am a plain blunt man ";

> For I have neither wit, nor words, nor worth,
> Action, nor utterance, nor the power of speech,
> To stir men's blood: I only speak right on.

But what a consummate speech Antony made, spite of his denial ! Simple words he used; but he used them so that he did sway men's minds. He has impressive phrases in varied contexts and tones—not elaborate phrases like Disraeli's when suggesting that Gladstone was " intoxicated with the exuberance of his own verbosity ", but phrases such as would be repeated by his hearers. He knew how effective the rhetorical question is—the question that does not await or need an answer, the statement more incisive because in the form of a question. You must know and greatly admire Antony's oration.

Indeed, the study of rhetoric is worth while. Wouldn't you rejoice if one could truthfully say of you what Ben Jonson said of the great Lord Bacon ?

> No man ever spake more neatly, more pressly, more weightily, or suffered less emptiness, less idleness, in what he uttered.

. . . His hearers could not cough, or look aside from him, without loss. He commanded where he spoke ; and had his hearers angry and pleased at his will. No man had their affections more in his power. The fear of every man that heard him was, lest he should make an end.

Milton, expounding the education needed for a boy, would have him taught " ornate rhetoric out of the rule of Plato ". " To which," he added, " poetry would be made subsequent, or indeed rather precedent, as being less subtle and fine, but more simple, sensuous, and passionate."

RHETORICAL QUESTIONS

(a) Voltaire had reached Frankfort. His niece, Madam Denis, came thither to meet him. He conceived himself secure from the power of his late master, when he was arrested by order of the Prussian resident. The precious volume was delivered up. But the Prussian agents had, no doubt, been instructed not to let Voltaire escape without some gross indignity. He was confined twelve days in a wretched hovel. Sentinels with fixed bayonets kept guard over him. His niece was dragged through the mire by the soldiers. Sixteen hundred dollars were extorted from him by his insolent gaolers. It is absurd to say that this outrage is not to be attributed to the King. Was anybody punished for it ? Was anybody called in question for it ? Was it not consistent with Frederic's character ? Was it not of a piece with his conduct on other similar occasions ? Is it not notorious that he repeatedly gave private directions to his officers to pillage and demolish the houses of persons against whom he had a grudge, charging them at the same time to take their measures in such a way that his name might not be compromised ? He acted thus towards Count Bruhl in the Seven Years' War. Why should we believe that he would have been more scrupulous with regard to Voltaire ?

(MACAULAY.)

(b) " Who is here so base that would be a bondman ? Who is here so vile that will not love his country ? I pause for a reply."
    " None, Brutus, none."

(SHAKESPEARE, *Julius Cæsar*.)

One example of emphasising a statement is to put it into the form of a question—a question the expected answer to which is at once forthcoming from the hearer. Such is a RHETORICAL QUESTION. Instead of " We are not downhearted " comes the insistent question " Are we down-hearted ? " and this meets the answering " No ". As you note from Macaulay's paragraph, a too frequent use makes the device lose a good deal of its effect.

RHYME (also spelled " RIME ")

(a) One speaks the Glory of the British Queen,
   And one describes a charming Indian Screen :
   A third interprets Motions, Looks, and Eyes ;
   At every word a Reputation dies.
   (POPE, The Rape of the Lock.)

(b) This is a spray the Bird clung to,
   Making it blossom with pleasure,
   Ere the high tree-top she sprung to,
   Fit for her nest and her treasure,
   Oh, what a hope beyond measure
   Was the poor spray's, which the flying feet hung to—
   So to be singled out, built in, and sung to !
   (ROBERT BROWNING.)

(c) He knew himself to build the lofty rhyme.
   (Lycidas.)

(d) Greek was free from rhyme's infection,
   Happy Greek by this protection
      Was not spoiled :
   Whilst the Latin, queen of tongues,
   Is not yet free from rhyme's wrongs,
      But rests foiled.
   (BEN JONSON, Fit of Rhyme against Rhyme.)

RHYME is the agreement in the end sounds of words : *joy* rhymes with *destroy* : *shutter* with *butter* : We all take delight in rhyme. Milton did, indeed, advance freedom from rhyme as a merit in *Paradise Lost*. " The jingling sound of like endings ", he calls rhyme ; and he adds, " a fault avoided by the learned ancients both in poetry and all good oratory ". But he himself delighted in rhyme ; and you would not have it absent from *L'Allegro* and *Il Penseroso* :

Come, and trip it as you go
On the light fantastic toe;
And in thy right hand lead with thee
The mountain nymph, sweet liberty;
And if I give thee honour due,
Mirth, admit me of thy crew,
To live with her, and live with thee
In unreproved pleasures free.

The rhyme is good when the last stressed vowel and any sounds following that vowel are the same in each of the rhyming words, but the sound preceding is different. Thus *smiled* and *wild* are good rhymes. But *loved and proved* are only half-rhymes; for the *o* in *loved* has not the same sound as the *o* in *proved*. Rhyme is also, as in (*c*), sometimes used for poetry in general. When the rhyme, as in (*a*), is one-syllabled (*Queen, Screen, Eyes, dies*), it is sometimes called a " male " or " masculine " rhyme. When the rhyme, as in (*b*), is of more than one syllable (*clung to, hung to, pleasure, measure*), it is sometimes called a " female " or " feminine " rhyme.

On occasions a poet adds what are called " internal rhymes " to his end rhymes. Look at *Spring, king, thing, ring, sting, sing*; *may, gay, day, aye, lay*; and *sweet, feet, meet, sit, street, greet*, in T. Nash's cheery song:

Spring, the sweet Spring, is the year's pleasant king,
Then blooms each thing, then maids dance in a ring,
Cold doth not sting, the pretty birds do sing
 Cuckoo, jug-jug, pu-we, to-witta-woo!
The palm and may, make country houses gay,
Lambs frisk and play, the shepherds pipe all day,
And we hear aye birds tune this merry lay,
 Cuckoo, jug-jug, pu-we, to-witta-woo!
The fields breathe sweet, the daisies kiss our feet,
Young lovers meet, old wives a-sunning sit,
In every street these tunes our ears do greet!
 Cuckoo, jug-jug, pu-we, to-witta-woo!

A poet like Browning can find rhymes in profusion. Others find a difficulty. So suggests Calverley:

Thro' the rare red heather we danced together,
 (O! love my Willie!) and smell for flowers:

246

I must mention again it was gorgeous weather,
Rhymes are so scarce in this world of ours.

RHYTHM (OF PROSE) : CADENCE

(a) I cannot praise | a fugitive and cloistered virtue, | unexer-
cised and unbreathed, | that never sallies out and sees
her adversary ; | but slinks out of the race | where that
immortal garland | is to be run for, | not without dust and
heat. |

(MILTON.)

(b) Arise, | shine ; | for thy light | is come, | and the glory |
of the Lord | is risen upon thee. | For, behold, | the
darkness shall cover the earth, | and gross darkness | the
people ; | but the Lord | shall arise | upon thee, | and his
glory | shall be seen | upon thee. | And the Gentiles |
shall come to thy light, | and kings | to the brightness |
of thy rising. |

(*Isaiah.*)

(c) But the iniquity | of oblivion | blindly scattereth her poppy |
and deals | with the memory of men | without distinction |
to merit of perpetuity. |

(SIR THOMAS BROWNE.)

You do not continue to talk on the one stress. You would be
disagreeably monotonous if you did. There is a natural rise and
fall—RHYTHM or CADENCE—of the stress. Whatever the sentence,
it has its rhythm ; but we apply the word, " rhythmical ",
particularly to a sentence that falls into pleasing groups of sounds.
Read aloud the passages above, and you will have a good idea of
what is meant by rhythmical prose. You may not quite agree
with the grouping given ; but your rendering will not differ
greatly.

Robert Louis Stevenson, who greatly admired the Milton
sentence, points out that the words of the phrase, " not without
dust and heat " all end with a dental (*t* or *d*) ; and he makes the
comment, " the singular dignity of the first clause, and the

hammer-stroke of the last, go far to make the charm of this exquisite sentence ".

Look, too, at this sentence of Burke's :

Little | did I dream | that I should have lived | to see such | disasters | fallen | upon her | in a nation | of gallant | men. |

The rhythm is not, as you see, the regular rhythm of poetry ; it is not the rhythm you have in lines like " As idle as a painted ship upon a painted ocean ". It is the rhythm belonging to what Dryden called " the other harmony of prose ". But how delightful it is ! Suppose we wrote the thought in this way : " I never thought that, the French being so chivalrous a people, she would there have met such misfortunes." That is quite passable as a sentence ; it is humdrum journeywork in English prose. Something is lacking, though ; the pleasing rhythm has vanished.

Perhaps you have not given much thought to the rhythm of prose. Yet you must often have been displeased in your own composition because of its jerking along like a wagon with un-greased wheels over rough ground—because of a flight of short unaccented syllables, or because of a huddle of heavy syllables. " It reads badly ", you say, and you set about remodelling it. Well, the remodelling will come easily if you closely study sentences such as the ones given for your examination.

To be sure, you must study more than a single sentence in order to appreciate the harmony of a paragraph. That passage of Burke's on page 242 is constantly quoted as a capital illustration of harmonious English prose. It begins with the sentence, " It is now sixteen or seventeen years since I saw the Queen of France, then the Dauphiness, at Versailles ; and surely never lighted on this orb, which she hardly seemed to touch, a more delightful vision." Look at the rhythm of phrases like : " glittering | like the morning | star, | full of life, and splendour, | and joy ", or like " But the age of chivalry | is gone." |

Examine, too, the rhythm of the closing sentence in Sir William Temple's *Discourse upon Poetry*. Read it aloud, and you will

248

agree that it owes much of its effect to its soothing rhythm, its "dying fall". Here it is:

When all is done, | human life is, | at the greatest and the best, | but like a froward child, | that must be played with | and humoured a little, | to keep it quiet | till it falls asleep, | and then the care is over. |

RIGHT WORD (THE)

(a) Bright is the ring of words
When the right man rings them ;
Fair is the fall of song
When the singer sings them,
Still are they carolled and said
On wings they are carried
After the singer is dead,
And the maker buried.

(ROBERT LOUIS STEVENSON.)

(b) He had brought himself to public scorn for lack of a word. What word ? they asked testily, but even now he could not tell. He had wanted a Scotch word that would signify how many people were in church, and it was on the tip of his tongue but would come no further. Puckle was nearly the word, but it did not mean as many people as he meant. The hour had gone by just like winking ; he had forgotten all about time while searching his mind for the word.

(BARRIE relates how *Sentimental Tommy* lost in the essay competition.)

What is the right word for our particular purpose ? It will be, at all events, a word of which we know the meaning. Moreover, it will be one that those to whom we speak or for whom we write will interpret in the required sense. It will serve to carry our thought unimpaired into the minds of others. Usually the choice among possible substitutes is a choice between better and worse ; it is not a choice between right and wrong. And perhaps we are unwise in acting as *Sentimental Tommy* did ; though we may know that a more effective expression exists, the need for getting something done compels us to accept the word ready to hand.

In our search after the right word we shall always consider our audience : the words we use to the child of six will, most likely, differ—and ought to differ—from the words we use to a meeting of town-councillors. It would seem, too, that this consideration of our audience will dictate the avoidance of both slang terms and of foreign phrases. The audience may lack understanding of phrases like " Tommy lifts his elbow too often " for " Tommy drinks too much ", like " scoop the kitty " for " win all the stake ", as well as of phrases imported from abroad.

See also the vigorous onslaught delivered by Robert South against fine phrases in sermons : it comes under the heading " *Verb* " on pages 300–1.

It would seem, too, that we shall give that audience no great trouble in getting at our meaning. Provided they do what we wish—carry the thought we intend to be carried—the simpler the words, the better. In a report upon an Indian tribe called " Gonds " the thought to be put into words was :

> Gonds drink, but seldom get drunk

Six words, you notice, the last five being words of the street and market place, words quite familiar to all of us. Is the verbiage of the official statement really an improvement ?—

> The members of this aboriginal tribe are notoriously addicted to the consumption of alcoholic stimulants, but rarely, if ever, prolong their potations to the point at which intoxication supervenes.

It is also worth notice that the line between what must be described as vigorous idiomatic English and what is slang cannot be drawn with any certainty. For example, which of these phrases having the preposition *on* are to be classed as slang ?—" on the cards " (i.e. liable to turn up) ; " on the carpet " (under consideration or under reprimand) ; " on the nail " (at once) ; " on the square "—or " on the level " (honestly) ; " go on the stump " (travel about making political speeches) ; " be on the fence " (be undetermined in opinion).

(See also the note on " *Simplicity* ".)

RISING RHYTHM. (See "Metre")

Were others angry, I excused them too ;
Well might they rage, I gave them but their due.
A man's true merit 'tis not hard to find ;
But each man's secret standard in his mind,
That casting-weight pride adds to emptiness,
This, who can gratify ? for who can guess ?
The bard whom pilfered pastorals renown,
Who turns a Persian tale for half-a-crown,
Just writes to make his barreness appear,
And strains, from hard-bound brains, eight lines a year ;
He, who still wanting, though he lives on theft,
Steals much, spends little, yet has nothing left :
And He, who now to sense, now nonsense leaning,
Means not, but blunders round about a meaning :
And He, whose fustian's so sublimely bad,
It is not poetry, but prose run mad :
All these, my modest satire bade translate,
And owned that nine such poets made a Tate.
How did they fume, and stamp, and roar, and chafe !
And swear not Addison himself was safe.

(POPE, upon some of his rivals.)

The lines here are made up of iambics, groups of two syllables, in which the first is unstressed, the second stressed : " Wĕre óth | ĕrs áng | rў Í | ĕx cúsed | thĕm, tóo | ". See also the examples of falling rhythm on pages 114–15.

S

SEMI-COLON and COMMA

These sentences help us to see when to use a comma, when a semi-colon :

(a) Give a man the secure possession of a bleak rock, and he will turn it into a garden ; give him a nine years' lease of a garden, and he will convert it into a desert.

(b) I saw her just above the horizon, decorating and cheering the elevated sphere she just began to move in ; glittering like the morning-star, full of life, and splendour, and joy.

(c) Sir, I have found you an argument ; but I am not obliged to find you an understanding.

(*d*) When bad men combine, the good must associate ; else they will fall one by one, an unpitied sacrifice in a contemptible struggle.

The COMMA marks off the smaller members of a sentence. The SEMI-COLON marks off more important parts. Look at these sentences of Macaulay—

Meantime the tide was rising fast. The *Mountjoy* began to move, and soon passed safe through the broken stakes and floating spars. But her brave master was no more. A shot from one of the batteries had struck him ; and he died by the most enviable of all deaths, in sight of the city which was his birthplace, which was his home, and which had just been saved by his courage and self-devotion from the most frightful form of destruction.

Two short sentences, the first and the third, need no internal stops. In the second sentence the comma marks a pause between two co-ordinate clauses, even though here many modern writers would dispense with the comma before *and*. Still, it is advisable to have it in order to make a difference between the *and* joining sentences and the *and* joining phrases, " the broken stakes and floating spars ", for instance. In the fourth sentence Macaulay wishes you to make a more impressive pause. He uses, therefore, a semi-colon, contenting himself with commas for the enumeration that follows. The semi-colon, you note, is not so heavy a stop as the full stop. When, as in the first example, the two sentences might have stood alone but are closely connected in meaning, the semi-colon seems appropriate. You will not have failed to notice, from your examination of current English prose, that the semi-colon is following the colon into disuse. You will read a whole leader in *The Times* without finding an instance.

SENTENCE

(*a*) Astonished grief had swept over the country.
     (SIMPLE SENTENCE.)

(*b*) When, two days previously, the news of the approaching end had been made public, astonished grief had swept over the country.
     (COMPLEX SENTENCE : the additional, or subordinate, part, " when, . . . public," is an ADVERBIAL CLAUSE.)

(c) The vast majority of her subjects had never known a time when Queen Victoria had not been reigning over them.

(COMPLEX SENTENCE: the part, "when Queen . . . them", defining as it does the noun "time", is an ADJECTIVAL CLAUSE.)

(d) That they were about to lose her appeared a scarcely possible thought.

(COMPLEX SENTENCE: the statement, "That they were about to lose her", serves as the subject of "appeared a scarcely possible thought".)

(e) So, taking care not to tread on the grass, we will go along the straight walk to the west front, and there stand for a while, looking up at its deep-pointed porches.

(COMPOUND SENTENCE: two sentences that might have stood separate are joined by the conjunction "and".)

Quite often we speak of the portion of writing from one full stop to another as a SENTENCE; and usually this answer satisfies the grammarians. The SENTENCE is the expression in words of a statement or a question or a command or a request, and it usually contains a subject and a predicate. The SIMPLE SENTENCE contains one subject and predicate: "I am speaking to you from the Cabinet Room at 10, Downing Street" is such a sentence. The COMPLEX SENTENCE contains one or more subordinate clauses: "This morning the British Ambassador in Berlin handed the German Government a final note stating that, unless we heard from them by 11 o'clock that they were prepared to withdraw their troops from Poland, a state of war would exist between us" is such a sentence. The subordinate clauses amplify the word "stating": the words "that . . . us" may be compressed into "this statement". That is, the clauses are equivalent to a noun. The parenthesis, "unless . . . Poland", is, you notice, the expression of a condition: it is what the grammarians call an adverbial clause. The COMPOUND SENTENCE contains more than one simple or complex sentence: such a sentence is this: "He had evidently made up his mind to attack Poland whatever happened; and, although he now says he put forward reasonable proposals which were rejected by the Poles, that is not a true statement."

Some sentences are loosely strung. It is as though the speaker, or the writer, is developing his thought as he gives it expression; and he adds a new fact, softens a previous assertion, suggests a fresh explanation. *And, but, though, if*—these conjunctions carry the thought along. In our formal business writing, where clear and concise expression is the desirable attribute, we shall avoid sentences that might end in more than one place. But for leisurely reading, for pleasant gossiping, the loose sentence is the natural vehicle of thought. See how Charles Lamb confides in you. He has no need to take you by the button-hole; you delight to hear him talk. Here, as instances of loose sentences, is a little of his playful study of himself:

Few understood him, and I am not certain that at all times he quite understood himself. He too much affected that dangerous figure—irony. He sowed doubtful speeches and reaped plain, unequivocal hatred. He would interrupt the gravest discussion with some light jest, and yet, perhaps, not quite irrelevant in ears that could understand it. Your long and much talkers hated him. That informal habit of his mind, joined to an inveterate impediment of speech, forbade him to be an orator, and he seemed determined that no one else should play that part when he was present. He was *petit* and ordinary in his person and appearance. I have seen him in what is called good company, but when he has been a stranger, sit silent, and be suspected for an odd fellow, till, some unlucky occasion provoking it, he would stutter out some senseless pun (not altogether senseless perhaps, if rightly taken), which has stamped his character for the evening.

Other sentences are closely built: till you reach the end, the mind cannot rest. It is as though thought and expression spring together complete. The writer has put pen to paper only when completeness is achieved. Here is such a well-girt sentence: " The reasonable requirement that parents of evacuated children should contribute to their maintenance comes to-day into force." Compare that period with this, in which the expansion of " requirement " is loosely attached : " The reasonable requirement comes into force to-day, that parents of evacuated children should contribute to their maintenance." The second is the kind of sentence you produce in your unstudied talks with your friends. The first betokens careful arranging so that no mistake shall arise in regard to the placing of the parts. Examine this sentence : " There is no valid reason why the requirement should adversely affect the dispersal of the children—provided, of course, that the administration is tactful and a fair view is taken of those on whom the charge is placed." You will agree that the proviso introduced by the dash shakes your mind from a state of rest. Your mind had been carried smoothly from " There " to " children ". You were prepared to acquiesce, or to deny ; and suddenly the proviso shoots up its head making you reconsider. Perhaps it would have been less disturbing if the sentence had begun with the proviso. Omit the patronising " of course ", and begin " Provided that the administration ".

Look at these two sentences from the same paragraph, and consider whether a tightening-up is desirable : " The evacuation scheme was not designed to relieve parents of natural responsibilities, nor should it be allowed to do so when the ability to pay is unquestionable."

Would it have been better to place the limiting clause " when . . . unquestionable " between " nor " and " should ". Here it is more closely knit : " The evacuation scheme was not designed to relieve parents of natural responsibilities ; nor, when the ability to pay is unquestionable, should it be allowed to do so." Read the two versions aloud, and ask yourself which is the better.

You must at all events agree that the second of the sentences sprawls in ungainly manner. It seems to call for a good deal of re-arrangement : " On the other hand, to ask too much from slender resources would undoubtedly induce parents to bring children home, and a workman's wages must be substantial to allow his parting with six shillings in respect of each child if the number should be three or more." You notice that at two points—at " home " and at " child "—the mind is at a stay long before the full stop heralds a rest. Doubtless you will like to try your hand at pulling the sentence together.

SESTET (at times spelled " SESTETTE "). (See " Sonnet ")

The Latin word for " six " is " sex " ; and " Sestet " is applied to a group of six lines of verse, more particularly to the last six lines of a sonnet on the Petrarchan model. See the example in the note on " Sonnet " (page 266).

255

SHALL or WILL ?

(*a*) " We shall pass by them presently." " But, if we only wait a few minutes, there will be no danger of our seeing them at all."

(JANE AUSTEN, *Pride and Prejudice*.)

(*b*) " I will see her," said Arthur. " I'll ask her to marry me once more. I *will*. No one shall prevent me."

(THACKERAY, *Pendennis*.)

That story of Barrie's is a good one. The clever young Scotsman had been offered what many eagerly desired, regular work as leader writer for a great newspaper. He is elated. But he quite successfully hides his elation ; and the Editor proceeds :

" By the way, you are Scotch, I think ? " " Yes," said Rob. " I only asked," the Editor explained, " because of the shall and will difficulty. Have you got over that yet ? " " No," said Rob, sadly, " and never will." " I shall warn the proof-readers to be on the alert," Mr. Rowbottom said, laughing, though Rob did not see why.

The Southerner very likely finds no difficulty in seeing why nor any difficulty at all in using the auxiliaries : " I never shall " would come trippingly to the tongue. " *Shall* " is his auxiliary of the future tense in the first person. (" When I read the several dates of the tombs, of some that died yesterday and some six hundred years ago, I consider that great day when we shall all of us be contemporaries and make our appearance together.") " *Will* " is the Southerner's auxiliary of the future tense for the second and third persons. (" Your choice will not ultimately fall on me.")

This general rule does not, as you know, conclude the matter. Thackeray was a Londoner ; and yet in his sentence you have *will* in the first person, and *shall* in the third. You have noted the reason for this deviation from the general rule : there is the expression of something more than the future tense. In the sentence " will " has its old sense of resolution. " I will see her " is " I am resolute to see her ". So you have it in Burke's sentence : " Gentlemen, I will see nothing except your former kindness, and I will give way to no other sentiments than those of gratitude."

" Shall " being used with the second or third person implies besides the futurity the sense of compulsion, of obligation. " Thou shalt love thy neighbour " is the injunction, the command that does not always bring about " Thou wilt love thy neighbour ". And notice the apt use of " shall " in the peroration of Lincoln's famous speech :

> We here highly resolve that these dead shall not have died in vain ; that this nation, under God, shall have a new birth of freedom ; and that government of the people, by the people, and for the people, shall not perish from the earth.

Look at an example or two. " They will probably return to-day fortnight " simply gives information ; " They shall return to-day fortnight " implies a determination on the part of the speaker to bring about the event. You ask one " Will you dine with me ? " " Won't I ? " is a more hearty acceptance of the invitation than " I will ", and this—indicating a promise—more to the point than " I shall ". Which of these is the simple statement, which the threat ? " I shall see him to-morrow, when he will tell me all about it ", " I will see him to-morrow, when he shall tell me all about it ".

And here is a capital instance from one of Mr. Churchill's war speeches : " We shall not fail or falter ; we shall not weaken or tire. Neither the sudden shock of battle nor the long-drawn trials of vigilance and exertion will wear us down." " Shall ", you agree—the matter-of-fact statement of futurity, needing no emphasis and put forward as admitting of no doubt—is much better than " will " for the first personal pronoun " we ". And " will " is better than " shall " as the verb attendant on " shock and trials " ; the calm simple declaration would be spoiled by " shall ". For " shall " would here suggest bluster.

SHOULD or WOULD ?

   (*a*) If you would sit thus by me every night,
       I should work better, do you comprehend ?

(ROBERT BROWNING.)

   (*b*) I should be in time if I hurried.
   (*c*) I would that my tongue could utter
       The thoughts that arise in me.

(TENNYSON.)

The distinction between "should" and "would" follows closely the distinction between "shall" and "will". To express the conditional mood, without other modification, we have "should" for the first person, "would" for the second and third. A writer to *The Times* puts the distinction cleverly:

I should like to endorse your correspondent's complaint of the growing misuse of "will" and "shall". In particular, I would protest against the common mistake that so many, even the announcers of the B.B.C., frequently make of saying "I would like to say", when they mean "I would say" or "I should like to say". "I would" means "I should like". "I would like to say" means, therefore, "I should like to like to say" or "I wished I liked saying", which is clearly not what they would say, and therefore not what they *should* say, as they obviously enjoy having their say. Quite recently a distinguished critic from Ireland, in taking us Englishmen to task for our mispronunciation of our own language, asked, "Would we understand Shakespeare if we had a record of his voice and could produce it in a gramophone?" Of course we would, if we could; but the question is whether we should.

Here is a little extract in which Dr. Johnson shows the distinction:

I would injure no man, and should provoke no resentment; I would relieve every distress, and enjoy the benedictions of gratitude. I would choose my friends among the wise, and my wife among the virtuous; and therefore should be in no danger from treachery or unkindness. My children should by my care be learned and pious, and would repay to my age what their childhood had received.

SILENT LETTERS

Salmon: Debt: Delight: Psalm: Deign: Rhyme.

These words all contain letters visible to the eye in writing or print, but inaudible to the ear: *l, b, gh, p* and *l, g, h, e*, have no effect upon the sound of the words. On the whole the letters of English words give reliable guidance to the sounds; but doubt often intrudes, and one of our spelling difficulties arises from this doubt. You know that curious collection—" Though the tough cough and hiccough plough me through."—devised to show how many sounds are attached to the combination *ough*. Words like *biscuits* (kits), *circuit* (serket), *salmon* (samn); *fissure* (fisher); *leopard* (lĕp); *yeoman* (yō); all present difficulties.

Very likely you have heard the story of the schoolmistress who seemed never to forget that she was a schoolmistress. She bought salmon, and the shopman wrote on her bill "sammon". This spelling she disliked, and she indicated it to the cashier, "Sorry, madam," said the cashier, "I've spoken before about his spelling. They don't teach them to-day in school like they used to do when you and me was young." And he altered the word to "psalmon".

The silent letter has at times some justification. It may help to connect the English word with its equivalent in another language. *Salmon* itself is an instance of this. Like many of our words denoting dishes for the table—*beef, mutton, veal, pork*, and so on—the word came in with the Normans; and, like modern French *saumon*, it remained here for long without an *l*. But when people began to study the origins of words and found that in Latin the *l* appeared—appeared because it represented a sound—they inserted the *l* in the English word too; and now we must write it under penalty of being thought either ignorant or careless. The words *debt* and *receipt* contain other instances of intruders intended to show origins. In the time of Chaucer *debt* had no *b*: much later than Chaucer we find the phrase "To paye large usury besides the due det". The learned, about the time when printing began to crystallise our spelling, introduced the *b* so that we should not overlook the connection of *debt* and *debtor* with the Latin *debitum*. In *debit* and *debenture* (the document giving evidence of *indebtedness*) the *b* is both seen and heard. So it is with *receipt*: in the first edition of Bacon's *Essays* we have "Every defect of the mind may have a special receit." The *p* was introduced to bring *receipt* into line with *receptacle* and *recipient*.

The silent *p*—in words like *psalm, psalter*, which came into the language at a very early date—is another result of a learned revision; it was adopted in order to show the Grecian origin of the words. On the other hand, in some words recently coined from the Greek, the *p* has always been present, though very likely never sounded. Such words are *psychology*, the study of the workings of men's minds and *pseudonym*, a fictitious name assumed by an author.

From the noun *nestling*, where the *t* is usually sounded, we have the verb " *to nestle* " where the *t* is silent. Other instances of *t* seen but not sounded are in the words, *bristle*, *thistle*, *jostle*, *castle*, *ostler*, *mistletoe*, *wrestle*, *apostle*, *bustle* (rhyming with *muscle*), *Christmas*, and *waltz* (which should rhyme with *false*, though the sight of the spelling induces at times the sounding of the *t*).

The silent letter that occurs more often than any other—the silent *e* in words like *whole*, *were*, *have*, *there*, *purpose*, *mere*, *alone* —originates in various ways and has various duties. At times it remains as a silent reminder of a lost inflexion. In some words the final *e* has the effect of making the preceding vowel long : contrast *răt and rāte*, *băr and bāre*, *sĭt and sīte*, *nŏt and nōte*, *cŭt and cūte*.

SIMILES

(*a*) As in the forests the leaves fall thick from the trees at the first frosts of autumn, or as the birds flock shorewards from the deep when the cold of the year sends them fleeing over the sea to sunny lands, so the shades stood, each praying for the first passage over, and they stretched out their hands in longing for the farther shore.

(VIRGIL, *Aeneid*.)

(*b*) His legions, angel forms, who lay entranced
Thick as autumnal leaves that strow the brooks
In Vallombrosa.

(*Paradise Lost*.)

(*c*) When I arose and saw the dawn,
    I sighed for thee ;
When Light rode high, and the dew was gone,
And noon lay heavy on flower and tree
And the weary Day turned to his rest
Lingering like an unloved guest,
    I sighed for thee.

(SHELLEY, *To the Night*.)

(*d*)   But what said Jacques ?
Did he not moralize the spectacle ?

260

O yes, into a thousand similes.
First, for his weeping into the needless stream ;
Poor deer, quoth he, *thou mak'st a testament*
As worldlings do, giving thy sum of more
To that which had too much : then, being there alone,
Left and abandoned of his velvet friends :
'Tis right, quoth he ; *thus misery doth part*
The flux of company.

(As You Like It.)

(*e*) He is quite unsocial ; his conversation is quite mono-
syllabical ; and when, at my last visit, I asked him what
o'clock it was, that signal of my departure had so pleasing
an effect on him that he sprang up to look at his watch,
like a greyhound bounding at a hare.

(So Dr. Johnson speaks of a visit to an
old schoolfellow.)

(*f*) Saul and Jonathan were lovely and pleasant in their lives,
and in their death they were not divided : they were
swifter than eagles, they were stronger than lions.

(Samuel ii.)

(*g*) As cold waters to a thirsty soul, so is good news from
a far country.

(Proverbs.)

(*h*) O my Luve's like a red, red rose
That's newly sprung in June ;
O my Luve's like the melodie
That's sweetly played in tune.

(Burns.)

" As the leaves fall " ; " as the birds flock " ; " as autumnal
leaves " ; " like an unloved guest " ; " than eagles " ; " than
lions " ; " as cold waters "—these are SIMILES or COMPARISONS.

When a teacher would have you imagine the new thing, he
links it with the old, the well-understood thing. He compares.
You thereby have time to ponder over the new idea ; and the
points of similarity are bound to make the new idea more vivid.
At times the image of the tangible thing is used to impress the
thought of the intangible thing :

Blessed is the man that findeth wisdom and getteth understanding : for the merchandise thereof is better than silver,

and the gain thereof better than gold ; it is more precious than pearls, and all things thou canst desire are not to be compared to her.

Professor Einstein, being asked whether science might some day convert matter into energy for practical purposes, doubted. An apt expression enables us to understand his doubt : " To release ", he said, " the energy of stores of atoms by bombarding with sub-atomic particles is like shooting birds in the dark in a country where there are very few birds."

To facilitate understanding is one reason—and a very important reason—for the comparisons and the similes that we meet with in our reading. Another reason there is. The well-devised simile adds to our enjoyment of the author. It may be that a tasteful ornament is introduced for its own sake and for the fun of the thing. For we need not give entire assent to Dr. Johnson's dictum : " A simile, to be perfect, must both illustrate and ennoble the subject." You cannot say that the simile in this couplet ennobles the subject,

> And like a lobster boiled, the morn
> From black to red began to turn.

This ingenious comparison is very different from the implied comparison in

> But look, the morn in russet mantle clad,
> Walks o'er the dew on yon eastern hill.

Still, in certain moods, you rejoice in such unexpected similes.

You know that sonnet of Keats in which he tells us of his intense delight upon finding an English translator able to give him what Homer wrote, and in Homer's manner. The sonnet begins, " Much have I travelled in the realms of gold ". The wonder of the new discovery, the sudden dawning of a new light on the glorious writings of ancient Greece, is vividly illustrated by other discoveries. You understand what a revelation to the mind there must have been, because you can readily understand the astonished wonder of the other discoverers. The poet " heard Chapman speak out loud and bold " :

> Then felt I like some watcher of the skies
> When a new planet swims into his ken ;

Or like stout Cortez, when with eagle eyes
He stared at the Pacific—and all his men
Looked at each other with a wild surmise—
Silent upon a peak in Darien.

The theme, that "the glories of our blood and state are shadows, not substantial things", is a familiar one. It gains renewed freshness by the comparison, the simile :

The Worldly Hope men set their Hearts upon
Turns ashes—or it prospers ; and anon,
Like Snow upon the Desert's dusty Face
Lighting a little Hour or two—is gone.

SIMPLICITY

(*a*) Give me a look, give me a face
That makes simplicity a grace.

(BEN JONSON.)

(*b*) "In that case," said the Dodo, solemnly rising to its feet, "I move that the meeting adjourns for the immediate adoption of more energetic remedies——"
"Speak English," said the Eaglet. "I don't know the meaning of half those long words, and what is more, I don't believe you do either."

(*Alice in Wonderland.*)

In our speaking and writing we seek the co-operation of our hearer or our reader, and we are unwise when we make that co-operation a hard task. It is discourtesy, too. Good manners as well as good sense prompt us to make our meaning easy of access. Making it so we strive after the grace of simplicity : we select the simple word rather than the difficult word when that simple word fully expresses our intended meaning. "Yes" is usually better than "the answer is in the affirmative" ; "his nose" better than "his prominent feature", "rats" better than "the whiskered vermin race".

The idea that simple directness calls for elaboration sometimes leads to strange pranks. Chaucer wrote the line.

The smiler with the knife under the cloak ;
Dryden expanded it into

Next stood Hypocrisy with holy leer,
Soft smiling and demurely looking down,
But hid the dagger underneath the gown.

Don't you agree that the one line of Chaucer has more effect on your mind than the three lines of Dryden?

The proverb is " Take care of the pence and the pounds will take care of themselves "; and we all grip its meaning at once. Yet the version was solemnly presented:

> The proverbial oracles of our parsimonious ancestors have informed us that the fatal waste of fortune is by small expenses, by the profusion of sums too little singly to alarm our caution, and which we never allow ourselves to consider together.

Mr. Churchill knows how effective the simple expression can be: witness the defiance, uttered during the dark days of 1940, of the German onslaught, " Let it rage and roar; we shall come through."

SLANG (JARGON)

(a) " This is a swell joint you've got here, Lady," said the steam-fitter. " The only thing that makes me sore is to think that all of this Hot-Dog you're throwing in comes out of the pockets of poor hard-working guys such as me."

" You wrong us," said the great Lady, in a tone of gentle sadness. " My husband never flimflams the poor labourer. All that he has made he has made by shifting the cut on the small stockholders."

(From GEORGE ADE'S *American Fables*.)

(b) *Tweeney* (anxiously): Have I offended of your feelings again, sir?
Crichton : A little.
Tweeney (in a despairing outburst): I'm full o' vulgar words and ways; and though I may keep them in holes when you are by, as soon as I'm by myself they comes in a rush like beetles when the house is dark. I says them gloating-like, in my head—" Blooming ", I says, and " All my eye " and " Ginger " and " Nothink ".

(From J. M. BARRIE'S *The Admirable Crichton*.)

With your familiars and for the fun of the thing you may use a jargon other than standard educated speech. It is a kind of secret language, readily interpreted by you and your intimates, but only guessed at by outsiders. " Don't funk answering," says Margaret; " This is a let-down for me "; " What did you do to the copper ? " And her mother, grieving at the colloquial " funk " and " let-down " and " copper " might ask her not to use such slang ; but the words to her friends were good currency.

Slang may be an intended mockery of formal propriety, a conscious offence against recognised usage. The user would have no difficulty in expressing the required meaning in terms that all would approve. But the slang term seems a much more lively mode of expression, and out it comes : a first-class ship in Lloyd's Register is A1 ; a dinner or person or place that is heartily approved of also is A1. The speaker has resolved ; he might say, " Well, I'll do it." But that is tame. So " Here goes " he says.

It is sometimes difficult to tell whether a word or a phrase is to be classed as standard English or as slang, the base coin of language. For a standard is something fixed, something by comparison with which other things are measured. A fixed language, however, would be a dead one ; and our language is very much alive, is constantly adopting new words, modifying old words. These words, for instance, *phiz*, *chap*, *cab*, *mob*, were once slang shortenings of *physiognomy*, *chapman* (or dealer), *cabriolet*, and *mobile vulgus* (the fickle multitude). Two of them, *cab* and *mob*, have now lived down their origin, and are recognised in polite society ; the other two are still absent from the visiting list. So the Roman soldiers in their talk used *testa* (a pot or shell) instead of the classical *caput* for head. *Testa* was certainly slang in Cæsar's day, but nowadays the ordinary word for head is *testa* in Italian and *tête* in French. Slang is like rebellion in this : that when it is successful none presumes to call it slang.

Here again is " grouse ", used as a verb in the sense of grumble. The dictionaries put the word down as " Army slang, origin unknown ". But to-day it has made its way into the leading articles of reputable newspapers : " The British taxpayer ", we were told after the introduction of the 8*s*. 6*d*. Income Tax Budget, " will grouse but he will pay " (*The Times*).

One very deplorable effect of using slang is that its user loses touch with the reality of things. " Where d'jer get it ? " asks one London urchin of another. " I knocked it orff " is the answer : " I stole it " would be self-condemnation, but very likely a salutary self-condemnation.

SOLECISM

(*a*) A wary man he is in grammar, very nice as to solecism or barbarism.

(DRYDEN.)

(*b*) Him and me is a pair I'm afraid.

(So Dora says in *Fanny's First Play*.)

" Speaking incorrectly " is the translation of the Greek adjective from which the noun " solecism " comes to us. The modern fashion is to use the word for an error or impropriety of any kind in writing or speaking. You have committed a solecism when in your composition there is a construction not sanctioned by good English usage : " Was you there ? " is an instance : the singular form *was* mates ill with the plural form *you*.

In the prose that imitates conversation, particularly in dramatic prose, you will find many solecisms. For in familiar talk we are not studious of grammatical correctness : " I believe most intensely in the dignity of labour," says Octavius in the best oratorial manner. But Straker is unimpressed, and he replies : " That's because you never done any, Mr. Robinson. My business is to do away with labour. You'll get more out of me and a machine than you will out of twenty labourers, and not so much to drink either."

" Regardless of grammar they all cried ' That's him ! ' " ; and it is indeed remarkable how, in the quick give and take of speech, we do offend against the formal rules of the grammar books.

SONNET

" Sonnet "—the original is " a little sound or song "—means in modern English a well-defined poetic form. It is a stanza complete in itself ; and it expresses one main idea in fourteen ten-syllabled lines in which the prevalent foot is the iambic. We have two widely different types of sonnet. The first, often called the Shakespearean, consists of three rhymed quatrains with a concluding rhymed couplet. Nor is there, as a rule, any interlocking in the rhymes of the quatrains. In Shakespeare's sonnets the three quatrains reiterate in varied forms the one idea, and the couplet comes with the clinching effect of an epigram. Look at this example :

When to the sessions of sweet silent thought
   I summon up remembrance of things past,
I sigh the lack of many a thing I sought,
   And with old woes new wail my dear time's waste;

Then can I drown an eye, unused to flow,
   For precious friends hid in death's dateless night,
And weep afresh love's long-since-cancelled woe,
   And moan the expense of many a vanished sight:

Then can I grieve at grievances foregone,
   And heavily from woe to woe tell o'er
The sad account of fore-bemoaned moan,
   Which I new pay as if not paid before.

But if the while I think on thee, dear friend,
All losses are restored and sorrows end.

That is : I lament the past ; I weep over the past ; I grieve over
the past ; I have present consolation.

The second type, at times called the Petrarchan Sonnet, is
quite different in build : it is quite different, too, in its effect.
It has the fourteen lines of iambic pentameter. But the usual
build is an octet of eight lines developing one idea ; and this is
followed by a sestet of six lines developing a kindred idea. Look
at this of Wordsworth's as an instance : it is his sonnet " Upon
Westminster Bridge " :

Earth has not anything to show more fair :
Dull would he be of soul who could pass by
A sight so touching in its majesty :
This City now doth like a garment wear
The beauty of the morning : silent, bare,   } Octet
Ships, towers, domes, theatres, and temples lie
Open unto the fields, and to the sky,
All bright and glittering in the smokeless air.

Never did sun more beautifully steep
In his first splendour valley, rock, or hill ;
Ne'er saw I, never felt, a calm so deep !
The river glideth at his own sweet will :   } Sestet
Dear God ! the very houses seem asleep ;
And all that mighty heart is lying still !

You will at times meet with a sonnet having another rhythm
than the iambic and another length of line than the pentameter.

Milton, always chafing against restrictions, uses the Petrarchan form ; but he sometimes makes his fourteen lines into a single unit. No break occurs between octet and sestet. Look at this " On His Blindness " :

When I consider how my light is spent
Ere half my days, in this dark world and wide,
And that one talent which is death to hide
Lodged with me useless, though my soul more bent } *Octet*
To serve therewith my Maker, and present
My true account, lest he returning chide,
Doth God exact day-labour, light denied ?
I fondly ask : But Patience, to prevent

That murmur, soon replies ; God doth not need
Either man's work, or his own gifts : who best
Bear his mild yoke, they serve him best : His state } *Sestet*
Is kingly ; thousands at his bidding speed
And post o'er land and ocean without rest :
They also serve who only stand and wait.

SOPHISTRY. (See " Fallacy ")

The argument seems to be sound ; it is, however, unsound, fallacious. The argument misleads those unable to detect where it fails. Such argument is SOPHISTRY. The Greek name signified a clever device or trick ; it was a display of ingenuity in reasoning. We now use " sophistry " or " sophism " to describe an argument deliberately intended to deceive.

Controversy arises. One of the contenders hits upon an ingenious argument , and it may well be, so enamoured of his ingenuity does he become, that he sacrifices common sense to it. Such sacrifice occurs now and again even on our judicial benches, and the sturdy common sense of the House of Lords may be requisite to brush away the sophistry.

That case of *Kirk* v. *Eustace* illustrates. A deed of separation secured to a wife a maintenance allowance. The husband died. Did that cause the allowance to cease ? Yes ; said two of the judges in the Court of Appeal. You cannot make the husband's estate liable. The arguments upon which they based their decision were curious. " The state of things ", said one Lord

Justice, "contemplated in a separation deed is the living apart of husband and wife. One being dead, they can hardly be said to be living apart." The deed, therefore, ceases to be operative. The other Lord Justice, agreeing with this decision, declared that the deed assumed conscious and deliberate action which, when the husband was dead, could not continue.

The reasoning, we must hasten to add, was not like that of Milton's Belial, deliberately devised to mislead others :

> his tongue
> Dropped manna, and could make the worse appear
> The better reason, to perplex and dash
> Maturest counsels.

Perhaps, in fact, we should not use " sophistry " ; for sophistry is argument framed so as to deceive others about the truth. It is not in strictness applicable to the argument that leads to self-deception. However that be, the House of Lords gave both arguments short shrift. The House agreed unanimously with the third, the dissenting Lord Justice, and declined to read into the deed anything other than a quite unambiguous covenant to pay the wife an allowance for her life.

SOUND : A FACTOR IN COMPOSITION

(a) And from the turf a fountain broke
And gurgled at our feet.
(WORDSWORTH.)

(b) All round the coast the languid air did swoon
Breathing like one that hath a weary dream.
Full-faced above the valley stood the moon ;
And like a downward smoke, the slender stream
Along the cliff to fall and pause and fall did seem.
(TENNYSON, *The Lotos Eaters*.)

(c) "The moral of that is," said the Duchess, " ' Take care of the sense, and the sounds will take care of themselves.' "
(*Alice in Wonderland*.)

(d) There is not in the whole book one single page of pure and vernacular English, one single period of which you forget the sense in admiration of the sound.
(MISS MITFORD'S severe censure of Scott's *Waverley*.)

In (a) you notice the predominance of the letters g and f.

The throat letter, the guttural *g*, seems peculiarly apt for words like " gurgle ", " gargle ", " struggle ", " wriggle "; the gushing *f* sound is similarly apt for words like " foam ", " froth ", " front ", " fount ", and Wordsworth makes his lines very effective by the use of the letters.

Tennyson, too, was keenly anxious about the sound of his words. " I had rather ", he said, " lose a thought than get two *s's* together." In *The Lotos Eaters* he wishes to give you, by the very sounds of the words he uses, the idea of drowsiness, of care-soothing sleep. How languidly each line of the passage above dies away in an *m* or an *n*! Coupled with the gentle rhythm of the lines it almost lulls you to rest; you feel that you can hardly reach the end of the long twelve-syllabled line that ends the stanza. Note how he plays on the *l* of *lotos* and the long *o* in these lines :

The Lotos blooms below the barren peat :
The Lotos blows by every winding creek :
All day the wind breathes low with mellower tone :
Thro' every hollow cave and alley lone,
Round and round the spicy downs the yellow Lotos-dust is
    blown.

Or read aloud these lines from another of Tennyson's poems. The aged Ulysses cannot rest from travel. He hears the compelling call of the sea ; and again he rouses up the men that had shared his exploits : don't you find that sound echoes sense in lines like ?—

The lights begin to twinkle from the rocks :
The long day wanes : the slow moon climbs : the deep
Moans round with many voices.

Note the expressive and apt words, *twinkle*, *wanes*, *moans*, *voices*. But the whole poem is admirable in this matter.

The beauty of passages—in prose no less than in verse— depends much upon the cunning arrangement of sounds. Study again, for one illustration, this wonderful passage :

Arise, shine ; for thy light is come, and the glory of the Lord is risen upon thee. For, behold, the darkness shall cover the earth, and gross darkness the people ; but the Lord shall arise upon thee, and his glory shall be seen upon thee.

And the Gentiles shall come to thy light, and kings to the brightness of thy rising. . . . The sun shall be no more thy light by day; neither for brightness shall the moon give light unto thee: but the Lord shall be to thee an everlasting light, and thy God thy glory. Thy sun shall no more go down; neither shall thy moon withdraw herself: for the Lord shall be thine everlasting light, and the days of thy mourning shall be ended.

Certainly, the meaning of this passage is important, very important. But concentrate your attention for a little while upon the sounds and the arrangement of them. Read the passage aloud two or three times. What makes the opening invocation so effective—the wonderful clarion call " Arise, shine ; for thy light is come " ? Don't you agree that the long vowel *i*, repeated four times in the seven words, is the cause ? This sound runs through the passage, now heard faintly and almost as though drowned in other vowel sounds, now ringing out in jubilant triumph. You hear it once only and far off in the second sentence—" For, behold, the darkness shall cover the earth, and gross darkness the people ; but the Lord shall arise upon thee, and his glory shall be seen upon thee." See how it recurs in the sentence : " And the Gentiles shall come to thy light and kings to the brightness of thy rising."

The undertone, the *or* sound of *Lord*, *glory*, *more*, *for*, gives the needed contrast and foil to the long *i* sound. Look at the dying close, where you have the bright, exhilarating sounds followed by those words insistent upon peace and rest : " The Lord shall be thine everlasting light, and the days of thy mourning shall be ended." You will yourself notice many other happy combinations of sounds. And when you have studied the passage thoroughly merely in regard to its sounds, you will go back to the thoughts expressed and be far better able to grasp them.

SOUND AND MEANING

> The trumpet's loud clangor
> Excites us to arms,
> With shrill notes of anger
> And mortal alarms

> The double double double beat
> > Of the thundering drum
> Cries " Hark ! the foes come ;
> Charge, charge, 'tis too late to retreat ! "
>
> > > (DRYDEN.)

You have formed the habit of discriminating among sounds. Now, this faculty of discrimination is not only greatly useful ; it also adds much to your delight in life. For it enables you the better to appreciate music and the poetry that is kin to music. Thus, you cannot fail to note how the sounds in the example suggest in themselves the meaning of the words ; and you enjoy the lines the more through noting.

Read aloud these seven lines from Tennyson's *Passing of Arthur* : he is speaking of Sir Bedivere, " First made and latest left of all the knights ", making his hazardous way as he carries the wounded king down the rocks towards the lake.

> Dry clashed his harness in the icy caves
> And barren chasms, and all to left and right
> The bare black cliff clanged round him, as he based
> His feet on juts of slippery crag that rang
> Sharp-smitten with the dint of armed heels—
> And on a sudden lo ! the level lake,
> And the long glories of the winter moon.

Isn't that an astonishing contrast between rough and smooth ? The sounds prominent in the lines about the perilous descent are explosive dentals (*t* and *d*) or labials (*p, b, f, v*) or harsh throat sounds (gutturals like *k* and *ng*). Why, in the first three lines you have no fewer than six *k* sounds : in *clashed, caves, chasms, black, cliff, clanged*. Try for yourself and note that these sounds —the dentals, pronounced by applying the tip of the tongue to the front upper teeth, the labials, formed by the complete or partial closure and then the sudden opening of the lips, and the gutturals—are all difficult sounds to make. And the poet cunningly combines them so that they do in fact sound harshly and in keeping with what is described. You are bound to notice, too, the staccato effect, the sounds cut short and not gliding smoothly into one another, of the first part, contrasted with the drawn-out effect—" sostenuto ", the musician calls it—of the close.

Then comes " Lo ! the level lake, and the long glories of the winter moon " with its succession of liquid sounds (*l*, *m*, *n* sounds that, as Ben Jonson says, " melt in the sounding, and are therefore called liquids, the tongue striking the root of the palate gently ").

In that sonnet of Shelley's beginning " I met a traveller from an antique land ", you have the same effect of contrast produced in much the same way. Shelley is describing the shattered statue with its vaunting inscription

> My name is Ozymandias, King of Kings,
> Look on my works ye mighty, and despair.

Then comes the impressive close with its contrast :

> Nothing beside remains : round the decay
> Of that colossal wreck, boundless and bare,
> The lone and level sands stretch far away.

The last line, with its alliterative *lone*, *level*, *sands*, *stretch*, its smooth syllables, its regular rise and fall, obliges you to see the desert stretching to the farthest horizon.

It is true that we are, on occasion, tempted to think a writer so attentive to sound as to trouble little about sense. When in 1942 the Copyright Bill was being debated a member quoted, to illustrate what trivial stuff the Bill was designed to protect, these lines of Wordsworth :

> I met Louisa in the shade
> And, having seen that lovely maid,
>   Why should I fear to say
> That she is ruddy, fleet, and strong,
> And down the rocks can leap along,
>   Like rivulets in May.

Still—though " Louisa was a lovely lass " might have sufficed —the lines are worth hearing for their sound.

SOUND and SYMBOL

(*a*) *comb* (rhyming with *home*) ; *climb* (rhyming with *time*) *psalm* (*sahm*) ; *ghost* (rhyming with *toast*) ; *sign* (rhyming with *fine*) ; *know* (rhyming with *blow*) ; *deign* (rhyming with *plain*) ; *scent* (where the initial sound is the same as in *sent*) ; *victuals* (pronounced *vittles*) ; *light* (rhyming with *bite*).

(The words given have a consonant symbol without a corresponding sound.)

(b) *can, kind, queen, thick, six* (five ways of representing the *k* sound ; *c, k, q, ck, x* (where it is one of the combination *ks*)) ; *fruit, philosophy* (two ways of representing the *f* sound) ; *zeal, rose* (two ways of representing the *z* sound) ; *soon, mice, practice, practise* (two ways of representing the *s* sound).

(The words given show inconsistency in the representation of consonant sounds.)

(c) *stable, ride, live, tongue, defence, mouse, toe* (in these words the final *e* is mute) ;

(d) *child, fly, height, eye, dye, guise* (six ways of representing the long *i* sound) ;

(e) *he, knee, yield, plead* (four ways of representing the long *e* sound) ; *she, measure, sink* (the *sh* in *she*, the *s* in *measure*, the *nk* in *sink* stand for three separate sounds for which the English alphabet has no separate symbol).

As the instances show, the English way of writing sounds is not a scientific way. One sound is represented in more than one way ; one symbol is not restricted to the representation of one sound. Note the inconsistency illustrated by the pairs of words, like in sound, different in look, that follow. In " With my bow and arrow " *bow* rhymes with *so* ; in " Orpheus with his lute made trees, And the mountain-tops that freeze, Bow themselves when he did sing " *bow* rhymes with *now*. In " gill of a fish " the *g* is as in *girl* ; in " a gill of beer " the *g* is as in *jilt*. In " A shadow lowered on the fields " *lowered* has the vowel of *now* ; in " Lower the flag " *lower* has the vowel of *so*.

Many efforts have been made to bring about the adoption of a more rational way of representing the sounds of our words. The late Poet Laureate, Robert Bridges, in *The Testament of Beauty*, made a few tentative innovations : here are a few lines from the poem :

Without thine ear, sound would hav no report,
Nature hav no music ; nor would ther be for thee
any better melody in the April woods at dawn
than what an old stone-deaf labourer, lying awake
o' night in his comfortless attic, might perchance
be aware of, when the rats run amok in his thatch.

Notice that he declines to write the mute *e* in *hav* and *ther*. But he retains, very wisely perhaps, the mute *e* in words like *thine* (where its function is to show that the preceding *i* is long and not like the *i* in *thin*), and also in *nature, aware,* and *awake*. And he, like so many spelling reformers, has not been greatly successful in inducing others to follow his example.

SPECIFIC TERMS. (See " **Concrete and Specific Terms** ")

SPELLING : A FASHION

The chief reporter was denouncing John Milton for not being able to tell him how to spell " deceive ". " What is the use of you," he asked indignantly, " if you can't do a simple thing like that ? " " Say ' cheat '," suggested Umbrage. So Kirker wrote " Cheat ".

(BARRIE, *When a Man's Single.*)

In some companies you had better rob a church than eat peas with your knife : to some folk you are more to censure for errors in spelling than for lack of thought. SPELLING, indeed, is no more than a convention, a fashion of the time. Yet, unless you are very eminent or very eccentric, you had better conform to the fashion.

" Words commonly misspelled " is a title affixed to lists laboriously compiled from the beginning of the nineteenth century, and examination of the lists shows how persistent some of the errors are. We recount the prevalent ones here, comforting you, however, by the assurance that none of the words that follow are other than those approved by orthographers. We give the correct forms only. This comforting assurance is needed because many are convinced—and there is sound reason for their conviction—that the one way to learn correct spelling is to observe correct spelling, to observe closely and to imitate. To look at errors is to invite yourself to make errors.

" Double or single ? " is often answered wrong. For it appears that, in the competition for relative frequency, *paralleled* and *accommodation* run one another close. The doubling of the last *l* in *paralleled* and the giving to *accommodation* only a single *m* are both deplorably frequent. Certainly, as regards the latter word, if we connected the word in our minds with " commodity " and " commodious ", we should not stray. In the word *harass* too, a doubled " r " often intrudes ; and because in " fill full " we have the doubled " l " many among us stumble over *fulfil*.

One word—*bus* with its plural *buses*—might have been expected to have a double *s*, like *fuss* and *puss* : it owes its simple *s* to the fact that it is a shorthand form of *omnibus*. The Latin ending has too much vitality to be modified. Besides, *buss* was already in the language. When we do, as we may, write *buss*, we should mean *kiss* ; and *busses* are *kisses*.

This matter of derivation, indeed, trips one up in a good many ways. We are apt to forget that when *vigour* and *valour* and similar words ending in " our " become adjectives the *u* disappears. Write *vigorous* and *valorous*. At times, though, the primary word is spelled correctly and a needless change is made in the derivative : the noun *synonym* retains its form when made into an adjective, *synonymous*.

Here is a short list of the nuisances in English spelling. Stop at this point, and persuade a friend to dictate them to you. If you make fewer than three mistakes in the twenty words presented, you may congratulate yourself ! You are among the " good spellers ".

acquiesce, aqueduct, embarrass, committee, moccasin, enforceable, collapsible, inveigle, concede, proceed, disastrous, separate, gauge, banister, disappoint, truly, seize, belief, leisure, desiccated.

Tradition is strong in this country. That is why the spelling of our words has, in the main, persisted since the days of the introduction of printing. The early printers did make some effort to be consistent in their representation of sounds by signs. The representation was far from perfect even then. It was decidedly better, though, than it is now. For, whereas the sounds of words have greatly changed since Caxton set up his printing press at Westminster, the spelling is substantially the same. Some changes have been effected. It is perhaps time more came about.

The symbols for both our consonants and our vowels vary to an astonishing and—to a foreigner at all events—a baffling extent. Here for example is the *k* sound. It masquerades in varied guises : *k* (*kiss, king, keen, book, like*) ; *c* (*can, catch, come, cup, cruel, secret, claim, act, distinct*) ; *ch* (*echo, anchor, school, ache*) ; *ck* (*thick, sick*) ; *q* (*queen, quit, quarrel, quart, requite, quash, squadron*) ; and *x* where it shares a representation with *s* (*example, luxury, six, fox*).

Now and then in our reading we lose something of what the writer intended by our failure to note a similarity of sounds under difference of sign. In the first seven lines of Wordsworth's fine sonnet, for example, the *k* sound is echoed throughout. How many *k* sounds do you find ?

> Tax not the royal Saint with vain expense,
> With ill-matched aims the Architect who planned
> (Albeit labouring for a scanty band
> Of white-robed Scholars only) this immense
> And glorious work of fine intelligence !
> —Give all thou canst ; high Heaven rejects the lore
> Of nicely-calculated less or more.

The eye discerns one only, in the word *work*. Read the lines aloud, though, and the ear listens to at least one in every line : *tax, expense, architect, scanty, scholars, work, canst, rejects, calculated*, eleven in all, since *architect* and *calculated* have each two *k* sounds.

And here are a few sentences that will illustrate our inconsistency in representing our vowel sounds. In " Peace hath her victories No less renowned than war ", the long *e* sound comes in *peace* as *ea* ; in " What a piece of work is man ! " the long *e* sound comes in *piece* as *ie*. In " Read the Will ! we'll hear it, Antony " *read* has the long *e* again as *ea* ; in a " reed shaken with the wind " *reed* has the long *e* as *ee*.

A good many of the strange spellings in English words arise from mistakes about the origin of words. In *Paradise Lost* you have the comparison of Satan's spear with " the tallest pine Hewn on Norwegian hills, to be the mast of some great ammiral ". Of the flagship, that is, the ship carrying the Admiral's flag. Milton's spelling is more consistent with the origin of the word than our " admiral ". The Arabian word *amir* (or *ameer*) means " commander "; the " ammiral " was the " Command-of-the-sea ". Some misguided scholar, though, thought that the word came from the Latin, that it must be connected with " admire " and " admiration " and " admirable ". So the *d* pushed itself in; and now none of us can avoid thinking of the admiral as a man to be admired—as, in fact, he very likely is.

This word " scent " is another with an intruding letter, the *c* that is visible but not audible. The French verb *sentir*, meaning " feel, perceive ", by other senses as well as by the sense of smell, is the origin of the word, and in early use there was no *c*. In *Hamlet*, for instance, there is the line : " But soft, methinks I sent the Morning's Ayre." The word " scent " is, in fact, connected with " sensitive " (feeling quickly and acutely), with " sense " (the power of feeling) and with " consent " (to feel as another feels). The mistaken notion that, in some way or another, the word was allied to " science " and " scientific " caused the appearance of the *c* which we must not now omit on pain of being thought very ignorant.

" Delight " is another interesting word. The *gh* is not sounded, and never has been sounded. Yet, because it was erroneously thought to be allied to " light " (in which *gh*, silent now, was formerly sounded) the *gh* presents a needless difficulty. *Delit* was the Old French word : Chaucer, speaking of the farmer's house in which it forever *snowed* of meat and drink, has " To lyven in delit was ever his wone." " Delight " is connected, not with " light " but with such words as " delectable ", " delicious ", " delicacies ".

SPELLING AND PRONUNCIATION (PROPER NAMES)

Beauchamp (bee-cham); Belvoir (bee-ver); Cholmondeley (chum-ley); Colquhoun (co-hoon); Keighley (keeth-ly); Keynes (kayns); Tollmache (toll-mash).

Both English vowels and English consonants despise consistency. The divergence between form and sound is bad enough in ordinary words ; it is appalling when it comes to proper names. *Menzies*, we learn, is pronounced *meng-is* or *ming-iz* ; and so it should be to keep touch with the old name. For the *z* has no *zed* sound. Its intrusion is due to the fact that printers in Scotland were—in the days of their poverty—obliged to eke out the scantiness of their resources by using one symbol for two letters : both *y* and *z* appear as the same character. That is why the Englishman is apt to go astray in names like *Dalziel* (which is to be pronounced *dee-ell*).

But then, we have heard the B.B.C. announcer give the name of Mr. Menzies, former Australian Prime Minister, as it is spelled. In fact the announcer was correct ; for Mr. Menzies does pronounce his name in conformity with its spelling. Perhaps he, or his immediate forebears, found the task of correcting mispronunciation a little wearisome—a little irritating, too. We should in truth be tolerant about the pronunciation of proper names. Often enough consistency cannot be expected. The great actor Kemble was once told about a bet upon the debatable question of how he pronounced " Coriolanus ". Was the first *o* long or short ? He came before the curtain and announced the play for the next evening. The play would be " Shakespeare's tragedy of *Cŏriolanus*, in which I myself shall have the honour of appearing as *Cōriolanus*."

"SPLIT" INFINITIVE

(*a*) Miss . . . has decided to again hold a Sale of Work at her home. She has felt it necessary to recently relinquish the S.P.G. Secretaryship.

(From " *Our Own Parish Magazine* ".)

(*b*) I do not believe God means us thus to divide life into two halves—to wear a grave face on Sunday, and to think it out of place to even so much as mention Him on a week-day.

(From Preface to *Alice in Wonderland*.)

(*c*) The Court may decree a dissolution of the partnership

279

when a partner has been guilty of such conduct as is calculated to prejudicially affect the carrying on of the business.

(From Section 35 of the Partnership Act, 1890.)

When an adverb, or other words, comes between *to* and the verbal part of an infinitive, you have what many condemn as " a split infinitive " : " to again hold " and " to recently relinquish " in (*a*) are examples.

It is curious how this fault—if fault it is—has in these days come to be regarded as a reliable test means of discriminating between good and bad writers of English. A split infinitive is to some people one of the deadly sins in writing ; and a good many other people in authority, oblivious maybe to more serious faults, do recognise a split infinitive when they see it, and are clamorous in reprobation. Until, therefore, you have gained an unassailable reputation as a writer, you had better not split your infinitives. And, indeed, a sentence in which a split infinitive occurs does usually grate upon a sensitive ear.

The infinitive consists nearly always of the word *to* along with the uninflected form of the verb : in the lines—

> The Gipsy crew,
> His mates, had arts to rule as they desired
> The workings of men's brains—

" to rule " is the infinitive ; in the line—

> And I myself seem half to know thy looks

" to know " is the infinitive, and the modifying " half " is not obtruded between the two words making up that infinitive. It needs a very urgent reason—a determination that the modifier shall certainly be understood to go with the infinitive—to diverge from that rule. Modifying words should be placed either before or after the infinitive, not inside it. Look at the sentence, " Maidens come to dance around the Fyfield elm by night." You must feel it to be a most awkward collocation to have " Maidens come to around the Fyfield elm by night dance." So we have such well-known phrases as " humbly to acknowledge ", " so to do ", " not to have done ", " with one accord to make our common supplications "—the modifying word or words, " humbly ", " so ", " not ", " with one accord " being outside the infinitive.

The fact that diligent search will unearth a split infinitive in writings of the best does not, you will admit, justify its habitual use. Nor does the fact prevent the feeling of awkwardness and restraint in reading. Here is Browning's (from *Fra Lippo Lippi*)

> You should not take a fellow eight years old
> And make him swear to never kiss the girls.

Perhaps it was a little of Browning's perversity, his deliberate flouting of convention, that made him write " to never kiss ", when " never to kiss ", is more natural—and reads better, too. And here are Byron's lines :

> To sit on rocks, to muse o'er flood and fell,
> To slowly trace the forest's shady scene,

Don't you think that " slowly to trace " would be better ? But a poet is quite prepared to sacrifice grammar for the sake of his rhythm.

Thus you would not venture to disturb the split infinitive in Herrick's song " To the Lark ", even though the noun is thrust between *to* and the verb form. Indeed, you could not ; for so doing, you would throw the verses out of gear. Here is the song ; the split infinitive might elude you on a casual reading, but you will find it :

> Good speed, for I this day
> Betimes my matins say,
>   Because I do
>   Begin to woo.
>   Sweet singing lark,
>   Be thou the clerk,
>   And know thy when
>   To say Amen.
>   And if I prove
>   Blest in my love,
>   Then thou shalt be

High Priest to me,
At my return
To incense burn,
And so to solemnise
Love's and my sacrifice.

About the specimen in Walt Whitman's note upon Thomas
Carlyle, for whom he had so great reverence, you may be doubtful. But you will enjoy the paragraph in which it occurs :

> And now that he has gone hence, can it be that Thomas
> Carlyle, soon to chemically dissolve in ashes, remains an
> identity still ? In ways perhaps eluding all the statements,
> lore, and speculations of ten thousand years—eluding all
> possible statements to mortal sense—does he yet exist, a definite
> vital being, a spirit, an individual—perhaps now wafted in
> space among those stellar systems, which, suggestive and
> limitless as they are, merely edge more limitless, far more
> suggestive system ! I have no doubt of it. In silence, of a
> fine night, such questions are answered to the soul.

STANZA

(*a*) Full many a gem of purest ray serene
The dark unfathom'd caves of ocean bear :
Full many a flower is born to blush unseen,
And waste its sweetness on the desert air.

(GRAY, *Elegy*.)

(*b*) Where are the songs of Spring ? Ay, where are they ?
Think not of them, thou hast thy music too,
While barréd clouds bloom the soft-dying day
And touch the stubble-plains with rosy hue ;
Then in a wailful choir the small gnats mourn
Along the river-sallows, borne aloft
Or sinking as the light wind lives or dies ;
And full-grown lambs loud bleat from hilly bourn ;
Hedge-crickets sing, and now with treble soft
The redbreast whistles from a garden-croft ;
And gathering swallows twitter in the skies.

(KEATS, *Ode to Autumn*.)

(c) *Amiens :* My voice is ragged : I know I cannot please you.

Jacques : I do not desire you to please me : I do desire you to sing. Come, more ; another stanza : call you them stanzas ?

(*As You Like It.*)

The Italian word " *stanza* " is a " stopping-place ". Applied to English verse forms, " stanza " means a group of verses arranged on a definite plan—a plan ranging from simple groupings of similar lines to quite elaborate groupings of varied lines. Here, for instance, is an intricate pattern of Herrick's :

Ah Ben !
Say how or when
Shall we thy guests,
Meet at those lyric feasts,
Made at the Sun,
The Dog, the Triple Tun ;
Where we such clusters had,
As made us nobly wild, not mad ?
And yet each verse of thine
Out-did the meat, out-did the frolic wine.

My Ben !
Or come again
Or send to us
Thy wit's great overplus ;
But teach us yet
Wisely to husband it,
Lest we that talent spend ;
And having once brought to an end
That precious stock,—the store
Of such a wit ; the world should have no more.

" A verse " is quite often used where " a stanza " would be perhaps more fitting ; indeed, the minister that asked his congregation to omit the " second stanza " of the hymn would be affected and a little ridiculous.

STRESS IN WORDS

The three aspects of a word are its spelling, its meaning, and its sound. One element of the sound is the STRESS. Upon which syllable in a many-syllabled word does the stress fall? And upon which words in a sentence does the stress fall?

Quite naturally, we stress in our speech the words to which we wish to call special attention. We may imply several meanings by varying the stress in such a question as " Did you get the problem right? " Stress " did " and you suggest a doubt; stress " you " and you express surprise; stress " right " and you seek information. By stressing a word usually unstressed you give it prominence as you do *a* and *the* in a sentence such as " Fox never wanted *a* word, but Pitt never wanted *the* word."

In single English words the main accent is normally at the beginning. These are instances : *báker, dáily, státesman, bédroom, wáistcoat*. Where a modifying prefix occurs the stress remains as in the unmodified word : *to-dáy, ashóre, forgíve, mistáke*, and so on.

A variation in the stress may be used, to indicate a change in meaning : a *gláss cáse* is a case made of glass ; a *gláss-cáse* is a case for holding glass ; a *bláckbird* is the name of species, a *bláck bírd* is a bird that is black.

The main trouble in regard to stress results from our tendency to shift the stress towards the beginning of words ; and this trouble is peculiarly incident when words have been introduced from other languages. The original stress may in time be made to conform to the English custom, and whether it is so made appears to be determined by capricious fashion. The adjective *cómparable* has the stress on the first syllable ; the noun *compárison* and the verb *compáre* have the accent on the second syllable. So with the adjective *sólid* and the noun *solídity* and the verb *solídify*.

There is, quite naturally, a dislike of many unstressed syllables together. This dislike accounts for variations such as follow : *líbrary* and *librárian* ; *músic* and *musícian* ; *hístory* and *histórian* ; *cóntroversy* and *controvérsial* ; *órigin* and *oríginal* ; *médicine* and *medícinal* ; *úniverse* and *univérsal*.

The most important distinction, often serving a useful purpose, is that some words being nouns or adjectives are stressed at the beginning, being verbs towards the end. We say " a farewell dinner " but " Farewell, Farewell ! " ; we say " an upstart " but " Upstarted Spurius " ; we say " the accent is on this syllable " but " He accented his words strongly " ; we say " the imports and exports of the country " but " the country imports wheat and exports coal " ; we say " a modern-language supplement " but " the father supplemented the son's allowance ". In the sentence, " Was he absent yesterday ? " the word " absent " has the stress upon the first syllable. In the sentence, " You must not absent yourself without leave ", the word " absent " has the stress upon the second syllable. When you speak of " an august monarch ", the stress in " august " is on the second syllable. When, however, you speak of the " month of August ", the stress is on the first syllable.

Here are a few words that call for care. " Laboratory ", say the dictionaries, consists of a first-stress syllable, followed by a flight of four unstressed syllables ; but before long, very likely, we shall, finding this flight a nuisance, stress the second syllable. And note the stressed syllable in *grimace, vagary, advertisement, decadent, despicable, formidable, impious, reveal, revelation.*

When the English accent falls, as it nearly always does, strongly on a syllable at the beginning of the word, then the unstressed part of the word is likely to be obscured. Thus, though they look different, the final syllables of *neighbour, doctor, colour,* sound the same as the final syllable of *butter.* This weakening often heralds loss ; so *fortnight* was once *fourteen-night,* and *butler* was once *botiler (bottler).*

STYLE

(a) The style of the Liturgy did not satisfy the Doctors of the Jerusalem Chamber. They voted the Collects too short and too dry ; and Patrick was entrusted with the duty of expanding and ornamenting them. In one respect, at least, the choice seems to have been unexceptionable; for if we may judge by the way in which Patrick paraphrased the most sublime Hebrew poetry, we shall probably be of opinion that, whether he was or was not qualified to make the Collects better, no man that ever lived was more competent to make them longer.

I will give a specimen of Patrick's workmanship: "He maketh me", says David, "to lie down in green pastures; he leadeth me beside the still waters." Patrick's version is as follows: "For as a good shepherd leads his sheep in the violent heat to shady places, where they may lie down and feed (not in parched, but in fresh and green pastures), and in the evening leads them (not to muddy and troubled waters, but) to pure and quiet streams; so hath he already made a fair and plentiful provision for me, which I enjoy in peace without any disturbance."

(MACAULAY.)

(*b*) Proper words in proper places, make the true definition of a style.

(SWIFT.)

(*c*) Style is the dress of thought.

(*d*) Style is a constant and continual phase or tenour of speaking and writing, extending to the whole tale or process of the poem or history, and not properly to any piece or member of a tale; but is of words, speeches, and sentences together; a certain contrived form and quality, many times natural to the writer, many times his peculiar by-election and art, and such as either he keepeth by skill or holdeth on by ignorance, and will not or peradventure cannot easily alter into any other.

(PUTTENHAM on "Style".)

Your STYLE is the manner that is characteristic of you. Applied to writing, style signifies the kind of expression, having regard to its clearness, its effectiveness, its beauty and so on. Here, for instance, are three little extracts that, you will agree, are in different styles.

(*a*) I suffered the utmost solicitude when I entrusted my book to the carrier, though I had secured it against mischances by lodging two transcripts in different places. At my arrival, I expected the patrons of learning would contend for the honour of a dedication, and resolved to maintain the dignity of letters by a hearty contempt of pecuniary solicitations.

(b) Lo! as I looked back for seventy leagues through the mighty cathedral, I saw the quick and the dead, that sang together to God, together that sang to the generation of man. All the hosts of jubilation, like armies that ride in pursuit, moved with one step. Us, that with laurelled heads were passing from the cathedral, they overtook, and, as with a garment, they wrapped us round with thunders greater than their own.

(c) I have eaten no vegetables, and only a very moderate quantity of meat; and it may be useful to my readers to know that the riding of twenty miles was not so fatiguing to me at the end of my tour as the riding of ten miles was at the beginning of it. Some ill-natured fools will call this " egotism ". Why is it egotism?

Look at the words chosen: in (a) a swarm of stately words remote from the talk of ordinary men, long-tailed Latin words in *-tion* and *-tude*; in (b) picturesque and poetic words in keeping with the impassioned prose; in (c) words current in the street and market place.

Look, too, at the build of the sentences: in (a) are carefully-balanced, well-girt, almost uniform sentences; in (b) are loose, rambling sentences, the poetic phrases coming impetuously as though struggling to overtake the thought; in (c) are straight-forward, precise, short sentences, disdaining to wander in search of ornament.

Here are three more extracts from the writers of (a), (b), (c). Would you care to couple the extracts?

(d) Cataracts and rapids were heard roaring ahead, and signs were seen far back, by help of old men's memories, which answered secretly to signs now coming forward on the eye, even as locks answer to keys. It was not wonderful that in such a haunted solitude, with such a haunted heart, Joanna should see angelic visions and hear angelic voices.

The voices whispered to her for ever, the duty self-imposed, of delivering France. Five years she listened to these monitory voices with internal struggles.

(e) If I had a village at my command, not a tea-kettle should sing in that village ; there should be no extortioner under the name of country shop-keeper, and no straight-backed, bloated fellow, with red eyes, unshaven face, and slipshod till noon, called a publican and generally worthy of the name of *sinner*. Well-covered backs and well-lined bellies would be my delight.

(f) He is surely a public benefactor who finds employment for those to whom it is thus difficult to find it for themselves. It is true, that this is seldom done merely for generosity or compassion, almost every man seeks his own advantage in helping others, and therefore it is too common for mercenary officiousness to consider rather what is graceful than what is right.

You probably coupled easily enough (f) with (a), (d) with (b), (e) with (c).

You readily perceive that, in speaking of style, you are not blaming one manner of writing and praising another. A simple style may be a delight to the readers ; but, then, so also may an ornate style. Here is what Dr. Johnson said in answer to Boswell's

We find people differ much as to what is the best style of English composition. Some think Swift's the best, others prefer a fuller and grander way of writing.

Johnson : Sir, the two classes of persons whom you have mentioned, don't differ as to good and bad. They both agree that Swift has a good neat style ; but one loves a neat style, another loves a style of more splendour. In like manner, one loves a plain coat, another loves a laced coat ; but neither will deny that each is good in its kind.

Perhaps, too, we err in looking upon a particular writer as master of one style only ; we err greatly in so looking upon Shakespeare and many another great writer. Why, in *Hamlet* you have a whole gathering of different styles. You have the grand style :

If thou didst ever hold me to thy heart,
Absent thee from felicity awhile,
And in this harsh world draw thy breath in pain,
To tell my story.

You have the lecture style :

O, it offends me to the soul, to hear a robustious periwig-pated fellow tear a passion to tatters, to very rags, to split the ears of the groundlings, who, for the most part, are capable of nothing but inexplicable dumb shows and noise. I would have such a fellow whipped for o'er doing Termagant ; it out-herods Herod. Pray you, avoid it.

You have the swift conversational style, this between Hamlet and Horatio, for instance :

Hamlet : Why, saw you not his face ?
Horatio : O yes ! my lord ; he wore his beaver up.
Hamlet : What ! looked he frowningly ?
Horatio : A countenance more in sorrow than in anger.

SUBJECT and PREDICATE. (And see " Sentence ")

(*a*) **Underneath this sable hearse**
Lies the subject of all verse.

(*b*) To be wise and love **exceeds man's might.**

(*c*)   **Him** the Almighty Power
Hurled headlong flaming from the ethered sky.

(*d*) The wicked industry of some libellers, joined to the intrigues of a few disappointed politicians, **have in their opinion been able to produce this unnatural ferment in the nation.**

The normal sentence consists of SUBJECT and PREDICATE : in the examples the predicate appears in the heavier type. It is the sentence that is the unit of thought : the study of grammar and composition is of value insofar as it enables us to compose better sentences. Words are our material for building a sentence. The sentence is a stage towards the finished article—letter, essay, report. The sentence may be a DECLARATORY one, making a clear statement (" The valiant never taste of death but once ") ; or an INTERROGATIVE one, asking a question (" How can I help England ? ") ; or an IMPERATIVE one, giving a command (" Ring out the false, ring in the true ") ; or an OPTATIVE one, expressing a wish (" Would I were with Edwin there ! ")

SUBJUNCTIVE MOOD. (See " Grammar ")

> It is not growing like a tree
>   In bulk, doth make Man better be ;
> Or standing long an oak, three hundred year,
> To fall a log at last, dry, bald, and sere :
>   A lily of a day
>   Is fairer far in May,
> Although it fall and die that night—
> It was the plant and flower of Light.
> In small proportions we just beauties see ;
> And in short measure life may perfect be.
>
> (BEN JONSON.)

A special form of the verb was once used in the dependent clause, a clause introduced by some such conjunction as *if* and *though*. In the lines above *fall* and *die* are in the subjunctive mood. In modern writing probably, in modern speech almost certainly, the indicative forms *falls* and *dies* would be used.

SUFFIX. (See " Prefix ")

SUPERLATIVES. (See " Comparison ")

SYLLABLE. (See " Length of Words ")

(*a*) Mon-o-syll-a-ble ; Di-syll-a-ble ; Pol-y-syll-a-ble.

(*b*) Tomorrow, and tomorrow, and tomorrow,
Creeps in this petty pace from day to day,
To the last syllable of recorded time ;
And all our yesterdays have lighted fools
The way to dusty death.

(*Macbeth*, V, VII.)

A SYLLABLE is a vocal sound (or sounds) uttered with a single effort, and forming either a word or an element of a word. The syllable has a vowel (or vowel-equivalent) and it may have also a consonant or consonants : in the line, " O come, all ye faithful ", *O* is a syllable in itself, *come* is a syllable, *faith-ful* is a disyllable.

There is an easy development in meaning (as in the Macbeth quotation) to " the smallest-part ". There is another development when, as so often in English, the noun is used as a verb, meaning " to utter " : in *Comus*, for instance, Milton has :

> Airy tongues, that syllable men's names
> On sands and shores and desert wildernesses.

By far the greatest number of words *in use*, in speech especially, are monosyllables : listen to the talk around you, and it is only at intervals that you hear a word of two syllables (disyllable), and only rarely a word of more than two syllables (polysyllable). The gradual change of English from an inflected to an uninflected language has brought about the preponderance of the single syllable word. There is, you will note, no such preponderance of single syllable words in the vocabulary of English—the full range of words as exhibited in the dictionary.

SYNONYMS. (See also " Words, Choice of ")

(*a*) Deliver us from all sedition, privy conspiracy, and rebellion.

(*Litany.*)

(*b*) Knowledge is proud that he has learned so much.
Wisdom is sorry that he knows no more.

(COWPER.)

(*c*) *Fluellen :* What call you the town's name where Alexander the Pig was born ?
Gower : Alexander the Great ?
Fluellen : Why ? I pray you, is not pig great ? The pig, or the great, or the mighty, or the huge, or the magnanimous, are all one reckonings, save the phrase is a little variations.

(SHAKESPEARE, *King Henry V.*)

(*d*) At her feet he bowed, he fell, he lay down.

(*Judges.*)

There are few instances of really substitute words; there are many instances of two or more words in the one language with the same general sense but with some slight shade of difference, or used in different contexts. SYNONYM is the learned word for such substitutes: " begin " and " commence ", " behaviour " and " deportment ", " snapdragon " and " antirrhinum " are pairs of synonyms.

The English language is rich in its possession of such groups of words, groups like *proud, dignified, haughty, arrogant, supercilious*. As you see, however, you would not, without considering the matter, substitute one of the group for another. " The proud peacock ", you say, as you see him spreading his gay feathers. It is not, " the dignified peacock "; the sight of the display amuses, not awes. You may be, quite rightly, proud of your achievements, proud of having overcome great difficulties. You would be quite wrong, though, if your achievements should make you supercilious—contemptuous, that is—of the achievements of others. And which of these synonyms—*sublime, majestic, grand, beautiful, pretty*—would you select to describe the *Falls of Clyde*. Shakespeare speaks of " The uncertain glory of an April day ". Isn't *uncertain*, in that connection, better than *fickle* or *changeable* or *passing* or *transitory* ?

So, too, you can separate the senses of the three nouns in (*a*). " Sedition " is the " sitting apart " in order to revile the Government; " privy conspiracy " is the plotting together engendered by such talk; " rebellion " is the outward movement against the Government. Shakespeare often makes a deal of fun by his using the variants that we call synonyms: " Shall I tell you a lie ? " asks Sir Hugh in *The Merry Wives of Windsor*—" I do despise a liar as I do despise one that is false; or as I despise one that is not true."

In our actual composition there is often a choice. The first expression may be good. The second that comes to mind may be better, though: and you do yourself wrong not to revise your composition. John Sand's first version (in Barrie's play *What Every Woman Knows*) was: " Gentlemen, the Opposition are calling to you to vote for them and the flowing tide, but I solemnly warn you to beware lest the flowing tide does not engulf you." " The second way is much better ", said the critic; and the second way was, " Gentlemen, the Opposition are calling to you to vote for them and the flowing tide, but I ask you cheerfully to vote for us and dam the flowing tide."

The synonyms often result from the fact that a word has been introduced from abroad where we already had a word to express the idea : *hearty* is the Old English, *cordial* is from the Latin ; *deadly* is the Old English, *mortal* from the Latin. So with *motherly* and *maternal* ; *lively* and *vivacious* ; *watery* and *aqueous*. At times the interloper has quite pushed out the native. Thus, the negative of *hope* was in Old English *wanhope*. Now *despair* has quite ousted *wanhope*. Charles Lamb writes " In hope sometimes, sometimes in despair, yet persevering ever."

It is noteworthy that for many of our adjectives corresponding to Old English nouns we have gone to Latin. The noun *eye* has the adjective *ocular* : noun *house*, adjective *domestic* : noun *land*, adjective *agrarian* ; noun *mind*, adjective *mental* ; noun *moon*, adjective *lunar* ; noun *son*, adjective *filial* ; noun *sun*, adjective *solar* ; noun *sea*, adjective *marine* ; noun *letter*, adjective *epistolary* ; noun *city*, adjective *urban*.

SYNTAX

It is not likely that any one will now see the game of fives played in its perfection for many years to come—for Cavanagh is dead, and has not left his peer behind him. It may be said that there are things of more importance than striking a ball against a wall ; there are things indeed which make more noise and do as little good, such as making war and peace, making speeches and answering them, making verses and blotting them, making money and throwing it away. But the game of fives is what no one despises who has ever played at it. It is the finest exercise for the body, and the best relaxation for the mind.

(From WILLIAM HAZLITT's Essay,
" The Indian Jugglers ".)

SYNTAX is arrangement. Above are four sentences, the syntax of which one could not improve. In other words, the arrangement of the sentences is such that (1) there is no ambiguity about the meaning and we reach that meaning with an economy of attention ; (2) the sentence reads well.

The questions we may profitably put to ourselves as we examine a sentence of a good writer, are first, *Why that word?* Next, *Why that order of words?* For, owing to the loss of inflexion, the order or arrangement—the syntax, that is—becomes of very great importance in English. An ill-arranged sentence may give an unintended meaning—at any rate to a perverse reader, intent upon fault-finding. How would you re-arrange this sentence, " Messrs. So-and-so's telescopes make clear and distinct objects almost invisible to the naked eye " ? Evidently, the intended meaning is " Messrs. So-and-So's telescopes make objects, almost invisible to the naked eye clear, and bright."

T

TAUTOLOGY (PLEONASM): and see " RELEVANCE '

(*a*) Heywood and Shirley were but types of thee,
　　Thou last great prophet of tautology ;
　　Even I, a dunce of more renown than they,
　　Was sent before but to prepare thy way.
　　　　　　　　　　　　　(DRYDEN, *MacFlecknoe.*)

(*b*) The Honourable Mrs. Jamieson has only just quitted me
　　and, in the course of conversation, she communicated to
　　me the intelligence that she had yesterday received a call
　　from her revered husband's quondam friend, Lord Maul-
　　ever. You will not easily conjecture what brought his
　　lordship within the precincts of our little town.
　　　　　　　　(Miss Jenkyns in *Cranford* writes her letter
　　　　　　　　　　　　　　　　　　　　in this style.)

(*c*) But now I am cabined, cribbed, confined, bound in
　　To saucy doubts and fears.
　　　　　　　　　　　　　　　　　　　(*Macbeth.*)

The Greek prefix *tauto* signifies " the same " ; the Greek word *logos* signifies " word ". TAUTOLOGY is the saying of the same thing over again. It may be a vice of style. It is when it springs

294

from the lack of a clear perception of the meaning of the words we use : you could not, for instance, justify expressions like " I would much rather prefer to walk " or, unless you want to summon smiles by the purposed reiteration, " This show is free, gratis, and for nothing." Dryden, in his strictures on his rival —his rival of whom he writes " Thy tragic muse gives smiles, thy comic sleep "—castigates the tautology as a vice. Yet it need not be : where, as in the Shakespeare quotation, intense feeling causes the mind to dwell upon an idea, its repetition in differing words may be quite effective. Nor need you blame the peculiarly English way of joining two or even three words, much the same in meaning, but with differing origins and calling up differing feelings, for the expression of one idea : you do well to keep your " hands from picking and stealing and your tongue from evil-speaking, lying and slandering " ; you are right to " acknowledge and confess your sins and wickedness ".

Pleonasm—the Greek word *pleon* means " more "—also denotes a superfluity of words. The extract from Miss Jenkyns's letter is an instance ; you prefer, for instance, to her second sentence something like " you could not guess what brought him here ", eight short words for sixteen, some long ; and surely you prefer the crisp " she told me " to the woolly " she communicated to me the intelligence."

" THAT " (PRONUNCIATION and FUNCTION)

The pronunciation of " that ", as of many other words, depends upon the use of the word. Read aloud the sentence " I swear that that is true " : you have pronounced the first " that ", the conjunction, with a different vowel sound and a different accent from the vowel sound and the accent of the second " that ", the demonstrative pronoun. Read Hamlet's line " Give me that man that is not passion's slave " : again you have two different sounds to the one group of letters. You stress the demonstrative adjective, " *That* man " ; you do not stress the relative pronoun in, " that is not passion's slave ".

As with many of our English words, this word seen in isolation cannot be described with certainty. We cannot tell what part of speech it is ; we cannot indicate its pronunciation. Look at these varied uses. In " Bless us ", cried the Mayor, " what's that ? " " That " is a pronoun, anticipatory of the name to be given. In Dickens's sentence, " I was on my guard for a blow, he was that passionate ", " that " must be described as a demonstrative adverb : it is, in fact, synonymous with " so ".

In " This is the house that Jack built " we have " that " with a differing pronunciation and a different function. It is now a relative pronoun. So it is in Milton's invocation to the nightingale,

> Sweet bird that shunn'st the noise of folly,
> Most musical, most melancholy !

With the same pronunciation, but used as a connecting link between two sentences, " that " is a conjunction in

> All arguments but most his plays persuade
> That for anounted dullness he was made.

So it is in both instances in the lines :

> I sometimes think that never blows so red
> The Rose as where some buried Cæsar bled ;
> That every Hyacinth the Garden wears
> Dropt in her Lap from some once lovely Head.

THIRD PERSON (FIRST PERSON : SECOND PERSON)

(a) Taking Cæsar's gown all bloody in his hand, he laid it open to the sight of them all, showing what a number of cuts and holes it had upon it.

(NORTH, Plutarch.)

(b) If you have tears, prepare to shed them now.
You all do know this mantle : I remember
The first time ever Cæsar put it on ;
'Twas on a summer's evening, in his tent,
That day he overcame the Nervii :
Look ! in this place ran Cassius' dagger through :
See what a rent the envious Casca made ;
Through this, the well-beloved Brutus stabb'd.

(SHAKESPEARE, Julius Cæsar.)

In pronouns the form used for the person speaking (*I, we,*) is FIRST PERSON : that for the person spoken to (*thou, you*) is SECOND PERSON ; that for the person or thing spoken of (*he, she, it*) is THIRD PERSON. There are usually corresponding distinctions in verbs : *I am, thou art, he is,* and so on. In (*a*) you have a narrative in the third person. In (*b*) you have the same narrative made dramatic by being put into the first and second persons : *he* becomes *I* ; *them* becomes *you* ; and so on. The English idiom when a first person pronoun and another are together is to postpone the first person : *You and I are aware : He and I were there.* The idiom of Latin, more in keeping with actuality, gives precedence to the first person, *Ego et tu.*

On occasions—which probably should be rare—a writer prefers to write in the third person : " Mrs. A. presents her compliments to Mrs. B. and regrets that she is unable to recommend as parlourmaid the girl about whom Mrs. B. writes."

You will be amused by its use in the letters below : you notice that when, as in No. 4, the spirits are strongly moved, the artificial form is deserted in favour of the more direct :

1. Lady Seymour presents her compliments to Lady Shuckburgh, and would be obliged to her for the character of Mary Steadman, who states that she had lived twelve months, and still is, in Lady Shuckburgh's establishment. Can Mary Steadman cook plain dishes well, and make bread, and is she honest, sober, willing, cleanly, and good tempered ? Lady Seymour will also like to know the reason she leaves Lady Shuckburgh's house. Direct under care to Lord Seymour, Meriden Bradley, Wiltshire.

2. Lady Shuckburgh presents her compliments to Lady Seymour ; her ladyship's letter dated October 28th, only reached her yesterday.

   November 3rd : Lady Shuckburgh was unacquainted with the name of the kitchenmaid until mentioned by Lady Seymour, as it is her custom neither to apply for, nor give, characters to any of the under servants, this being always done by the housekeeper, Mrs. Cough, and this was well known to the young woman. Therefore Lady Shuckburgh is surprised at her referring any lady to her for a character. Lady Shuckburgh, keeping a professed cook, as well as a housekeeper in her establishment, it is not very probable she herself should know anything of the abilities or merits of the under servants : she is therefore unable to reply to Lady Seymour's note. Lady Shuckburgh cannot imagine Mary Steadman to be capable of cooking anything except for the servants' hall table. November 4th.

3. Lady Seymour presents her compliments to Lady Shuckburgh, and begs she will order her housekeeper, Mrs. Cough, to send the girl's character. Otherwise another young woman will be sought for elsewhere, as Lady Seymour's children cannot remain without their dinners because Lady Shuckburgh, keeping a professed cook and housekeeper, thinks a knowledge of the details of her establishment beneath her notice. Lady Seymour understands from Steadman that, in addition to her other talents, she was actually capable of cooking food for the little Shuckburghs to partake of when hungry.

4. Madam—Lady Shuckburgh has directed me to acquaint you that she declines answering your note, the vulgarity of which she thinks beneath her contempt, and although it may be a characteristic of the Sheridans to be vulgar, coarse, and witty, it is not that of a lady, unless she chances to have been born in a garret and bred in a kitchen. Mary Steadman informs me that your ladyship does not keep either a cook or a housekeeper, and that you only require a girl who can cook a mutton chop ; if so I apprehend that Mary Steadman, or any other scullion will be found fully equal to the establishment of the Queen of Beauty.
       I am, Madam, Your Ladyship's, etc.,
                         ELIZABETH COUGH.

Perhaps it is well to explain, in regard to the allusion in Mrs. Cough's letter, that Lady Seymour was grand-daughter of Sheridan (who wrote *The School for Scandal*). And Lady Seymour had been chosen as Queen of Beauty at a tournament, and this fact may have rankled.

TRIAD

(a) But little do men perceive what solitude is, and how far it extendeth ; for a crowd is not company, and faces are but a gallery of pictures, and talk but a tinkling cymbal, where there is no love.
                         (BACON, *Essay on Solitude*.)

(*b*) O, what a noble mind is here o'er thrown !
The courtier's, soldier's, scholar's, eye, tongue, sword ;
The expectancy and rose of the fair state,
The glass of fashion and the mould of form,
The observed of all observers, quite, quite down.

(*Hamlet.*)

(*c*) The purpose of playing . . . was and is, to hold as 'twere,
the mirror up to nature ;
to show virtue her own feature,
scorn her own image,
and the very age and body of the time his form and
pressure.

(*Hamlet.*)

(*d*) There are no fields of amaranth on this side of the grave :
there are no voices O Rhodope ! that are not soon mute,
however tuneful : there is no name, with whatever emphasis of passionate love repeated, of which the echo is
not faint at last.

(LANDOR.)

A TRIAD is a group of three—three related thoughts expressed
together, three facts supporting and illuminating one another.
With some writers—Bacon in his *Essays* is one—there seems to
be an irresistible tendency to compose these groups ; and very
effective the containing sentences are. Look at these instances
from a single page of Bacon :

Studies serve for delight, for ornament, and for ability.
Their chief use for delight, is in privateness and retiring ;
for ornament, is in discourse ; and for ability, is in the
judgment and disposition of business. . . .
Crafty men condemn studies, simple men admire them,
and wise men use them. . . .
Some books are to be tasted, others to be swallowed, and
some few to be chewed and digested. That is, some books
are to be read only in parts ; others to be read, but not
curiously [i.e. carefully] ; and some few to be read wholly,
and with diligence and attention.

In (*a*), you will agree, the group *crowd . . . faces . . . talk*
reads well ; so does in (*b*) the groups of single nouns, *courtier's,*
soldier's, scholar's, and of the parallel phrases, *the expectancy . . .*
the glass . . . the observed.

TROCHEE. (See " Metre ")

> Why so pale and wan, fond lover?
>   Prythee, why so pale?
> Will, when looking well can't move her,
>   Looking ill prevail?
>   Prythee, who so pale?
>
> Why so dull and mute, young sinner?
>   Prythee, why so mute?
> Will, when speaking well can't win her,
>   Saying nothing do't?
>   Prythee, who so mute?
>
> Quit, quit, for shame! This will not move,
>   This cannot take her,
> If of herself she will not love,
>   Nothing can make her:
>   The devil take her!
>
> (SIR JOHN SUCKLING.)

The prevailing foot of this lyric is a group of two syllables, the first more strongly accented than the second. The lyric, that is, consists of TROCHEES: " Trochee trips from long to short ", says Coleridge. The strong accent of our verse replaces the long syllable of classical verse.

V

VERB

" I speak the words of soberness ", said St. Paul; and " I preach the gospel not with the enticing words of man's wisdom." This was the way of the Apostles' discoursing of things sacred. Nothing here of " the fringes of the North-star "; nothing of " Nature's becoming unnatural "; nothing of " the down of angels' wings ", or " the beautiful locks of cherubims ": no starched similitudes, introduced with a " thus have I seen a cloud rolling in its airy mansion " and the like. No; these were sublimities above the rise of the apostolic spirit. For the Apostles, poor mortals, were content to take lower steps and to tell the world in plain terms, "that he who believed should be saved, and that he who believed not should be damned". And this was the dialect which pierced the conscience, and made the hearers cry out, "Men and brethren, what shall we do?" It tickled not the ear, but sunk into the heart: and, when men came from such sermons, they never commended the preacher for his taking voice or gesture; for the fineness of such a simile, or the quaintness of such a sentence: but they spoke like men conquered with the overpowering force and evidence of the most concerning truths; much in the words of the two disciples going to Emmaus, "Did not our hearts burn within us while he opened to us the scriptures?"

In a word, the Apostles' preaching was therefore mighty and successful because plain, natural, and familiar, and by no means above the capacity of their hearers: nothing being more preposterous than for those who were professedly aiming at men's hearts to miss the mark by shooting over their heads.
(ROBERT SOUTH'S *attack on the ornate language of Jeremy Taylor and his imitators : for a specimen of what is attacked see "Ornate Speech".*)

The VERB is the part of speech that is used to express doing or being: in the passage above *speak, said, preach*, are examples of verbs that express doing; *was, were*, are examples of verbs that express being. When a verb is transitive it needs an object in order to complete the statement made: thus in "It tickled not the ear", *tickled* is a transitive verb in the active voice, and *ear* is the object. The intransitive verb makes in itself the complete statement: thus in "Did not our hearts burn within us?" *did burn* is an intransitive verb.

The verbs expressing being usually have a complement: thus in "The Apostles were content to take lower steps", the complement of the verb *were* is *content to take lower steps*.

VERBIAGE : VERBOSITY. (See "Tautology")

A man is VERBOSE—Adam Smith talks about a "verbose attorney"—when he uses an unnecessary number of words. "He draweth out the thread of his verbosity finer than the staple of his argument" is Shakespeare's description of one such.

There is VERBIAGE, an abundance of words without any real need, as when " In many cases the answers lacked care " is written instead of the more effective " Often the answer lacked care " or " Many answers lacked care " ; or when " It was evident that he was dismayed at the news " is written rather than " Evidently he was dismayed at the news ". Here is Ben Jonson's instance : " I came to the stairs, I took a pair of oars, they launched out, rowed apace. I landed at the Court Gate, I paid my fare, went up to the presence, asked for my Lord. I was admitted." All this is only " I went to the Court and spake with my Lord."

VERS LIBRE (FREE VERSE)

(*a*) Many are the sayings of the wise,
    In ancient and in modern books enrolled,
    Extolling patience as the truest fortitude ;
    And to the bearing well of all calamities,
    All chances incident to man's frail life,
    Consolatories writ
    With studied argument, and much persuasion sought,
    Lenient of grief and anxious thought :
    But with the afflicted in his pangs their sound
    Little prevails, or rather seems a tune
    Harsh, and of dissonant mood from his complaint :
    Unless he feel within
    Some source of consolation from above,
    Secret refreshings, that repair his strength,
    And fainting spirits uphold.

                  (MILTON, *Samson Agonistes*.)

(*b*) I think I could turn and live with animals, they are so
        placid and self-contained ;
    I stand and look at them long and long.
    They do not sweat and whine about their condition ;
    They do not lie awake in the dark and weep for their sins ;
    They do not make me sick discussing their duty to God ;
    Not one is dissatisfied—not one is demented with the
        mania of owning things ;
    Not one kneels to another, nor to his kind that lived
        thousands of years ago ;
    Not one is respectable or industrious over the whole earth.

              (WALT WHITMAN, *The Beasts*.)

FREE VERSE (Vers Libre) passes from one metre to another in accordance with what the poet considers the requirement of his thought. Our ear hardly gets accustomed to one metre before it is broken and another metre substituted.

VOCABULARY ; ACTIVE and PASSIVE. (See also "Words : Choice of ")

(*a*) After this, it was noised abroad that *Mr. Valiant-for-truth* was taken with a Summons, by the same *Post* as the other, and had this for a Token that the Summons was true, *That his Pitcher was broken at the Fountain.* When he understood it, he called for his Friends, and told them of it. Then said he, I am going to my Father's, and though with great difficulty I am got hither, yet now I do not repent me of all the Trouble I have been at to arrive where I am.

(JOHN BUNYAN, *The Pilgrim's Progress.*)

(*b*) The notice which you have been pleased to take of my labours, had it been early, had been kind : but it has been delayed until I am indifferent, and cannot enjoy it ; till I am solitary, and cannot impart it ; till I am known, and do not want it. I hope it is no very cynical asperity not to confess obligations where no benefit has been received, or to be unwilling that the public should consider me owing that to a Patron, which Providence has enabled me to do for myself.

(From SAMUEL JOHNSON's letter to the Right Honourable the Earl of Chesterfield.)

Your vocabulary is your range of language, the record of the words you use in expressing your thoughts. This is the narrow sense of the word, a sense that may be called your " active vocabulary ". The range differs greatly in speakers and in writers. Look, for instance, at the contrasted examples above : you agree that Bunyan's consists of words current on everyone's tongues, Johnson's contains many words you will not hear in street and market place.

The much wider sense of " vocabulary " is the " passive vocabulary ", the record of the words you understand when you hear or see them. Your active vocabulary is very likely but a small part of your passive vocabulary, just as you may be able to read French quite well and yet be very ill able to express your thoughts—whether in writing or in speech—in French.

You extend your vocabulary, the stock of words at your disposal, to a small extent by acquiring new words. You extend it to a much greater extent by adapting old words to new meanings. A real or a fancied resemblance makes the old word seem applicable to the new idea. " Leaf of a tree ", you know ; you have no difficulty in understanding the lament " My way of life is fallen into the sere, the yellow leaf ". It is easy to transfer the name to a single thickness of folded paper, the " leaf of a book ", whence we have the figurative extension, " to turn over a new leaf " (to mend your ways), " to take a leaf out of a person's book " (to imitate him). And you transfer the names to other things, because they resemble the leaf in being thin sheets—the " goldleaf ", the " leaf " inserted into an expansible table, the " leaf " of a shutter. Instead of burdening ourselves with new words we adopt the old and interpret it " with a difference ". There is this new verb " to bale out ", for instance, meaning " to make a parachute descent from a damaged aeroplane ". You may not find it yet in your dictionary ; yet the strange happenings of war have made it current everywhere : the imagination of its first user, likening the escaping airman to a bale of goods emerging from the carrying vessel, has added a new word which, for its purpose, is hardly likely to be displaced.

The topic of this fancied talk between Dr. Johnson and Coleridge is the fit vocabulary of poetry :

Johnson : Why, yes, sir : Wordsworth has certainly discoursed of that, and he has endeavoured to persuade me that there is no difference between the proper language of poetry and the common speech of the rudest and meanest of mankind. Am I to understand, sir, that the object of your Romantic Movement was to substitute the jargon of Giles and Hodge for the higher discourse in which the poet has in all ages sought to express himself ? What is the notable discovery of the new school that he should aim at a style of diction as much below that of a cultivated reader as he has hitherto striven to rise above it ?

Coleridge : Give me leave to explain, Dr. Johnson. The promoters of the Romantic Revival proposed to themselves a twofold aim. They sought at once to reform the language of the poetry and to renew its spirit. They not only called on the poet to free himself from the trammels of a frigid and conventional vocabulary, but they invited him to come closer to Nature, and to view her with his own enkindled eye instead of through the dim and distorting glass which an outworn poetical tradition had too long interposed between the human vision and its objects.

(TRAILL, *The New Lucian.*)

VOWEL. (See " **Consonant** ")

W

WHO or WHOM ? (See "**Coiloquialism** ")

(*a*) My little ones crept about me the other evening to hear about their great grandmother Field, who lived in a great house in Norfolk.

(*b*) Children love to listen to stories about their elders when *they* were children ; to stretch their imagination to the conception of a traditionary great-uncle whom they never saw.

In these instances, from Lamb's essay " Dream Children ", *who* is the nominative relative ; *whom* is the objective relative. Consider these instances :

1. To the English he was a goodly and gallant gentleman, who had never turned his back upon an enemy, and was remarkable in that remarkable time for his constancy and daring.
2. Sir Richard commanded the master gunner, whom he knew to be a most resolute man, to split and sink the ship.

(*Whom* is clearly the word : " he knew *him* to be a most resolute

man ".) We must admit, though, that there is a growing reluctance to say " whom ", though one does write " whom " without
qualms. The writing of " whom " instead of " who " is less
frequent. But in a *Times* crossword the question was, " Whom
does she become when the Chatelaine stops talking ? "

WIT AND HUMOUR

    (*a*) Queen Mab has been with you. . . .
        She is the fairies' midwife and she comes
        In shape no bigger than an agate-stone
        On the forefinger of an alderman,
        Drawn with a team of little atomies
        Athwart men's noses as they lie asleep :
        Her waggon-spokes made of long spinners' legs ;
        The cover, of the wings of grasshoppers ;
        The traces, of the smallest spider's web ;
        The collars, of the moonshine's watery beams ;
        Her whip, of cricket's bone ; the lash of film ;
        Her waggoner, a small gray-coated gnat.
                (Mercutio in *Romeo and Juliet*.)

    (*b*) Honour pricks me on. Yea, but how if honour prick me
    off when I come on ? how then ? Can honour set-to a
    leg ? No. Or an arm ? No. Or take away the grief of
    a wound ? No. Honour hath no skill in surgery, then ?
    No. What is honour ? A word. What is that word,
    honour ? Air. A trim reckoning ! Who hath it ? He
    that died o' Wednesday. Does he feel it ? No. Doth
    he bear it ? No. It is insensible then ? Yes, to the
    dead. But will it not live with the living ? No. Why ?
    Detraction will not suffer it. Therefore I'll none of it :
    honour is a mere scutcheon : and so ends my catechism.
            (Falstaff in *King Henry IV, Part I*.)

" Wit " and " humour " were once by no means interchangeable ; they denoted different things. Wit included the humorous
statement that evokes laughter. Falstaff, whose argument against
temerity is our instance of humour, would speak of himself as
a wit, not as a humorist : " The brain of this foolish-compounded
clay, man, is not able to invent anything that tends to laughter
more than I invent or is invented on me : I am not only witty

in myself, but the cause that wit is in other men." Humour at the outset meant temperament, manner—the exhibitions of the temperament not always moving to laughter : " I'll curb her mad and headstrong humour," says Petruchio in *The Taming of the Shrew*.

To use " wit " and " humour " as perfect synonyms—perfectly interchangeable terms for causes of laughter—is nowadays common, and any attempt to distinguish between the two will not affect the matter. Pathos will, however, often accompany playfulness in humour : " I can ", says Falstaff, " get no remedy against this consumption of the purse : borrowing only lingers and lingers it out, but the disease is incurable."

In wit the stress is upon ingenuity, upon the cleverness of its creator. Sprightly remarks—" flashes of merriment that were wont to set the table on a roar "—smart repartees, fanciful comparisons, gay talk of any kind, these are wit. Mercutio, whose poetic fancies we give as an example, is the typical wit.

Wit wins your admiration and applause ; humour delights you and makes you lose your troubles in another's. Wit and laughter go together. Laughter goes with humour, too, but tears also may.

WORDS

(*a*) What do you read, my lord ?
Words, words, words.

(*Hamlet.*)

(*b*) I tell you there is no word yet coined and no melody yet sung that is extravagant and majestical enough for the glory that lovely words can reveal. It is heresy to deny it : have you not been taught that in the beginning was the Word ? That the Word was with God ? Nay, that the Word was God ?

(G. B. Shaw, *The Dark Lady of the Sonnets.*)

A word is, in the first place, a sign made by the tongue—a vocal gesture. In the second place, a word is a sign made by writing —by marks that are understood to represent vocal gestures. Those hearing the sounds, or seeing the writing, may gather thought from doing so. In the third place, a word has a meaning. We may study any one or all three aspects of the word.

The sound, or vocal gesture, may be like the whistle of birds and the cry of animals, and express thought in a vague manner. Such sounds can, in some instances, be only approximately shown in writing. Thus, to express vexation we may make a clicking sound, by placing the tongue against the teeth and then suddenly withdrawing it. The *tut !* in writing only remotely symbolises this. We make a sharp *s* sound to urge on a dog, a soft *s* sound to dictate silence, an explosive sound (as though expelling something distasteful) to show contempt or scorn. We ask our readers' complacence when we indicate these as *ss ! sh ! pooh !*

We call such sounds, often involuntary and meaningless, INTER-JECTIONS or EXCLAMATIONS. They are hardly real words. Real words are the sounds that can be combined so as to express, by means of a sentence, a definite thought.

WORDS : CHOICE OF. (See also "Synonyms")

(a) " I forget what this here word is ? " said Sam, scratching his head with the pen, in vain attempts to remember.

" Why don't you look at it then ? " inquired Mr. Weller.

" So I *am* a lookin' at it," replied Sam, " but there's another blot. Here's a ' c ' and a ' i ' and a ' d '."

" Circumwented, p'raps," suggested Mr. Weller.

" No, it ain't that," said Sam, " circumscribed ; that's it."

" That ain't as good a word as circumwented, Sammy," said Mr. Weller, gravely.

" Think not ? " said Sam.

" Nothin' like it," replied his father.

" But don't you think it means more ? " inquired Sam.

" Well, p'raps it is a more tenderer word," said Mr. Weller, after a few moments' reflection. " Go on, Sammy."

(CHARLES DICKENS, *Pickwick Papers.*)

(b) Many people would have called her a fat woman, but Mr. Polly's innate sense of epithet told him that plump was the word.

(H. G. WELLS, *The History of Mr. Polly.*)

(c) How well could I have spared for thee, young swain,
    Enow of such as for their bellies' sake,
    Creep and intrude and climb into the fold.

                           (MILTON, *Lycidas*.)

And here is Ruskin's comment on the last line :

Do not think Milton uses those three words to fill up his verse, as a loose writer would. He needs all the three ; specially those three, and no more than those—" creep ", and " intrude " and " climb " ; no other words would or could serve the turn, and no more could be added. For they exhaustively comprehend the three classes, correspondent to the three characters, of men who dishonestly seek ecclesiastical power. First, those who " creep " into the fold ; who do not care for office, nor name, but for secret influence, and do all things occultly and cunningly, consenting to any servility of office or conduct, so only that they may intimately discern and unawares direct, the minds of men. Then those who " intrude " (thrust, that is) themselves into the fold, who by natural insolence of heart, and stout eloquence of tongue, and fearlessly perseverant self-assertion, obtain hearing and authority with the common crowd. Lastly, those who " climb ", who, by labour and learning, both stout and sound, but selfishly exerted in the cause of their own ambition, gain high dignities and authorities, and become " Lords over the heritage ", though not " examples to the flock ".

(d) I cannot praise a fugitive and cloistered virtue, unexercised and unbreathed, that never sallies out and sees her adversary, but slinks out of the race where that immortal garland is to be run for not without dust and heat.

                           (JOHN MILTON.)

No doubts assail you here. Of course, some words are better for your purpose than others ; of course the great writers, of prose as well as of poetry, have achieved their greatness very largely because they have chosen well. Much, very much, has been written concerning the choice ; much will continue to be written. For the subject is of perennial interest.

You have at your disposal in the English language a multitudinous gathering of words : the *Oxford Dictionary* marshals and defines nearly half a million. You will never need to use, or even to understand, a great many of these words. What consideration should guide you in your choice of those you must use ? Read again the Milton sentence above. There is much more than the skilful choice of words worthy of note—worthy of emulation as well—in Milton's sentence. You have a musical cadence throughout the sentence ; the rise and fall of the stresses give you much of the delight that poetry does. The words to express the lofty thought are, however, our present concern. Of many of these words you are certain to say : " I should not have selected that word " ; but you will go on to say : " How well it suits the thought to be expressed ! " So you may watch these expert players, at hockey perhaps or billiards ; one player makes a quite unanticipated movement, does what you would never have thought of, and admiring, you say, " Only a genius would have done that."

Look at the adjectives descriptive of " virtue ". " Fugitive " —" timidly fleeing from conflict "—you might have hit upon. " Cloistered ", however—" quietly secluded from danger "—is far from the ordinary ; but how clear-cut is the image that it brings into your mind ! The two participles, " unexercised and unbreathed ", carrying on and emphasising the description, are noteworthy, too. The more general " unexercised " prompts to the more special, more vivid, " unbreathed " : it is this, the unusual word, that gives you the picture of the warrior warmed to the conflict going with renewed vigour upon his foe.

Here, again, is the antithesis—the contrast between " sallies out and sees her adversary " and " slinks out of the race '. The robust " sallies out " is an effective contrast to the furtive " slinks out " : " to sally "—" to make a sudden rush from the beleaguered place upon the enemy ", suggests courage ; " to slink " suggests cowardice. Doubtless you notice, too, how the echo of the sounds in the two verbs—the *s* and *l* sounds—adds force to the antithesis.

The poetic " immortal garland " is, no doubt, unsuited for commonplace talk or writing. It is quite in keeping with the passionate plea that Milton is making. So is the phrase giving a vigorous and striking close to the sentence " not without dust and heat ".

Choice is out of the question often enough. One word, and one word only, is requisite. It would be lost labour to seek for substitutes for your well-understood terms like " Bill of Lading ", " Invoice ", and the like ; or for the essential linking words of our speech. Deliberate choice, however, is often possible. Look at these few sentences from John Bright's speech on the Russian War :

> I cannot but notice that an uneasy feeling exists as to the news which may arrive by the very next mail from the East. I do not suppose that your troops are to be beaten in actual conflict with the foe, or that they will be driven into the sea ; but I am certain that many homes in England in which there now exists a fond hope that the distant one may return— many such homes may be rendered desolate when the next mail shall arrive. The Angel of Death has been abroad through-out the land ; you may almost hear the beating of his wings. There is no one, as when the first-born were slain of old, to sprinkle with blood the lintel and the two side-posts of our doors, that he may spare and pass on ; he takes his victims from the castle of the noble, the mansion of the wealthy, and the cottage of the poor and lowly.

Clearly, a passage like that is worth close study. All manner of questions present themselves. Consider one or two. " Rendered desolate " is the orator's choice : why does he prefer the adjective " desolate " to any of the possible substitutes, " wretched ", " miserable ", " sorrowful ", " unhappy ", " un-fortunate " ? You will answer that he wished to emphasise the loss of the loved one ; and none of the other words would bring out with effect the idea of being left alone. " The beating of his wings " is the phrase. Is " beating " better than " flapping ", " rustling ", " throbbing ", " sounding " ? Yes, you say ; none of the possible substitutes gives, as " beating " does, the idea of the menacing sound. " Spare and pass on ", " castle of the noble ", " mansion of the wealthy ", " cottage of the poor and lowly "—all these are notable phrases.

We must remember that meaning is not the only consideration dictating choice. Sound matters, too. Read aloud this beautiful passage and ask yourself wherein its beauty lies :

> Or ever the silver cord be loosed, or the golden bowl be broken or the pitcher be broken at the fountain, or the wheel broken at the cistern ; then shall the dust return to the earth as it was ; and the spirit shall return unto God who gave it.

The beauty lies, you answer, very largely in the sounds of the words, the vowel sound in particular. Examine them a little closely. The first " or ", we had better note, is a form of " ere ", so that " or ever " is " before ever ". Well, now : there is the contrast between the short sounds prominent in the first phrase " Or ever the silver cord ", and the long *o* tolling like a bell through the second phrase " the golden bowl be broken ". Then the short and the long sounds are mingled, " pitcher be broken at the fountain ", " wheel broken at the cistern ". Any number of other noteworthy points emerge as you read and re-read the passage.

It is an old controversy whether the sense or the sound of words is more to be considered. Here is one that prides himself on his plain way of speaking—and of writing. " *Ficum voco ficum* : I call a spade a spade ", he says, " I do not use words for their own sake but simply to convey ideas. I would have you regard not how I write but what I write." Here is another careful in his choice of words, neat in his speech, ever alert to avoid awkward sounds like " Burke's works " or " one wonders ".

Certainly the purpose of language is to communicate ideas, and the words that communicate the ideas most speedily and with least loss are the best.

True it is, too, that a writer may use words to hide the want of thought. The harassed reporter, hard put to it for a story, is often obliged to string together words void of thought. For space clamours to be filled. " It is understood ", he writes, " that the position in the Tea Market in Mincing Lane has been recently the subject of much discussion. Following some un-usual events, it is believed that the Tea Association has taken certain action." This leaves the reader as he was before except with admiration of the ingenuity that has made bricks without straw. In truth, though, you cannot dissociate sound from sense. The idea to be conveyed is the important matter ; but in conveying the idea, you will instinctively consider the manner of conveyance also. An old author writes : " When you see a fellow careful about his words and neat in his speech, know this for a certainty, that man's mind is busied with toys, there's no solidity in him. As he said of a nightingale, *vox es, praeterea nihil*,—' a voice thou art and nothing else '." Still, it should be our purpose—as, indeed, it was with the author quoted—to regard the method as well as matter.

The words used have a meaning and a sound. They also take on a colouring from their context. That word " dear ", for example, means little or nothing in our conventional opening of a letter " Dear Sir ", " Dear Madam ". It has meaning enough when in other unions : " I could not love thee, dear, so much, loved I not honour more ". See what a wholly unintended effect is given by the accidental omission of a companion word in this notice. The watchmaker is advising his customer of the completion of repairs :

DEAR MADAM,
We have pleasure in advising you that the article kindly left for repair is now ready.

We are, Dear
Yours truly,

Of the great W. E. Gladstone, a fluent and exhaustive speaker, it used to be said that he never was in want of a word. " Shall I be short and concise ? " he asked his leader, Sir Robert Peel, when about to speak for the Government, then passing through troubled waters. " No," said Peel, willing to confuse the issues before the House, " be long and diffuse " ; and none could so effectively obey as Gladstone.

Of Gladstone's great rival, Benjamin Disraeli, the commendation was that he was never in want of *the* word—the apt phrase to fit the occasion. Both capacities—the capacity to make a little sense the pretext for many words, and the capacity to condense into a few apt works the essence of a matter—have their function. It is the second, though, that merits cultivation.

WORDS (NEW)

> In words, as fashions, the same rule will hold;
> Alike fantastic, if too new, or old;
> Be not the first by whom the new are tried
> Nor yet the last to lay the old aside.
>
> (POPE.)

We should look in vain through all the plays of Shakespeare and his friends for the words *steam-engine* or *aeroplane*, or *psychology* or *economics* or *quotas* or *tariffs*. *Listening-in* and *radio* and *broadcasting* are all new names for new things. So are *television* (which ought to be *long vision*, for *tele* is Greek and *vision* is Latin,) *the films*, and other words that would have made Shakespeare stare and gape. In the sentence " Scenes from *The Tiger* were televised yesterday afternoon " we have a brand-new verb that would have confounded the men and women of Queen Victoria's day.

A dictionary of a living language like English becomes incomplete even as it is being prepared. For new words are ever entering and finding a permanent place in the language. The new words may be deliberately coined in order to express an idea that formerly needed no expression. You have very likely found the strange word " kilowatt " on the electricity bill. " kilo " you know to be the Greek word for " thousand "; " Watt " you know as the name of the boy that watched the steam pushing up the kettle-lid and later on invented the first practical steam engine. But how has the union of the incongruous elements been effected ? How has the ingenious Scotsman acquired the Greek prefix ?

Well, the Board of Trade has made a regulation that the electricity used shall be charged for in units called " Kilowatt Hours ". " Watt " was the name given, in honour of the great Scotsman, to denote a unit of activity or power. This unit corresponds to the rate of work represented by a current of one " ampere " under a pressure of one " volt ".

That word " volt " is another word deliberately adopted, this time in memory of a clever Italian called Volta, who died in 1826 and who discovered much that we now put to practical use. We measure the electric force at a point in " volts "; and we speak of its " voltage ". Just as water flows from a high level to a low level, so the electric force flows along the conducting cables from a point of high voltage to a point of low voltage. One volt sends a unit of current; and this unit is called an " ampere ", often shortened to " amp ". There is the word by which another famous scientist, the French electrician Ampère, is kept in memory. If you have studied physics you will have learnt that " An ampere is the current that one volt can send through one ohm." In that last word " ohm " we have a memorial to yet another great student of science. He it was who showed how to determine with accuracy the resistance offered to the flow of electricity.

In these four monosyllables, therefore—watt, amp, volt, ohm —we pay tribute to the memory of the Scotsman Watt, the Italian Volta, the Frenchman Ampère, and the German Ohm.

During the momentous days of the World War strange expressions in abundance, denoting the strange things of the War, were thrust upon our notice. Look in a pre-war dictionary : you will seek in vain for terms like *asdic, jeep, bren, bulldozer, maquis, blitz,* and a host of other that for a while became unhappily familiar to us. Some will not outlive the occasion that gave them birth and become permanent denizens of the language. Others will. *Pluto* (Pipe Line Under The Ocean) will be forgotten along with the extraordinary feat it named ; for the atomic bomb has made it obsolete. *Radar* (*RA*dio *D*etection *A*nd *R*anging) is, however, bound to stay ; for its peace-time developments have entered into the daily life of men. The atomic bomb itself has brought many terms in its train—*neutrons, isotopes, electrons, nuclear, cyclotron* and others.

It is often difficult at times to trace the origin of the words we use. " Brazil, where the nuts come from " is an expression that is often heard. Of course, you say, the nuts take their name from the country. On the contrary, the country takes its name from the nuts. " Brazil ", denoting the red wood of an East Indian tree, a wood much prized by dyers, was in the English language long before Columbus, boldly committing his ship to the trade wind sweeping to the West, reached America. " The Portuguese ", the report tells us, " named the country ' Brazil ' from the red wood of that name."

To be sure, a good many of the things bought and sold bear the names of the places where they originate, where perhaps they are still made or grown. *Calico* is the cotton-cloth first imported from the East, quite possibly from Calicut, the Indian city on the Malabar coast. The woollen fabric of long-staple fleece, made from well-twisted yarn, bears the name of the Norfolk parish Worsted; there can be no doubt at all that the place preceded the commercial commodity. Our word *florin*—the one concession we have to decimal coinage—is also connected with the name of a place, with Florence, where the gold coin introduced by Edward III was first issued. It has a more remote origin, however, for, like *florist*, it is connected with *flos*, the Latin name for flower. The original florin had the figure of a lily stamped upon it.

You have read how Falstaff described his cramped and very uncomfortable position when he was hidden in the dirty-clothes basket: " Compressed, like a good bilbo, in the circumference of a peck, hilt to point, heel to head." The sword-makers of Bilbao made weapons so well-tempered that they could be bent point to hilt; and *bilbo* became a name for such a sword as Othello's : " It is a sword of Spain, the ice-brook's temper." That strange abbreviation—O.K.—which now comes glibly from many speakers, has actually received judicial notice. We may now all of us—even the most fastidious—use the barbarous abbreviation with a quiet conscience. We may actually speak of " okaying " documents. It may indeed soon be that the man who, wishing to give his certificate of the correctness of the details submitted to him, shall write " all correct ", will be judged affected and pedantic. He had far better follow the crowd and write O.K. For the Judicial Committee of the Privy Council, our most august tribunal, has interpreted the term. It has been presented at Court and received its own certificate of respectability ; it is now O.K. to use it. Does it mean, as one of the litigants claimed, " all correct ", or, as the other claimed, " so be it ? " The first, decided their Lordships with surprising unanimity ; and Lord Russell, delivering the judgment said :

> The origin of this commercial barbarism is variously assigned. The general view is that the letters O.K. came from America and represent a spelling, humorous or un-

educated, of " all correct " ! Another view is that they represent the Choctaw word " okeh ", which signifies " so be it ". But the only conclusion possible is that the letters on delivery orders and invoices mean that the details in those documents are correctly given.

Another interesting example is " regatta ", which still after many years retains its foreign look. When in Tudor times it made its first appearance in English it signified the yearly boat-races on the Grand Canal at Venice. It was one of the Italian introductions that many people here disliked extremely, at which indeed Shakespeare—though he uses the foreign newcomer quite freely—pokes genial fun. Some of his fellows appeared as though they " had been at a great feast of languages, and stolen the scraps ". Or, as Queen Elizabeth's schoolmaster very sensibly says : " He that will write well in any tongue must follow this counsel, to speak as the common people do, to think as wise men do. Many English writers have not done so, but—using strange words as Latin, French, and Italian—do make all things dark and hard." Still, a good many of these " ink-horn terms " served a useful purpose, and have survived to become indisputably English. We should not cast about for another word than " regatta "—defined in an Italian dictionary as " a strife or contention or struggling for the mastery "—to describe those pleasant social events where boat—and yacht—races are ancillary to the entertainment.

It comes to this, the point we have so often noted. Language originates in usage, in what people are accustomed to do. Reason may insist, may prove up to the hilt, that such and such a usage is quite erroneous. Custom prevails for all that. The language goes on its way unperturbed by the pedants. In time custom makes the wrong term or the illogical expression a recognised inmate of the language. There is this name " black-out ", for instance. For the new and deplorable thing a new name had to be found or coined ; and, in some subtle way, people hit upon " black-out ". Newspapers and official publications alike agree in calling " lights-out " a " black-out ". " Lights-out " would have been a truer term ; and we have all heard it again and again at school or camp. " Black-in " would really have said what was intended. Perhaps, too, we might justify the word by saying that " out " means here " utterly, fully ", as it does in " play out " or " fight out " or " Work out your own salvation with fear and trembling ".

Z

ZEUGMA

Kill the boys and the luggage.

(Fluellen in Henry V.)

In their haste, speakers may yoke one word *kill* with two others, with only one of which it is applicable. This yoking is sometimes called by the Greek name for " yoking ", ZEUGMA. The hearer, in interpreting the hurried utterance, must himself supply an appropriate word, as in the instance, " plunder " or " destroy ". The joining together of two inconsistent metaphors is a species of zeugma.

Printed in Great Britain by
Butler & Tanner Ltd.,
Frome and London